SECURITY WITH SOLVENCY

SECURITY WITH SOLVENCY

Dwight D. Eisenhower
and the Shaping of the
American Military Establishment

Gerard Clarfield

Westport, Connecticut
London

Library of Congress Cataloging-in-Publication Data

Clarfield, Gerard H.
    Security with solvency : Dwight D. Eisenhower and the shaping of
the American military establishment / Gerard Clarfield.
      p.   cm.
    Includes bibliographical references (p.   ) and index.
    ISBN 0–275–96445–0 (alk. paper)
    1. United States—Military policy. 2. United States. Dept. of
Defense—Appropriations and expenditures. 3. United States—
Politics and government—1953–1961. 4. Eisenhower, Dwight D.
(Dwight David), 1890–1969. I. Title.
UA23.C5584   1999
355′.033573—dc21   98–50241

British Library Cataloguing in Publication Data is available.

Library of Congress Catalog Card Number: 98–50241
ISBN: 0–275–96445–0

First published in 1999

Praeger Publishers, 88 Post Road West, Westport, CT 06881
An imprint of Greenwood Publishing Group, Inc.
www.praeger.com

Printed in the United States of America

The paper used in this book complies with the
Permanent Paper Standard issued by the National
Information Standards Organization (Z39.48–1984).

10 9 8 7 6 5 4 3 2 1

For Julie

Contents

Photo essay follows page 146.

Introduction

During his years in the White House, Dwight Eisenhower demonstrated a real passion for frugality especially when it came to supporting the military establishment. At the time, some believed that he had fallen under the spell of the many conservative businessmen who he had appointed to positions of influence in the government. A careful reading of the documentary record, however, demonstrates that Ike was an instinctive fiscal conservative whose belief that military spending should be controlled and limited can be traced back at least to the period of the Great Depression. Ike took it as an article of faith that too much spending on the military could disrupt a free economy. The objective, he believed, should be to strike a balance between the nation's security requirements and its economic well-being. The best method of achieving these goals was to eliminate the waste, overlap, and redundancies found in the military establishment by unifying the services.

In the nineteenth century it had been reasonable to establish a clear separation between the Army, which operated exclusively on the North American continent, and the Navy. However, by the beginning of the twentieth century modern technologies, especially the airplane, began to blur distinctions between the services. Moreover, World War I made it clear that future military operations would require close coordination between ground, air, and naval forces. These developments, along with the huge costs of modern warfare, led many including Ike to conclude that the military could operate more effectively and at lower cost if the services were unified.

Though unification was considered briefly in the early 1920s, the armed services remained separate entities down to the beginning of World War II. When the Japanese launched the attack on Pearl Harbor that plunged the United States into war, the services were, to all intents and purposes, as separate as they had been a century before.

The World War II experience, which highlighted the inadequacies of the existing military organization, gave new vitality to the concept of unification. In 1943 Army Chief of Staff General George C. Marshall called for the creation of a single cabinet level department to replace the War and Navy departments. Three branches would exist under this new arrangement—the Army, the Navy, and an independent Air Force. A fourth agency would be responsible for purchasing supplies common to all. Marshall's proposal also called for the creation of a powerful chairman who would outrank the other members of the Joint Chiefs of Staff (JCS). The chairman's job would be to resolve differences among the chiefs when they could not achieve unanimity among themselves. He would also have the power to present the secretary and the president with clear, unambiguous advice based on the national interest, not on the parochial concerns of the services.

The Navy, fearing that unification would result in the elimination of the Marine Corps as well as its air arm, refused to support Marshall's ideas. When the Navy blocked action at the JCS level, the War Department carried the battle to Congress only to be thwarted once again. The legislators refused to take any action until the war had been brought to a successful conclusion. Thus it was not until October 1945 that the political battle over unification began in earnest. A few weeks later Eisenhower replaced Marshall as army chief of staff and became the principal spokesman for unification. He remained the driving force behind the movement for the next thirteen years.

As army chief of staff, Eisenhower was a major player during the debate that led to the enactment in 1947 of the original National Security Act. As far as he was concerned the new law, which left the services autonomous and created a virtually powerless secretary of national defense, was a hopeless abortion, a Frankenstein's monster that would not bring unity. Two of the law's only redeeming features, he believed, were that it created a single, albeit powerless, secretary who might be made more powerful by future changes in the law and that it established an independent Air Force. Even that achievement was marred by the fact that in the future the Army would have to contend for its share of a shrinking budget with not one but two high profile, elite services. The only thing worse than duplication, Eisenhower thought, was triplication; and that was precisely what the National Security Act produced.

In December 1948, Eisenhower, who had several months before left his post as army chief of staff to assume the presidency of Columbia University, returned to Washington as an advisor to the new secretary of national defense, James Forrestal. In this capacity he again attempted to advance the cause of unification. First, he aided in the formulation of a set of amendments to the National Security Act that, when enacted in the summer of 1949, created a chairman for the JCS and expanded the secretary's powers. As the informal head of the JCS he attempted to use the budget process to create a greater degree of unity among the services and develop a single, agreed upon military strategy to be implemented in the event of war with the Soviet Union. He failed for two reasons. First, declining revenues made it impossible for President Truman to endorse a defense budget sufficient to achieve the stated goal. Moreover, even given the growing intensity of the cold war crisis, the services could not agree on a single strategic concept. At length, Eisenhower wound up his efforts, presented the new secretary of defense, Louis Johnson, with a defense budget for 1951 that he himself pronounced hopelessly inadequate, and returned to his post at Columbia.

In 1950, following the outbreak of the Korean War, the Truman administration's attitude regarding defense spending underwent a dramatic shift. The lid on spending came off as the cold war appeared to enter a new, more violent phase. In 1952, when Eisenhower ran for the presidency, he did so in part because the Truman administration's huge and, he believed, wasteful spending program was leading the nation down the path to economic disaster. He was also motivated by the fact that many of the problems he had tried to address in 1949 persisted. The services remained locked in an unrestrained and unseemly rivalry for the lion's share of the budget and refused to agree on a set of clearly defined and limited roles and missions. The members of the JCS also continued to act more as "special pleaders" for their particular services than as a group interested in providing the secretary of defense with sound military advice. The defense secretary did not have the authority he required to effectively run his department.

As president, Eisenhower sought to rein in government spending, 70 percent of which was going to the military, by advancing the cause of unification. Toward these ends Secretary of Defense Charles E. Wilson created a special committee headed by New York's Nelson Rockefeller and charged it with the responsibility for planning a large scale reorganization of the Pentagon. Reorganization Plan Six, the result of the Rockefeller Committee's work, augmented the power of the secretary of defense while reducing the influence of the JCS as well as the service secretaries. It did not represent the radical change that, under other circumstances, Eisenhower might have sought. With the Korean War still going on the time was not right for what would have amounted to a set of highly controversial changes. More importantly, Eisenhower was able to implement Plan Six under terms of the Executive Reorganization Act of 1949, which gave the president the power to reorganize executive departments with only limited congressional involvement. A more complete reorganization of the armed services would have required a full-scale legislative effort. Eisenhower, a participant in the long and bitter struggle that preceded the enactment of the original National Security Act, had no desire to begin his administration by engaging in a similar battle. Instead, he took what he could get, no doubt hoping that a more powerful secretary of defense, working with a new and carefully selected JCS, would be able to bring about some positive changes.

Eisenhower's hopes were soon dashed, however. The administration's search for a new, less expensive military strategy, which resulted in the New Look with its heavy emphasis on nuclear striking power, alienated the Army and to a lesser extent the Navy. Leaders of both services argued that Eisenhower was preparing the country to fight the type of war that was least likely to occur, while leaving open the possibility that, because the New Look de-emphasized the importance of conventional arms, the United States would not be prepared to deal with small-scale aggressions. Eisenhower's efforts to control military spending also alienated the Air Force, which, even though it was the main beneficiary of funding under the New Look, was unable to achieve the force goals established in 1950.

Before the end of 1956 the resistance of the armed services to administration policies led Ike to conclude that another round of reforms was necessary. In the autumn of 1957, following the launching of Sputnik by the Soviet Union, he thought the time was right to seek basic change. However, Congress, led by Carl Vinson and Richard Russell, chairmen respectively of the House and Senate Armed Services Committees, refused to give Eisenhower everything that he sought. Nevertheless, the 1958 Defense Reorganization Act represented a major shift in power inside the defense establishment. It eliminated the service secretaries from the chain of command that now ran from the secretary of defense directly to the unified commands. In the future the service departments would only be responsible for raising, training, and equipping forces that were then to be turned over to the unified commanders, who reported directly to the secretary of defense. The JCS was also reformed. Deputy chiefs were given responsibility for the day-to-day operation of each service branch and the chiefs' were denied all command responsibilities. Their principle task became to serve as the defense secretary's staff.

The 1958 law did not achieve all of the objectives championed by Eisenhower. Clearly, unification remained a long way off. Even so, more than any other single individual, Eisenhower was responsible for transforming what had been an inefficient postwar military establishment into a centralized organization with a secretary of defense who enjoyed truly extraordinary powers. Nor did Eisenhower's influence end there. In 1986, when Senators Barry Goldwater and Sam Nunn decided that the time had come for the next major effort at reorganization, they brought ideas advanced earlier by Eisenhower still closer to fruition. The Goldwater-Nichols Act came close to transforming the chairman of the JCS into the powerful chief of staff of the armed forces that Eisenhower had wanted while further reducing the power and influence of the JCS. It also required a new level of cooperation among the services. "Jointness" was now mandated by law. In these regards Eisenhower's vision of a military establishment dominated by a powerful secretary of defense working in concert with an equally powerful chief of staff of the armed forces has come close to fruition as has his call for coordination of the activities of the separate services.

In writing this book, I have incurred numerous debts. I could not have produced this manuscript without the support of the Research Council of the University of Missouri, which helped with significant funding. I would also like to thank the staff at the Eisenhower Library, especially Dr. James Layerzapf, for help in finding needed materials. The archival staffs at the Truman Library, the Western Manuscripts Division of the State Historical Society of Missouri, and the Modern Military Branch of the National Archives provided equally important help. I would also like to thank Dr. Linda McFarland, whose work was important to me as was the friendly encouragement of several of my colleagues including Steve Bradford and David Wakefield. Finally, I must acknowledge the important contribution made by my wife Julie. First, she put up with me as I produced who knows how many drafts of this manuscript. (Anyone who says writing on a computer saves time should watch me.) Second, because she is far more adept at dealing with the whims and fancies of the computer than I am, she was, on too many occasions to count, able to come to my rescue when all seemed lost.

SECURITY WITH SOLVENCY

"The Foundation of Military Strength Is Economic Strength."

On September 25, 1952, as he was about to leave on a month-long, twenty-six state campaign swing, General Dwight D. Eisenhower, the Republican candidate for president, addressed a rally at the Baltimore armory. In one sense the speech was traditional campaign fare, replete with attacks on the failings and inadequacies of the Truman administration. However, at the same time, Eisenhower was discussing issues that had long been a matter of concern to him, the future of the American military establishment and the strength of the domestic economy. America, Eisenhower believed, faced two equally serious dangers: the threat posed by the Soviet Union and the danger of economic collapse, which he saw as a distinct possibility if the United States continued to sink huge sums into the defense establishment. America's challenge, he told that Baltimore audience, was to achieve "security with solvency." [1]

As Eisenhower saw it, defense spending, which then exceeded $60 billion annually, had gone out of control because of a lack of "far-sighted direction" on the part of President Truman and his advisors. History demonstrated, he said, that it was either feast or famine for the American military. The American people spent unstintingly during the two world wars: but after each conflict, military budgets had been cut to the bone leaving the military unprepared and the country inadequately defended. With the coming of war in Korea, funding again skyrocketed, with predictable results. "[F]renzied expansion" produced duplication, waste, high taxes, a growing federal deficit, and worrisome inflation. This boom-and-bust cycle was bad for the military and bad for the country. America had to find a method of reducing costs while "maintaining its defensive power." [2]

Eisenhower's prescription for reform involved a program of defense spending that would protect the integrity of the economy while providing for the necessary minimum needs of the armed services. He knew that such an approach was certain to arouse the ire of military leaders and that "[s]pecial interests in the armed services" had in the past played Congress and the president off against one another to the disadvantage of the public. To control this tendency he called for close cooperation between Congress and the White House. Some in the armed forces were apparently under the impression that there was no limit to what the government could spend on weaponry; but Ike insisted that there had to be limits. "We cannot pretend to do everything in every field all the time," he said.[3]

The emphasis that Eisenhower placed on the importance of striking a balance between the needs of the military establishment and the health of the national economy was not something that he or his advisors dreamed up for the political wars of 1952. On the contrary, this was a deeply felt and long-standing concern. For example, in March 1933 at the height of the Great Depression, he wrote that President Roosevelt ought to seek a balanced federal budget even if it meant draconian cuts in the already anemic military establishment and in his own inadequate salary.[4] Six years later while serving in the Philippines as an aide to General MacArthur, he informed President Manuel Quezon that a large-scale effort was "desperately needed" if the islands were to be properly defended. Yet at the same time he recommended only a modest program and warned that spending too much on defense could wreck "the very thing" the spending was designed to secure, "the stability and security of the nation."[5]

Thirteen years and a devastating world war later, Eisenhower had not altered his opinions. As the former supreme commander of NATO forces in Europe he was, of course, familiar with the basic national security policy as outlined in NSC 68/2. Fundamental to that document was the assumption that when Moscow had achieved "a sufficient atomic capability to make a surprise attack" it "might be tempted to strike" and that the United States ought therefore to be fully prepared for war by 1954 when, it was calculated, the Soviets could have an arsenal of as many as two hundred atomic bombs.[6] Ike rejected the fundamental assumptions underlying NSC 68/2, telling his friend, the financier Bernard Baruch, that he did not agree with those who "have insisted that we could identify our point of greatest danger as 1952, or 1954, or any other year." Nor did he "believe that the Soviets would in their own best interests deliberately provoke global war." Therefore, he wrote, "I feel that we should figure out our strength objectives and push toward them steadily, but always having in mind that we must retain a strong and solvent economy." The "foundation of military strength is economic strength," he wrote. He also thought that "a bankrupt America is more the Soviet goal than an America conquered on the field of battle."[7]

Central to Eisenhower's hopes for controlling military spending over the "long haul" was his commitment to the unification of the armed services. World War II had proven that the day of separate land, sea, and air operations was over. Every major military operation undertaken during the war had involved all three services acting in concert. That being the case there could be no question that "effective coordination of the services in war requires central planning in time of peace." If unification could be achieved, waste and duplication might be eliminated and defense costs sharply reduced. Unhappily, the 1947 National Security Act had only made matters worse, it not only had failed to unify the services but it also had created an independent air force. As a result there were now "three services in place of the former two . . . going their separate ways." Because Congress had not seen fit to provide the secretary of defense with the requisite power to rein in the military, "the end result has been not to remove duplication but to produce triplication." As president, Eisenhower intended to do something about this.[8]

Eisenhower's commitment to the unification of the armed services was in large measure the result of his personal experiences during and immediately following World War II. Up to the day of the Japanese attack on Pearl Harbor, no serious attempt had been made to coordinate the activities of the Army and Navy. On the contrary, for the most part the War and Navy departments functioned independently of one another. Each had its own cabinet-level secretary, developed its own budget proposals, and had its own independent relationship with Congress. Nor was any serious attempt made to encourage the services to coordinate their activities. Thus, for example, the Army was home to the Army Air Corps and operated its own troop transports, while the Navy had its own air as well as ground forces. As late as 1938, *Joint Action of the Army and Navy*, which spelled out established policy, called for nothing more than limited forms of voluntary cooperation between the services. As a result cooperation was at best problematic.[9]

One result of this unfortunate arrangement was that during the interwar years competition for the limited funds ensued. The Navy, the elite service with powerful friends in Congress and the White House, consistently fared better than the Army. By 1939 the situation had become grotesquely unbalanced. In that year the Navy, which ranked third in the world behind those of Britain and Japan, was spending more on the construction of a single battleship than the Army had in its entire equipment budget.[10]

Eisenhower, like most other career officers, was frustrated by the Army's second-class status. At one level his feelings were highly personal. Even during World War II, after he had risen to become Supreme Commander of Allied Forces in Europe, it disturbed him that naval officers were paid more than army officers of comparable rank, and that when on temporary assignment they received twice as much in per diem pay. At the same time, he saw this lack of a uniform pay policy as symptomatic of a more basic problem, for he believed that the country was ill-served by a system that failed to produce a balanced defense establishment, one capable of operating with equal effect on land and sea, and in the air.

In December 1941, Army Chief of Staff General George C. Marshall appointed Eisenhower, who was well acquainted with the military situation in Southeast Asia and the Far East, deputy chief of the War Plans Division for the Far East and the Pacific and promoted him to the rank of brigadier general. A talented staff officer and strategic planner, Eisenhower rose quickly in Marshall's estimation and was soon promoted again, this time to head the Army's Operations Division.[11]

During these early months of the war, Eisenhower, who idolized Marshall, had ample opportunity to watch, learn, and think about the importance of military organization at the highest levels. Among the lessons he learned during this time was how crucial it was to establish a central authority with the power to control the different branches of the service.

Very early in the war Marshall and Eisenhower began work on an administrative initiative that was designed to facilitate the decision-making process and coordinate the activities of the services. In 1941 Marshall and Admiral Harold Stark, chief of naval operations, held talks aimed at creating a "permanent joint general staff" for plans and operations to be headed by a single chief of staff who would outrank the service chiefs and would have ultimate decision-making authority. Had this been done the services would have been brought under a single, unified command. Modern warfare, Marshall and Eisenhower both believed, required nothing less.[12]

On January 28, 1942, Marshall brought this idea to the Army and Navy Joint Board, which, only days later, was superceded by the newly created Joint Chiefs of Staff (JCS).[13] By this time Stark had gone to London and Admiral Ernest King, a fierce defender of the Navy's autonomy, had replaced him. When King raised objections to Marshall's proposal, it was referred to the Joint Planning Committee where Eisenhower represented the Army and the redoubtable Admiral Kelley Turner spoke for the Navy.[14]

Eisenhower thought that administrative reform was absolutely essential. The JCS was a committee that could not make decisions unless its members agreed unanimously on a particular course of action. It was intolerable that a single service chief could block the entire decision-making process. There was a war going on, the Allies were not doing well, and the closest possible coordination of effort was vital. On this subject Eisenhower was adamantine. Of all possibilities the worst was that a military establishment might be paralyzed because of its inability to make a decision. In wartime, he later remarked to a congressional committee, any decision was better than none at all.[15]

Eisenhower, who doubtless believed he had logic and reason on his side, had no luck converting Admiral Turner to his point of view. Interservice politics doomed these talks to failure. Since the 1920s, air power advocates, the most famous of whom was General Billy Mitchell, had been loudly demanding independence for the Army Air Corps while at the same time proclaiming that modern aircraft made navies obsolete. By the time Eisenhower and Turner sat down to talk, the airmen, supported by the Army, had made considerable progress toward their primary goal of service independence. Moreover, General Henry "Hap" Arnold, the chief of staff of the Army Air Force (AAF), was a sitting member of the JCS. Admiral King, who reflected the views of the Navy's hierarchy, feared that the Navy would be marginalized within the organizational structure that Marshall proposed, outvoted, and stripped of its air and ground forces by an Army-AAF alliance.[16] It is not surprising then that Eisenhower and Turner were unable to come to an agreement or that Marshall's proposal went into limbo. That was precisely what Admiral King intended.

This as well as other difficulties with the Navy, especially a disagreement between the War and Navy departments over control of land-based aircraft engaged in antisubmarine warfare, caused Eisenhower to reflect on what Major General Fox Conner had once told him about the difficulties of working with foreign allies. In his diary Ike noted that Conner had not told him the whole story for he might "well have included the Navy." "What a gang to work with," he exclaimed.[17] Eisenhower was particularly angry with the grotesquely brusque Admiral King whose policies, he believed, were endangering the war effort. "One thing that might help win this war," he wrote, "is to get someone to shoot King. He's the antithesis of cooperation, a deliberately rude person" and "a mental bully."[18] For the first but by no means the last time Eisenhower had come face to face with what Secretary of War Henry L. Stimson described as "the peculiar psychology of the Navy Department, which frequently seemed to retire from the realm of logic into a dim religious world in which Neptune was God, Mahan his prophet, and the United States Navy the only true Church"; and he had lost.[19]

Defeated in one arena, Marshall and Eisenhower sought greater centralization of authority in another where, fortunately, they could count on the Navy's support. In the days before America entered the war, as Marshall ruminated on his World War I experience, he concluded that some method had to be found to coordinate Allied military operations. This had not been the case in World War I, and Marshall did not look back on that experience fondly.[20] The only reasonable course of action, he believed, was to create unified commands in which a single supreme commander would have ultimate authority and responsibility in each theater of war.

At the time the like-minded Eisenhower saw the Southwest Pacific region as desperately in need of a unified command. In those dark December days of 1941 and early 1942, as the Japanese swept into the Pacific and across Asia, American, British, Dutch, and Australian forces were all engaged in various parts of the Pacific. Although there existed a certain amount of cooperation between these widely disbursed forces, Eisenhower was convinced that no amount of voluntary cooperation would allow them to function at "maximum efficiency." The area of operations was too vast, the forces involved too complex. Some one individual, he believed, should be in command of all land, sea, and air forces in the region. In a long memorandum to Marshall, he noted that the "strength of the allied defenses in the entire theater would be greatly increased through single, intelligent command."[21]

The ARCADIA Conference between American and British military leaders was going on in Washington when Eisenhower wrote that memorandum. At the December 28 meeting, with the conferees having already agreed to create the Combined Chiefs of Staff (CCS) to run the war at the highest level, Marshall argued that unity of command at the theater level was absolutely essential.[22] The British, however, were unenthusiastic. They viewed the American proposal as novel and untested. Moreover, the idea that British forces might serve under American command, or that officers of one service might find themselves subordinated to officers of another, seemed to them quixotic at best.[23] Then too, there were the political aspects of such a proposal to be considered. A theater commander, especially an American with that much power, might take it upon himself to interfere in Britain's political affairs, for example, those in sensitive India. President Roosevelt had made no secret of his anticolonial sentiments; and the subcontinent was restive. Britain would certainly not want American military men mucking about in its internal affairs. All things considered, the British preferred a command structure in which autonomous local commanders reported to the CCS where decisions on strategy and tactics could be worked out. This was, as Eisenhower described it on more than one occasion, command by committee, and was in his judgment the antithesis of sound military practice.

Marshall and Eisenhower left that meeting aware that convincing the British to accept unity of command was going to be difficult. In an attempt to make the case, Eisenhower drafted instructions to a hypothetical supreme commander for the Southwestern Pacific Theater of War. This document created unity of command but carefully circumscribed the power of the theater commander in both the military and political spheres. The purpose of these rigid restrictions, Eisenhower wrote, was to convince the British that unity of command posed no threat to their imperial interests and that "great profits would result" militarily from such an arrangement.[24]

By using Eisenhower's draft instructions and recommending a British general, Sir Archibald Wavell, for the command, Marshall was able to convince the British to go along. Eisenhower was pleased. "Good start," he remarked in his diary, "but what an effort. Talk-talk-talk."[25]

Eisenhower confronted a similar problem when, following the collapse of the Wavell Command, he became involved in efforts to establish a unified command for the entire Pacific Theater. In this instance, however, difficulties arose as a result of internal differences between the Army and Navy. The original plan called for a single Pacific Theater commander. It soon became clear, however, that General Douglas MacArthur, the ranking Army general in the area, would not subordinate himself to a naval commander. The Navy was just as reluctant to place its Pacific operations under MacArthur's command. As a result, two theaters of operation were created. The one in the Central Pacific was commanded by Admiral Chester Nimitz, and a second one in the Southwest Pacific was headed by General MacArthur.

This compromise was far from satisfactory. Later in the war, as Allied forces converged upon Japan and the geographic area in which American forces operated shrank, the weakness of this arrangement became apparent. The Army-Navy conflict meant that two commands could not be collapsed into one. Washington was forced to bow to MacArthur's ego, the Navy's insistence on independence, and the growing influence of the AAF. The result was an unsatisfactory compromise in which Admiral Nimitz was placed in command of all naval forces, MacArthur controlled Army ground forces, and General Carl Spaatz commanded the strategic bombing campaign. Co-

ordination of land, sea, and air activities became a matter of voluntary cooperation, which was often illusory.[26]

The Anglo-American dispute over unity of command took on a new urgency in 1942 as preparations went forward for an assault on Hitler's Fortress Europe. In May, while in London on an inspection trip, Eisenhower
attended a meeting of the CCS at which the main order of business was a
discussion of the command organization for the French invasion. Eisenhower insisted that "single command was essential and that committee
command [which the British favored] could not conduct a major battle." He
did not get very far with this line of argument, however, and left the meeting
aware that the British remained wedded to their own views. "It is quite apparent," he wrote, "that the question of high command is the one that is
bothering the British very much and some agreement, in principle, will have
to be reached at an early date in order that they will go ahead wholeheart-
edly to succeeding steps."[27]

On returning to London several weeks later, Eisenhower discovered that
"little if any real progress" had been made "in the formulation of broad decisions affecting the operation as a whole." In an off-the-record conversation,
General Paget of the British Army told him: "If we could only have the organization you have here, we could settle these matters in a morning. As it is
we constantly go over the same ground and no real progress has been
made." At that point, Eisenhower reported to Marshall that he took it upon
himself to force "decisive action."[28]

In 1942, British doubts notwithstanding, Eisenhower was appointed supreme commander of Allied forces in the Mediterranean Theater of Operations. His experience in heading up Operation TORCH, the invasion of
North Africa, convinced him that a unified command was essential to the
success of modern military operations.

During TORCH Eisenhower learned not only from his success, but also
from his own early inability to exercise complete control over air operations, a failure that proved costly to the ground forces. AAF doctrine held
that the primary purpose of the air arm was to secure control of the air and
carry out the strategic bombing raids that air enthusiasts believed would
bring victory in war. It is not much of an exaggeration to state that the airmen believed land operations were a waste of time and resources, that victory could be achieved through air operations alone. It comes as no surprise,
then, that tactical air support for ground forces was a low priority as far as
the airmen were concerned but high on the list of services that ground commanders expected. Because of AAF indifference, Eisenhower's ground
forces took heavy losses in Tunisia during the early stages of the North Afri-

can operation. Though AAF cooperation improved during the Italian campaign and once the Allies landed in France, this problem persisted to the end of the war.[29]

Despite the overall success of TORCH, the British remained opposed to the unified command concept. At the Casablanca Conference held in January 1943, Prime Minister Winston Churchill and his military advisors convinced President Franklin Roosevelt to endorse their method of command for the upcoming operations in Sicily and Italy. Ike simply refused to accept this. He informed Marshall that he considered attempts by the CCS to interfere with his subordinates "a definite invasion of my own proper field" and that "no attention will be paid to such observations." "It is my responsibility," he went on, "to organize to win battles."[30] Ike did not confront the problem directly, however. Instead he found ways of circumventing the CCS. "Through his own efforts—by force of his own personality and by the internal administrative arrangements he perfected," one historian has written, "he created the unified command organization that the CCS had denied him in a formal directive."[31] This was the last time during the war that the British or anyone else challenged Eisenhower's judgment on this matter. Unified commands had proven themselves.

Beyond his commitment to unity of command, Eisenhower also believed that teamwork was essential to a successful military operation. This view was the product of his military education as well as personal experience. At West Point he was taught to consider himself part of a system that was larger than any individual. Taking the German General Staff as its model, the Army sought to instill in its officers the view that they were replaceable and interchangeable. Leaders would naturally emerge. It was the team, not the individual, that was important. Eisenhower never forgot these lessons, which were reinforced by his experiences on the football field. As a star player for West Point until a knee injury put a premature end to his career, and later as a successful football coach, he learned and learned again the vital importance of teamwork.[32]

During the war Eisenhower faced two major obstacles as he worked to establish the sort of team he envisioned. First, Britons and Americans had to rise above their innate national prejudices. Second, soldiers, sailors, and airmen had to set aside their parochial views, learn to think of their services as part of a larger whole, and come to trust and rely upon one another. His solution to these problems was to bring the members of his staff into constant, intimate contact with each other. He wanted his people to "think war, plan war, and execute war twenty-four hours a day, or at least all of our waking hours." In this way trust and a team spirit were forged. Those who would not or could not adjust were weeded out.[33]

Eisenhower's efforts paid off. In 1942, with the North African campaign under way he confided to his diary that "through months of work we've rather successfully integrated the forces and the command staffs of British and American contingents." "Every element of my command—all United States and British services—are working together beautifully and harmoniously."[34] Later, Eisenhower recalled that at first "officers of the two nationalities were apt to conduct their business in the attitude of a bulldog meeting a tomcat." Over time, however, their "discoveries of mutual respect and friendship developed a team that in its unity of purpose, devotion to duty, and absence of friction could not have been excelled if all its members had come from the same nation and the same service."[35]

In September 1943, Lord Louis Mountbatten, who had just been appointed Supreme Allied Commander for the Southeast Asia Theater of War, asked Eisenhower's advice on how to organize his new command. The general's long, detailed response serves as a brilliant summation of his mature thinking on the subject. It is notable that first and foremost he emphasized the importance of breaking down the suspicions and distrust that inevitably divided men of different nationalities and services. Genuine "unity in an allied command," he wrote, "depends directly upon the individuals in the field." This, he said, involved "the human equation," which the theater commander had to deal with on a daily basis. "Patience, tolerance, frankness, absolute honesty in all dealings, particularly with all persons of the opposite nationality, and firmness, are absolutely essential." Because new problems inside a command grew up like mushrooms, he wrote, *the thing you must strive for is the utmost in mutual respect and confidence among the group of seniors making up the allied command.*"[36]

As far as organizational structure was concerned, Eisenhower assumed Mountbatten would have three commanders in chief under his overall command, one for air, one for ground forces, one for naval elements. The theater commander's job was to set the objectives his subordinates were to achieve and to be certain they had the requisite resources to do the job. Committed to decentralization at the operational level, he believed the theater commander should allow each of his subordinates a "great degree of independence in his own field." The system could not work any other way, which was why it was so important that all members of the team trust and have confidence in one another.

This did not mean that the theater commander had little or nothing to do. On the contrary, strategic coordination public relations, logistics, civil affairs, communications with the CCS—all of these functions and more were his responsibility.[37] Eisenhower admitted that his description of a theater commander in no way approximated the popular image of a military leader, but neither was he "a figurehead or a nonentity." He was "in a very definite sense the Chairman of a Board" with "very definite executive responsibilities." Ike recognized that the administrative structure he described did not always run smoothly. However, an alternative such as the British system in which several autonomous commanders in chief reported to the CCS, itself a committee of equals, was unworkable. Unified commands were not perfect, but they functioned. If the gears of the machine sometimes ground, it was up to the theater commander to use his "personality and good sense" to get things back on track and "make it work."[38]

Eisenhower's wartime experience directly influenced his thinking regarding the form that America's postwar military establishment should take. If Britons and Americans could shed their nationalist prejudices and service loyalties to join together under the sheltering umbrella of a unified command structure, certainly the same should be true of American officers operating in a peacetime environment and separated only by service distinctions. If unity of command worked well at the theater level, it would, in his judgment, prove even more useful at the national level where he envisioned replacing the War and Navy departments with a single department, an umbrella cabinet-level agency that controlled three subordinate coequal units—the ground, air and naval forces.[39]

Eisenhower was not the only one thinking these thoughts. On the contrary, on November 3, 1943, General Marshall put a plan before the JCS that called for the creation of a single cabinet-level department that would have responsibility for national defense. The Army, Navy, an independent air force, and a general supply agency would become subordinate units under a single secretary of war. A general staff made up of four chiefs of staff would be headed by a "Chief of Staff to the President" who would outrank the other members of the JCS and have ultimate decision-making authority. In this way the JCS would be transformed from a committee of equals where unanimous agreement was required into a body that could take expeditious decisions.[40]

Marshall made his proposal because in numerous ways the JCS had been unable to resolve service differences, even under the pressure of wartime conditions. The result, he contended, had been waste, duplication, and inefficiency. The Marine Corps, for example, had grown from a tiny force of some 25,000 men with a limited role to become a duplicate army of 500,000 officers and enlisted personnel with its own tactical air units. The Navy and the AAF remained caught up in a fierce dispute over the Navy's insistence on operating long-range land-based aircraft. The Army and Navy were at odds because the Navy refused to operate troop transports. Marshall concluded as a result of these and numerous other difficulties that a system that had functioned badly in wartime would not function at all once peace was restored. If something was not done before the end of the war, he feared that the armed forces would once again find themselves in the same institutional muddle that existed prior to Pearl Harbor.

Marshall's unification proposal was also intended to avoid a repetition of the situation that pertained during the interwar period when the Army fared so badly in the battle of the budget. Marshall assumed that if the services were combined in a single department, the secretary of that department would strive to create a balanced military establishment, and that budgets would be designed so that each branch would have the wherewithal to carry out its assigned roles and missions. He deplored "the present system, or lack of system" wherein "two separate executive departments compete for annual appropriations." The nation's security was a "single problem," he said, and could not "be provided for on a piecemeal basis." Congress "should have the opportunity of passing on a balanced program that makes provision at one and the same time for all the needs of the armed forces." National security, in his judgment, demanded a properly funded military establishment in which land, sea, and air forces were all closely integrated.[41]

Marshall might have achieved unification at or even before the end of the war but for the Navy's continued opposition. After Admiral King blocked action at the JCS level, the War Department took the issue to Congress but was again thwarted. With the war still to be won, a special House subcommittee chaired by Representative Clifton Woodrum of Virginia decided against taking any action. Instead, on learning firsthand of the deep divisions that separated the armed services, the committee suggested that the JCS undertake a special study of unification, the results of which could be used to guide Congress at war's end.[42]

The JCS Special Committee for Reorganization and National Defense (the Richardson Committee), which traveled some 18,000 miles in all theaters of war to survey opinion, interviewed Eisenhower in 1944, not long after the Normandy invasion. Not surprisingly the Supreme Commander strongly endorsed service unification and the creation of a chief of staff of the armed forces. These changes, he said, would "promote efficiency in combat operations and . . . avoid unconscionable duplications involving unnecessary expense both financially and in manpower." A strong advocate of strategic air power, he was particularly insistent that the AAF should be made into an independent and coequal branch of the service. One of the major lessons of the war, he thought, was "the extraordinary and growing influence of the airplane in the waging of war." Air power alone could not win victories, but, he said, "no great victory is possible without air superiority."[43] Ike also made the point that the prewar policy of developing separate budgets for the Army and Navy simply would not do. National security would depend upon integrated planning that took into account the needs of all the services. Therefore, service budgets should be developed "as a whole through a combined body and approved by the President."[44]

Characteristically, Eisenhower also emphasized the importance of keeping the cost of the military establishment under control. For that reason if for no other, he believed that the functions to be performed by the separate services, their roles and missions, should be carefully delineated in order to avoid waste through overlap. He correctly predicted that once the wartime emergency was over Congress would revert to its prewar patterns, sharply reducing its support for the military. Therefore, the only way to retain a respectable peacetime military establishment was to convince the public that it was a sound investment and that public money was being used wisely. It was "mandatory," he told the committee, "that economy be made the watchword of the whole effort."[45]

Eisenhower's views, widely held in Army and AAF circles, were also popular at the time among many naval officers. For example, both Admirals Chester Nimitz and William "Bull" Halsey, when interviewed by the Joint Committee, endorsed unification. Nimitz was quite specific, telling the committee: "I favor a single Secretary of the Armed Forces with a complete elimination of civilian secretaries for Army, Navy, and Air Force." It would be better, he said, "to have a single Commander of Armed Forces who has all the authority and responsibility for issuing a directive."[46] The idea of unifying the armed services was so widely accepted that Eisenhower later claimed he had met no one who opposed it until the fall of 1945 when he returned to the United States.[47]

Its exhaustive work done, the JCS Special Committee for Reorganization and National Defense divided 3–1 in favor of a plan that was in many ways similar to the one originally proposed by General Marshall, with air, naval, and ground forces becoming coequal parts of a single cabinet-level department. Admiral James Otto Richardson, the chairman of the committee and the lone holdout, filed a brief minority report in opposition. Richardson was especially concerned by the thought of so much power concentrated in the hands of a single chief of staff and was strongly opposed to the creation of an independent air force.[48]

Only days after the majority and minority reports were presented to the JCS, the details of the majority report were leaked to Hanson Baldwin, syndicated columnist of the *New York Times,* who published the story under the headline "Front Leaders Approve Army-Navy Merger." Noting the extraordinary efforts the committee had made to sample opinion in all theaters of war, Baldwin quoted "informed sources" as indicating that in general the opinion of those surveyed was "remarkably favorable." Baldwin specifically mentioned Eisenhower, Douglas MacArthur, and Admirals Nimitz and Halsey as all favoring unification.[49]

The report and the Baldwin story came as a stunning surprise to Admiral King, who strongly opposed unification. He blocked an AAF attempt to publish the report in its entirety, challenged its reliability by claiming that Admirals Nimitz and Halsey had been misrepresented, and saw to it that Rear Admiral M. F. Schoeffel, the Navy representative on the Joint Committee who had joined with two generals in drafting the majority report, was sent far from Washington to sea duty in the Pacific.[50]

Admiral Nimitz, had not been misunderstood by the committee. He had simply been out of touch with the political situation as it was developing in Washington, and with the views of Admiral King and the Navy hierarchy. On returning to the United States he reversed himself, telling Congress: "I now believe that the theoretical advantages of such a merger are unattainable, whereas the disadvantages are so serious that it is not acceptable. For this change of opinion I make no apology, since it represents my conviction based on additional experience and further study of the proposal and its current implications."[51]

Because Admiral King refused to endorse the majority report of the Joint Committee, the JCS was for a second time unable to make a recommendation. This was not the end of the matter, however. Unification was a popular idea both with the public and in Congress where it was thought vast savings might result if the services could be made to operate more efficiently. It also had the unswerving support of the Army and the AAF. It is not surprising, then, that once the war had ended, the fighting between the Army, Navy, and AAF erupted in earnest.

On October 17, 1945, the Senate Military Affairs Committee opened hearings on two bills, each calling for the unification of the armed services. Predictably, the hearings made front-page news with important generals and admirals, whose names had only recently been associated with great wartime victories, now trading verbal punches. General Marshall and Secretary of War Robert Patterson, himself a winner of the Silver Star and the Distinguished Service Medal for heroism during World War I, both made strong statements in support of reform. Patterson denounced the "waste" as well as the "conflict, overlapping, and duplication" that had characterized the procurement policies of the War and Navy departments during the war. Patterson claimed that "billions" could have been saved if instead of two departments competing for resources there had been "a single Department of the Armed Forces." The lesson of the war, he continued, was that the services "must operate as a single team under single direction which has responsibility and final power of decision over all."[52] Marshall was especially critical of the way the JCS functioned, pointing out how difficult it was to make decisions because of the requirement for unanimity among the chiefs. Even under the "stress of war," he said, the JCS did not function well. At times, agreement had been reached only after "long delays" and "numerous compromises." Marshall feared that in peacetime, "without the impetus of war," even this level of cooperation would prove impossible. He also deplored the current approach to budgeting in which the services testified before separate congressional committees regarding their financial needs. Not only did this place them in a competitive rather than a cooperative environment, but it also denied Congress the opportunity to pass "on a balanced program that makes provision at one and the same time for all the needs of the armed forces."[53]

Later in the hearings General J. Lawton Collins, deputy commanding general and chief of staff of the Army's ground forces, brought before the committee the War Department's plan for the unification of the services. In his autobiography Collins makes the point that this proposal, which was similar to Marshall's earlier plan, was not intended to create a single service "but to integrate the management of the three autonomous services. . . . The Navy would retain its Fleet Air Arm and Marine Corps, but the land-based Air Forces would achieve parity with the Army and Navy for the first time."[54]

Secretary of the Navy James Forrestal, the first witness to testify in opposition to unification, had long since decided that the Navy could not afford to simply oppose reform. In September 1944, he told "King, Nimitz and Company that as of today the Navy has lost its case and that either in Congress or in a public poll the Army's point of view would prevail." He concluded, therefore, that the Navy could not "be in the position of merely taking the negative in this discussion, but must come up with positive and constructive recommendations" that nevertheless preserved the Navy's autonomy, its air arm, and the Marines.[55]

The proposal that Forrestal now placed before Congress was in large measure based on the work of Ferdinand Eberstadt who had, at the secretary's request, produced an apparently plausible alternative to unification. An old school chum and business associate of Forrestal, Eberstadt had considerable credibility in Washington, having served as chairman of the Army-Navy Munitions Board and vice chairman of the War Production Board. More to the point, however, he also happened to be a former vice president of the Navy League, a fiercely partisan organization, which since its founding in 1902 had lobbied hard on behalf of the Navy.[56]

Working with a staff of about two dozen naval officers, Eberstadt produced a 251-page report that rejected unification, writing that it was an ineffective panacea for what ailed the national security establishment. Contrary to the Army's argument, he insisted that cooperation among the services had been excellent during the war. What the country really needed, he wrote, was a greater degree of coordination between military and foreign policy planners. Basing his thinking on that assumption, Eberstadt designed a national security establishment that was intended to fracture the Army-AAF alliance while preserving the Navy's autonomy. The Eberstadt Plan rejected the idea of a single chief of staff on the ground that such a job was beyond the capabilities of any single individual. Similarly, it dismissed the idea of a single unified department. Instead, it called for three separate, autonomous departments, the Army, the Navy, and an independent Air Force, each with its own cabinet-level secretary. Where once there had been two competing services, Eberstadt would create three. Under the Eberstadt plan the military services, the State Department, and those agencies responsible for mobilizing the country's human and material resources, as well as the scientific and intelligence communities, would all be brought to work together through a number of committees, the National Security Resources Board, the Munitions Board, the Central Intelligence Agency, and the National Security Council. The last of these was to function as an umbrella agency "for maintaining active, close and continuous contact between the departments and agencies of our government responsible for our foreign and military policies and their implementation."[57]

In essence the Eberstadt Plan created an elaborate system of interlocking joint committees with no command structure at the top. The three military departments would have equal representation on the committees and unanimous agreement would be required before any recommendation could be passed on to the president. The armed services would remain independent of one another, their roles and missions unclear and overlapping. As before the JCS would be leaderless, unable to arrive at decisions when unanimity proved impossible. In only one significant way did the Eberstadt proposal differ from what Forrestal proposed to Congress. The Navy secretary was not yet willing to endorse the creation of an independent air force.[58]

Eisenhower, who was about to replace Marshall as the Army's chief of staff, and who had been monitoring these developments from his post in Europe, disagreed with virtually every aspect of the Eberstadt Plan. He rejected as absurd the idea that had so many naval officers in an uproar, that somehow if the services were unified in a single department the Navy would be "swallowed up." He had commanded land, sea, and air forces in the Mediterranean and northern Europe and, he insisted, his "viewpoint has been as much naval and as much air as it has been ground." Success in war, he insisted, depended upon being able to coordinate the activities of all three. Otherwise, he wrote, "our operation would have failed." He recalled how difficult it had been early in the war with "each service fighting for itself and its requirements and quite certain that no one else was concerned in them." The services had to learn to cooperate in peacetime so that if war came they could immediately begin to function as a well-oiled machine. There would be no time for the services to find "by experience that the others regard it as a friend and part of the team rather than one of the enemies in the operation."[59]

Eisenhower blamed the system that kept the services separate and distinct for the difficulties he and other theater commanders had encountered in developing a cooperative spirit. When men in the different services spent the majority of their careers isolated from one another, he observed, "it is pretty difficult to develop . . . team play." He was particularly critical of the service academies where interservice rivalry and competition were overemphasized. "If I had my way," he told one congressional committee, "I would trade classes between Annapolis and West Point." At some point in the curriculum, he thought, each class ought to be required to spend a year at the other school. Young officers needed to be taught that their first loyalty was to "the Government of the United States, this Nation, first of all," not to their branch of the service.[60] All sides had to "get it into our heads that no one of these services is complete within itself—to the other two, the whole program of preparation must be a balanced one." War required teamwork, "and teamwork is not possible among people that [sic] are mutually suspicious."[61]

On November 12, 1945, Ike, who emerged from the war as the most popular military figure of the century, flew into Boston to a hero's welcome. After a busy day that included participating in the city's annual Armistice Day parade, a press conference, a formal dinner, and a speech before the American Legion's annual convention, he boarded a train for Washington.

Two days later, in a Senate hearing room jammed to overcapacity by reporters and interested bystanders, he testified before the Military Affairs Committee in support of the unification of the armed services. His remarks made
the first page of the *New York Times* and left the Navy looking like the pro-
verbial "dog in the manger."[62]

Eisenhower told Congress that during the war "hard experience" had
proven "that the nation's security establishment is . . . a single fighting team,
composed of three services each supplementing the other in proper balance." Unity of command had not been achieved quickly or easily. At Pearl
Harbor in December 1941, he noted, unity of command had not been the
rule and the result had been one of the greatest military disasters in this nation's history. Referring to his own difficulties in gaining control of air operations during the early stages of the North African campaign, he observed
that he too had problems to iron out before a unified command was established, and that these had to be dealt with during actual operations "when
lives were at stake." "In my opinion," he continued, "those difficulties grew
directly from the traditional separation of the Army and Navy, which is the
inevitable outcome of the present organization of our military departments.
Separation at the top necessarily fosters separation all along the line."[63]

Because Eisenhower testified weeks after the hearings had begun, he
had the opportunity to rebut many of the arguments put forward by those
who opposed unification. Thus, for example, Forrestal, Eberstadt, and others had claimed that War Department estimates notwithstanding, there was
no proof that unification would save money, that it put too much power in the
hands of a single secretary, that it created an overcentralized system that no
single cabinet-level secretary could control, and that the proposal to create a
general staff headed by a presidential chief of staff smacked of "Prussianism." Eisenhower rejected all of these arguments. In comparing the Eberstadt Plan with the War Department's proposal, he estimated that given
unification "you could develop a more efficient fighting force . . . with 75%
of the men that you would have if you had separate forces." "With integration," he said, "we can buy more security for less money. Without it we will
spend more money and obtain less security." Nor could he accept Forrestal's
claim that a single secretary would be unable to manage the entire military
establishment. If that were true, he pointed out, "no man has the capability
to assume the Presidency." He noted that he himself had commanded
5,000,000 men and women in the land, sea, and air forces of not one but several countries during the war. As for the claim that unification smacked of
"Prussianism," Eisenhower thought that was absurd. In fact, he noted, one
of the great weaknesses of the German war machine was its distinct lack of

unity. "One of the major contributing factors to the Nazi defeat was the utter lack of unified direction over the Luftwaffe and the Wehrmacht, both in the Mediterranean and in Europe."[64]

Eisenhower had not been back in the United States long before he concluded that the issue would not soon be resolved. Passions had been aroused. Emotions ran too deep. Convinced that nothing could be accomplished as long as the unification question was before the public, he told friends in the Navy: "As far as I am concerned, in public I keep my mouth shut. From now on we talk about this among ourselves."[65]

Though the hearings before the Senate Military Affairs Committee continued for another month, when they recessed nothing had been resolved. The battle over unification was entering its second year and still there was no legislation on the books. Yet Eisenhower held to his vow of public silence. In a letter to Navy Secretary Forrestal, he remarked: "So far as unification is concerned, I have been for a long time stubbornly insistent on my right to keep my mouth shut." He had spoken his mind, he said. He would say no more in public.[66]

Ike meant what he said. If unification was to come about, he felt certain the terms of an agreement would have to be worked out privately, by direct talks among service leaders. As army chief of staff he hoped to calm jittery nerves and create the environment of mutual trust that was essential if the national security establishment was to begin acting like the team he envisioned. In a sense Eisenhower believed he was revisiting problems he had encountered as supreme commander of Allied forces in Europe. In this case, however, it was the armed forces of the United States that would have to learn to live together in harmony.

NOTES

1. *New York Times* (hereafter cited as *NYT*), 26 Sept. 1952.

2. Ibid.

3. Ibid.; entry for 18 Oct. 1951, Robert A. Ferrell, ed., *The Eisenhower Diaries* (New York: Norton, 1981), 201–203.

4. Entry for 10 March 1933, Eisenhower's "Red" Diary, the Kevin McCann Papers, Box 1, Eisenhower Library (hereafter cited as EL).

5. Eisenhower to the President of the Philippines, 8 Aug. 1940 (drafted in 1939), Whitman File, Eisenhower's Papers as President, Box 10, EL. For more on Eisenhower's fiscal views, see Herbert S. Parmet, *Eisenhower and the American Crusade* (New York: Macmillan, 1972), 36.

6. For a copy of NSC 68, see Department of State, *Foreign Relations of the United States, 1950* (Washington DC: GPO, 1975), 1:234–92. See also John

Lewis Gaddis, *Strategies of Containment: A Critical Appraisal of Postwar American Security Policy* (New York: Oxford University Press, 1982), 89–126; Saki Dockrill, *Eisenhower's New Look: National Security Policy, 1953–1961* (New York: St. Martin's Press, 1996), 19–47.

7. Eisenhower to Baruch, 30 June 1952, Whitman File, Administration Series, Box 5, EL; Baruch to Eisenhower, 30 June and 4 July 1952, ibid. See also Gaddis, *Strategies of Containment*, 133; Fred Kaplan, *The Wizards of Armageddon* (1983; reprint, Stanford: Stanford University Press, 1991), 176.

8. Ibid.; *NYT*, 26 Sept. 1952.

9. Charles J. Hitch, *Decision Making for Defense* (Berkeley: University of California Press, 1965), 13.

10. Demetrios Caraley, *The Politics of Military Unification: A Study of Conflict and the Policy Process* (New York: Columbia University Press, 1966), 58. For a description and analysis of how the Army deteriorated in the years after World War I, see Forrest C. Pogue, *George C. Marshall: Education of a General* (New York: Viking, 1957), 3: 203–20. See also Russell F. Weigley, *A History of the United States Army* (New York: Macmillan, 1967), 396–404.

11. Stephen E. Ambrose, *Eisenhower: Soldier, General of the Army, President Elect, 1890–1952* (New York: Simon and Schuster, 1983), 1:131.

12. Forrest C. Pogue, *Marshall: Organizer of Victory* (New York: Viking, 1973), 4:299–300; Curtis W. Tarr, "Unification of America's Armed Forces" (Ph.D. diss., Stanford University, 1962), 64–69.

13. The JCS was established by order of the president and without legislative sanction. The president's purpose was to create an organization that would be able to deal on equal terms with the British Chiefs of Staff. In this regard it is important to note that the members of the JCS had to be in unanimous agreement before any policy could be implemented.

14. Tarr, "Unification," 69; James F. Schnabel, *The History of the Joint Chiefs of Staff* (Wilmington: Michael Glazier Inc., 1979), 1:239–40. Anticipating disagreements between the Army and Navy, Marshall tried to convince President Roosevelt to appoint a chairman for the JCS who would have the power to decide issues when the services could not agree. Roosevelt was not enthusiastic about this idea. Ultimately, he did appoint Admiral William D. Leahy to be chairman of the JCS, but he refused to grant him the power Marshall believed essential. See Pogue, *Marshall: Organizer of Victory*, 298–300.

15. Senate Committee on Military Affairs, *Hearings on S. 84 and S. 1482, Department of the Armed Forces, Department of Military Security, 79th Cong., 1st sess.,* 17 October—17–December, 1945 (Washington DC: GPO), 365–66: Schnabel, *History of the Joint Chiefs of Staff,* 1: 239–40.

16. Robert G. Albion and Robert H. Connery, *Forrestal and the Navy* (New York: Columbia University Press, 1962), 252–53.

17. Ferrell, *Eisenhower Diaries,* 47–48. Major General Fox Conner, West Point, Class of 1898, had served as G-3 at General John J. Pershing's headquar-

ters during World War I. See also Vincent Davis, *Postwar Defense Policy and the U.S. Navy* (Chapel Hill: University of North Carolina Press, 1965), 7.

18. Ferrell, *Eisenhower Diaries*, 50.

19. Henry L. Stimson and McGeorge Bundy, *On Active Service in Peace and War* (New York: Harper, 1947), 506.

20. For a brief description of the difficulties the Allies encountered in World War I, see Weigley, *History of the U.S. Army*, 419.

21. Eisenhower to Marshall, December 1941, in Alfred D. Chandler, Jr., Stephen E. Ambrose, Louis Galambos et. al., eds., *The Papers of Dwight D. Eisenhower,* 17 vols. (Baltimore: Johns Hopkins University Press, 1970—96), 1: 23–25. (hereafter cited as *EP*)

22. Eisenhower, memo for the file, 28 Dec. 1941, ibid.; see also Eisenhower to Marshall, 26 Dec. 1941, "Draft instructions to Supreme Commander, Southwestern Pacific Theater," ibid., 28–31.

23. Eisenhower to H. H. Arnold, 1 May 1943, ibid., vol. 2, 107.

24. Eisenhower to Marshall, 26 Dec. 1941, ibid., vol. 1, 26; see also Grace P. Hayes, *The History of the Joint Chiefs of Staff in World War II: The War against Japan* (Annapolis: Naval Institute Press, 1982), 47–52; Stephen Ambrose, *The Supreme Commander: The War Years of General Dwight D. Eisenhower* (Garden City: Doubleday, 1969), 25.

25. Eisenhower, diary entry, 2 Jan. 1942, *EP*, vol. 1, 35.

26. Hayes, *History of the Joint Chiefs of Staff,* 88–104; Eisenhower's memo to the JCS, 9 March 1942, *EP*, vol. 1, 176–80; Eisenhower to General George H. Brett, 10 March 1942, ibid. The inadequacies of this arrangement showed up immediately as there was no coordination between naval and AAF air operations over Japan.

27. Eisenhower to Marshall, 11 May and 30 June 1942, *EP*, vol. 1, 292, 366–68; Dwight D. Eisenhower, *Crusade in Europe* (Garden City: Doubleday, 1948), 67.

28. Eisenhower to Marshall, 30 June 1942, ibid., 366–67; Eisenhower to Connor, 4 July 1942, ibid., 369.

29. Eisenhower to Arnold, 1 May 1943, ibid., vol. 2, 1106–1107; J. A. Huston, "Tactical Use of Air Power," *Military Affairs* vol. 14: 1950, 167–68; Ambrose, *Supreme Commander*, 313. For more on Eisenhower's difficulties in controlling the AAF, see Max Hastings, *Overlord: D-Day & the Battle for Normandy* (New York: Simon and Schuster, 1984), 40–42, 269–71.

30. Eisenhower to Marshall, 8 Feb. 1943, *EP*, vol. 2, 944.

31. Ibid., xxiv; Ambrose, *Supreme Commander*, 163.

32. Ambrose, *Eisenhower*, 1:43–54.

33. Ibid., 80–81.

34. Eisenhower, diary entry, *EP*, vol. 2, 679.

35. Eisenhower, *Crusade in Europe*, 67.

36. Eisenhower to Mountbatten, 14 Sept. 1943, *EP*, vol. 3, 1420–24.

37. Ibid.

38. Ibid.

39. For a complete statement of Eisenhower's views, see Eisenhower to George, 25 July 1945, *EP*, vol. 4, 214–17; see also Eisenhower to Edward "Swede" Hazlett, Jr., 27 Nov. 1945, in Robert Griffith, ed., *Ike's Letters to a Friend* (Lawrence: University of Kansas Press, 1984), 28–31.

40. Caraley, *The Politics of Military Unification,* 24; Tarr, "Unification," 177.

41. Senate Military Affairs Committee, *Hearings on S. 84 and S. 1482,* 79th Cong., 1st sess., 50–51; Pogue, *Marshall, Organizer of Victory,* 364–65. AAF leaders supported Marshall's plan primarily because it called for the creation of an independent Air Force, co-equal with the other two branches of the service. This had been the goal of the airmen since the 1920s and the days of General Billy Mitchell.

42. Caraley, *The Politics of Unification,* 26–30; Albion and Connery, *Forrestal and the Navy,* 250, 259–60; Davis, *Postwar Defense Policy and the Navy,* 44.

43. Eisenhower to George, 25 July 1945, *EP*, vol. 6, 214–17.

44. Ibid.

45. Ibid.

46. Senate, Committee on Military Affairs, *Hearings on S. 84 and S. 1482,* 79th. Cong., 1st sess., 383–84. See also E. B. Potter, *Nimitz* (Annapolis: Naval Institute Press, 1976), 402. It is interesting to note that in 1953, after he had retired, Admiral Nimitz helped draft the 1953 reforms that in fact did much to advance the cause of unification.

47. Eisenhower to Hazlett, 27 Nov. 1945, *EP*, vol. 6, 555.

48. For a summary history of the work of the Joint Committee, including an analysis of the reasoning behind its recommendations, see JCS, 749/14, 30 May 1945, Records of the Joint Chiefs of Staff, 1942–1945, in CCS 040, Central Decimal Files, Box 20, Modern Military Branch, National Archives (hereafter cited as NA). A summary may be found in Caraley, *The Politics of Military Unification,* 35–36. For a brief description of the differences between Marshall's thinking and the committee's plan, see Eisenhower to George, 25 July 1945, *EP*, vol. 6, 215–16 n. 1.

49. Reprinted in the *Washington Post,* 3 April 1945.

50. Memorandum for the JCS, Serial: 4036, 8 May 1945, CCS 040, Central Decimal Files, Box 20, NA; JCS 749/19, 11 Sept. 1945, ibid.; JCS Info Memo 432, 25 Aug. 1945; Memorandum by Commanding General, AAF, 9 Sept. 1945, ibid.; Charles Sucey to General McFarland, 31 Aug. 1945, ibid. Admiral King also demanded an investigation into the leaking of the Joint Committee's report. See "Unauthorized Disclosures Concerning Pacific Command Directive and Special Committee Report," 11 June 1945, ibid.

51. U.S. Congress, Committee on Military Affairs, *Hearings on S. 84 and S. 1482,* 79th Cong., 1st sess., 383–84; *Time,* 26 Nov. 1945. Nimitz's quick turnabout cost him his credibility on the issue.

52. House, Committee on Military Affairs, *Hearings: Department of Armed Services, Department of Military Security*, 79th Cong., 1st sess., 9, 11, 14.

53. Ibid., 50–51; *Time*, 29 Oct. 1945, 29.

54. The Collins Plan called for the creation of a single department headed by a secretary of the armed forces. It also called for four subordinate agencies, the Army, the Navy, the Air Force, and an Agency for Common Supplies. Each service would have a chief of staff. There would also be a chief of staff of the armed forces. These four would sit as the Joint Chiefs of Staff. The four agencies would report to the secretary through the chief of staff of the armed forces, whose job it would be to bring clear, unambiguous advice to the secretary and the president. J. Lawton Collins, *Lightning Joe: an Autobiography* (Baton Rouge: Louisiana State University Press, 1979), 337; see also U.S. Congress, Senate, Committee on Military Affairs, *Hearings on S. 84 and S. 1482*, 79th.Cong., 1st sess., 155–180; Eisenhower to Marshall, 4 Oct. 1945, *EP*, vol. 6, 373 n. 1.

55. Forrestal to Hoyt, 2 Sept. 1944, to Walsh, 27 May 1945, Walter Millis, ed., in *The Forrestal Diaries* (New York: Viking Press, 1951), 60–61; Davis, *Postwar Defense Policy and the U.S. Navy,* 101. For a complete analysis of the thinking behind the Navy's opposition to unification see Caraley, *The Politics of Military Unification,* 87–108.

56. For more on the League, see Armin Rappaport, *The Navy League of the United States* (Detroit: Wayne State University Press, 1962).

57. U.S. Senate, Committee Print 1281, 79th Cong., 1st sess., 5–6. The Eberstadt Plan did not have the complete support of the Navy's hierarchy where opposition to an independent Air Force remained very strong.

58. Ibid., 99; *Time*, 5 Nov. 1945. Forrestal's strategy failed. When senators on the committee began questioning him about how the system of interlocking committees would work, he had no answers, saying only that the question was under study. *Time* concluded from this that "the Navy had no plan: it was just against the Army plan."

59. Eisenhower to Everett "Swede" Hazlett, 27 Nov. 1945, in Griffith, *Ike's Letters to a Friend,* 27–29.

60. U.S. Congress, House Committee on Expenditure in the Executive Departments, *Hearings on H.R. 2319*, 79th Cong., 1st sess., 299; see also Eisenhower to General Henry S. Aurand, 26 Dec. 1945, *EP*, 7: 681; Eisenhower to General Maxwell D. Taylor, 21 Aug. 1947, *EP*, 9:1886–87.

61. Eisenhower to Hazlett, 27 Nov. 1945, in Griffith, *Ike's Letters to a Friend*, 29.

62. *NYT*, 17 Nov. 1945; U.S. Congress, Senate, Committee on Military Affairs, *Hearings: Department of the Armed Services, Department of Military Security*, 79th. Cong. 1st sess., 359 –81.

63. Ibid.

64. Ibid.; *Time*, 26 Nov. 1945, 26–27. *Time* received Eisenhower's testimony with great enthusiasm while at the same time noting that the Navy "had no ade-

quate plan to replace or revise the present system of divided administration and command."

65. U.S. Congress, House Committee on Expenditures in Executive Departments, *Hearings on H.R. 2319*, 79th Cong., 1st sess., 289.

66. Eisenhower to Forrestal, 13 April 1946, *EP*, 7: 1001.

2

"Our Problem Should Be Solved on the Basis of What Is Best for National Security."

In December 1945, only days after Eisenhower was sworn in as army chief of staff, Representative Andrew J. May, chairman of the House Military Affairs Committee, introduced a bill that was intended to kill the War Department's hopes for unification. The bill called for the creation of an independent air force with a cabinet-level secretary and a new "United States Aviation Academy" but proposed no other reforms.[1]

The May bill was timed to take advantage of AAF frustration and crack the alliance between the Army and the airmen. AAF leaders supported the War Department's unification proposal because it promised coequal status with the Army and Navy under the rubric of a single cabinet-level department, and because they needed the Army's support to achieve their goal. However, by December 1945, Congress had demonstrated that unification was not going to come easily if it came at all. This led some AAF officers to conclude that the time had come to change tactics. As one of Air Force General Carl Spaatz's aides put it, unification might be "the desirable ideal but the coordinate position of air is of prime importance and a third department as proposed in the May bill will solve this and other pressing air questions." When Secretary of War Patterson publicly criticized the May proposal, this same aide advised Spaatz to enter a vigorous protest to Eisenhower and demand the right to express a separate AAF view in support of May's bill.[2]

AAF leaders including General Spaatz and Chief of Staff Henry "Hap" Arnold, who was then on the verge of retirement, no doubt sympathized with those who saw the May proposal as offering the long sought-after prize of service independence. They also had good reasons for cleaving the alliance with the Army. Immediately after moving to the Pentagon, Eisenhower acted to cement his relationship with the airmen. He met with members of the AAF staff and reiterated his commitment to them and to the principle that America's "fighting forces should rest on a three-legged stool, with each leg equally important: Navy, Army and Air Forces." On the next day he told his own staff that while there was much that could not be done until Congress passed unification legislation, he was determined to act "exactly as if we were going to have that law." Furthermore, he said, if legislative reform efforts failed, "we must go just as far as we can . . . to carry out the basic idea." Toward that end he announced that within the War Department "the Air commander and his staff" were to be considered "an organization coordinate with and co-equal to the land forces and the Navy."[3]

If Arnold and Spaatz believed they had a powerful and reliable friend in Eisenhower, they also understood that the fastest way to transform him into an opponent was to seek Air Force independence outside the context of unification. Eisenhower believed the only thing that could possibly be worse than having two autonomous military departments was to have three. If the AAF took the bait being dangled by Congressman May, the airmen had to face the possibility that Ike would ally himself with the Navy and use his vast prestige to oppose the proposal. He might well win, setting back the cause of Air Force independence for the indefinite future. It only made sense, then, to reject the May proposal and continue the fight for unification.

When the May bill came before the House Committee on Expenditures in the Executive Departments, the committee chairman, Carter Manasco, asked for the War Department's opinion of the bill. A letter approved by Eisenhower and AAF Chief of Staff "Hap" Arnold, and signed by Acting Secretary of War Kenneth Royall, opposed the May proposal and pointed out that the real question was "whether the most effective use of all our military arms can be obtained in three separate independent departments or in one under unified direction." The War Department, the letter continued, "is firmly convinced that maximum economy can only be realized through the unity of a single department."[4] Faced with the united opposition of all elements within the War Department, Manasco let the May proposal die in committee.

With the May bill out of the way, Eisenhower set out to see what could be done to improve relations with the Navy and perhaps achieve through direct talks some of the reforms he had hoped to bring about through unification. His first step, so very reminiscent of his management of relations between Britons and Americans during the war, was an attempt to stem the flood of derogatory, anti-Navy speeches, remarks, and comments coming from Army and AAF sources. Toward that end he issued a general order to all senior commanders urging them to "avoid" even "the appearance of criticizing a sister service." It was especially important, he explained, that "in preparing statements, issuing releases, citing examples and the like, complete impartiality between the services be maintained."[5]

Eisenhower, an enormously likable man, had what a reporter once described as an "absolutely unique ability to convince people that he has no talent for duplicity." Even Field Marshall Sir Bernard Montgomery, who so often disagreed with him, paid homage to Eisenhower's charm. Ike, he remarked, had "the power of drawing the hearts of men towards him as a magnet attracts the bits of metal. He merely has to smile at you, and you trust him at once."[6] Now Eisenhower tried to put these skills to use once again, hoping to make the new chief of naval operations (CNO), Admiral Chester Nimitz, his partner in an attempt to achieve needed reforms.[7]

Born in Fredericksburg, Texas, the son of a hotel keeper, Nimitz showed no early signs of interest in a naval career. In fact the service academy that first attracted his attention was West Point. Even this was a matter of happenstance, the result of a chance meeting with two young cadets who stopped at his mother's hotel on their way east. Following this encounter Nimitz sought an appointment at West Point. He ended up at Annapolis because there were no vacancies at the Military Academy and his congressman suggested the Naval Academy as an alternative.

Despite the rather circuitous route he took in arriving there, the soft-spoken Texan turned in a superb performance at Annapolis. Graduating seventh in a class of 114, he went on to a long and successful career in the submarine service and as a naval strategist. In 1939 as chief of the Bureau of Navigation, Nimitz handled a variety of major administrative problems associated with a rapidly expanding navy, in the process impressing the chief of naval operations, Admiral Harold Stark, Secretary of the Navy Frank Knox, and the president as well. Hardly a week after the disaster at Pearl Harbor, Knox gave Nimitz an extraordinary vote of confidence, dispatching him to Hawaii where he replaced Admiral Husband Kimmel as commander of the Pacific Fleet. Nimitz did not disappoint. He infused hope and confidence where despair had been the ruling emotion and went on as supreme commander in the Central Pacific to head the Navy's successful island-hopping campaign against the Japanese.[8]

Eisenhower was hopeful that together he and Nimitz could heal some of the wounds suffered during the recent clash over unification and bring about some essential reforms. In a letter to a close friend he described the new CNO as not only "a man of . . . ability and devotion to duty" but also "a friendly soul with whom it is a pleasure to work." He did not know, he wrote, whether Congress would pass a unification law, but, he continued, "I have no doubt that he and I will succeed in instituting a lot of reforms that are badly needed."[9]

Unfortunately, few of the collaborative efforts undertaken by Eisenhower and Nimitz turned out well. Consider, for example, a matter that greatly concerned Ike, the means by which the services were then attempting to coordinate their activities. The war, which created the need for collaboration on a scale never before imagined, saw the proliferation of joint boards, committees, and commissions on which Army, Navy, and AAF officers worked together to integrate the activities of the three branches. When the fighting stopped at least 170 of these ad hoc groups existed with more being established for the purpose of handling problems associated with demobilization.[10] For a variety of reasons these committees and boards functioned inefficiently when they functioned at all. In the first place officers assigned interservice responsibilities tended to give the greater part of their energies to their own service while allowing their work on the joint agencies to slide. Moreover, joint boards could produce results only when all sides agreed on a course of action, and agreement was difficult to achieve on issues that were of a sensitive nature to one or another of the services. Finally, on paper each of these boards and commissions reported to a "next higher joint superior" where at least theoretically decisions were to be made. In actual practice, Ike explained, "there is a vast field in which indecision and doubt prevail." As a result, important issues were often ignored and altogether too many routine matters were left in limbo. The situation was so confused, he wrote, that the service secretaries were often left in ignorance of important matters that directly concerned them.[11]

In Eisenhower's judgment unification offered the only sound solution to the enormous organizational problems the services faced. Of course the Navy was not willing to go that far. Nimitz did suggest, however, that they create a "Joint Secretariat" that would provide "coordinated supervision on all subjects in which the two Secretaries have a common interest." Ike told Secretary of War Patterson that he thought this a worthwhile proposal. Patterson, perhaps more suspicious of the Navy's purposes than Eisenhower, rejected the proposal. In the end all that Eisenhower and Nimitz could do was establish the Joint Committee of Ground, Air and Navy as a model "to show how all the various agencies engaged in joint work could be properly headed up so that . . . the whole work was properly organized and supervised." Creating a model that would serve as an example showed good intentions but was hardly a substitute for true reform.[12]

Sometimes, cooperative efforts failed because of opposition on the part of subordinate officers. This was the case with regard to a proposal Nimitz made for closer collaboration between Army Intelligence and the Office of Naval Intelligence. When the admiral first made his suggestion, Eisenhower jumped at the idea, assigning Major General Howard A. Craig to work with Admiral Thomas B. Inglis, director of Naval Intelligence, on the problem. Despite this promising start, by mid-summer the Army had given up on the idea. Eisenhower's deputy, General Thomas Troy Handy, more than hinted at the reason for this when he informed Secretary of War Patterson that it was both his and Eisenhower's view that "complete integration of Army and Navy intelligence activities cannot . . . be affected by anything short of unification." While progress had been made, Handy explained, "the development of a completely satisfactory system" would "take time and . . . have to be based on the development of a greater degree of mutual confidence and trust" than was currently the case.[13]

Even on issues less sensitive than intelligence gathering it sometimes proved impossible to get lower-echelon officers to cooperate. A case in point revolved around a pet idea that Eisenhower advanced throughout his career, the creation of a close connection between West Point and Annapolis. "War," Eisenhower wrote to his closest personal friend, Edward "Swede" Hazlett, Jr., "is a matter of teamwork, and teamwork is not possible among people who are mutually suspicious." Indeed, he argued, "perfect teamwork can be achieved only among friends." For this reason, he thought, "the closest possible kind of association among the" officers of the three services "is mandatory." That association ought logically to begin with the youngsters attending the service academies, but the exact opposite was the case. The academies encouraged an intense rivalry that generated a strong element of distrust. Communication between the two schools was virtually nonexistent, and once commissioned, the officers of each service went their separate ways. How surprising was it then that when called upon to work together later in life these same youngsters were unprepared?[14] He was convinced that "unless we start with our young 17 year old boys to promote the feeling that each of us is a member of our country's armed forces and not merely an exponent of some particular technical or specialized profession, we shall never succeed in developing the kind of unification that can give us the maximum in security with the minimum in cost."[15]

Eisenhower wanted to change the way in which young officers were trained. He thought the curricula of West Point and Annapolis should be as close to identical as possible and that West Point cadets ought to spend their third year at Annapolis while the midshipmen attended West Point. If the service academies coordinated their curricula and arranged for exchanges, he said, "[j]oint boards later on would have acquaintances and friends as their members, rather than rivals." He thought that even if unification was someday achieved, it would solve only part of the problem, that "the inter-mingling of the services during their educational years is a long term ap-proach. "[16]

Eisenhower also believed that each branch of the service ought to desig-nate a group of young promising officers in the thirty-to-thirty-five-age group "for general all around training and that these should be freely trans-ferred around among the three services." At about age fifty some of these, those obviously headed for high command, should be commissioned "offi-cers of the Armed Forces, completely severing connection with any particu-lar branch." The commanders of the future, he thought, should be those, "regardless of service, who have demonstrated a capacity to deal with sub-jects of the broadest scope; whose reputations and experience give proof that they will never forget for an instant the relationships existing between fighting forces in the field and the complex economic, political and social problems of the area in which they may be called upon to operate."[17]

During his term as army chief of staff, Eisenhower resolved to make a start toward the big changes in the training of officers that he envisioned. In 1946 he and Nimitz arranged for an exchange program in which cadets and midshipmen traded places for a few three-day weekends. In the following year students from the two schools participated in some combined amphibi-ous operations. That was as far as cooperation went. When Eisenhower pro-posed a full-scale exchange program for third-year students at the service academies, he hit a stone wall in the person of Admiral James L. Holloway, Jr., superintendent of the Naval Academy. A dedicated defender of the An-napolis tradition, Holloway rejected Eisenhower's proposal in a blunt re-sponse that left Ike fuming. According to a very angry Eisenhower, Holloway considered his idea "the ultimate in ridiculousness."[18] Even so, Ike refused to give up. Seven months after his run-in with Holloway he urged General Maxwell Taylor, the superintendent at West Point, to see what he could do to make the curricula for the second and third years at the academies "practically identical." He also suggested that Taylor see to it that "at least a few instructors from each academy" exchange places.[19]

Ike also made a stab at dealing with what was to become one of the most controversial inter service issues of the entire cold war era, the question of weapons development, which at the time was being carried on separately by each of the services. Virtually everyone of consequence in the War Department deplored the fact that those running Army research programs refused to collaborate with their Navy counterparts. Secretary of War Patterson noted that guided missile research, which was being carried on independently by the Army, Navy, and AAF, was an area of particular concern. Eisenhower agreed, admitting that "he just could not understand why the Army would not take advantage of Navy research and profit from it." He told the secretary that "time after time" he had "pushed joint action" and that he would try once again "with the idea of eliminating some of the present duplication."[20]

Nimitz and Ike did in fact join in an effort to encourage greater interservice cooperation in the field of research and development. The result was the new Joint Research and Development Board. Chaired by Dr. Vannevar Bush, former head of the wartime National Defense Research Committee, the board was charged with creating "a strong, unified, integrated and complete research and development program in the field of national defense." It was also supposed "to eliminate unnecessary or wasteful duplication or overlapping."[21] The new board had impressive-sounding responsibilities, but it had no power to affect changes or require cooperation. It could only make recommendations and these were not likely to be taken seriously when an individual service saw its interests threatened.

If Eisenhower had only the most limited success in addressing relatively minor matters of mutual interest with the Navy, he had none whatsoever when attempting to deal with those issues that motivated him to champion unification in the first place—the need for an integrated defense budget, balanced force levels, and a clear and precise definition of the roles and missions to be carried out by each of the services. These were questions the Navy was not prepared to discuss, insisting instead on its traditional go-it-alone approach.

In June 1945, in keeping with this tradition, and without informing the War Department, Secretary of the Navy James Forrestal submitted to Harold D. Smith, director of the Bureau of the Budget, a peacetime budget proposal for the 1947 fiscal year that called for a naval establishment of 659,880 officers and enlisted personnel including a Marine Corps of 110,000 men.[22] This was precisely the way business had been conducted before the war when the budget of each service was prepared and approved without considering the needs of the military establishment as a whole. Had Franklin Roosevelt, a notorious Navy partisan, still occupied the White House he might well have approved Forrestal's proposal. However, in the summer of 1945 Harry S. Truman sat in the Oval Office and he, along with

Budget Director Smith, viewed the Navy's budget as "entirely too ambi-tious and . . . utterly out of the question in relation to the total Government program."[23]

Truman made no response to the Forrestal proposal until August, after the first atomic bombs had fallen on Hiroshima and Nagasaki. He then for-warded it to the JCS with a set of extraordinary instructions. The chiefs of the three services were to evaluate the Navy's budget proposal in terms of the country's overall peacetime military needs and "in light of our interna-tional commitments for the postwar world, the development of new [nu-clear] weapons and the relative position of the services as a result of these factors." [24]

The president also asked the chiefs to produce a single integrated budget for the entire military establishment, one that would establish the size and composition of all the services and that took into account the effect new technologies, especially the atomic bomb and modern long-range aircraft would have on national needs. When Truman made that request public and announced that he was going to send Congress an integrated defense budget based on "necessity" and "cost," *Time* magazine immediately saw the sig-nificance of what he proposed. "This in itself," *Time* wrote, "was merger of a kind in advance."[25] Unification might not be a legislative fact in 1945, but Truman made it clear that for purposes of deciding upon postwar budgets and force levels he wanted each service to consider itself one element in a larger whole.[26]

Before returning from Europe, Eisenhower had taken the position that because the public was unlikely to support a large peacetime military estab-lishment, the Army and AAF should seek a small force of roughly 325,000 regular officers and enlisted personnel. These regular forces would be backed by a large trained reserve that was to be produced by a program of Universal Military Training that Congress had yet to create. In December 1945, however, he adopted an entirely different position, approving a budget that called for an army of 886,000 and a seventy-group air force with 400,000 officers and enlisted personnel. The total force would amount to 1,286,000.[27]

Eisenhower's change of heart was, no doubt, a result of a number of con-siderations. Above all, he was reacting to the fact that though months had passed since the president had made his requests, the JCS had made no progress in developing an integrated defense budget and the Navy was sticking to its June budget and force-level proposals. Ike considered the Navy's plan excessive and noted, too, that "there must be considerable du-plication and overlapping between the Army Air and Army Ground Forces on the one hand and the Naval Air and Marine Corps plans."[28] He was not going to propose a regular force of 325,000 for the Army and AAF while the Navy was pushing for a force twice that size. Given President Truman's call for a single integrated defense budget, interservice negotiations seemed inevitable. He wanted to enter those talks with a proposal that left room for bargaining and compromise.

To strengthen his negotiating position, Eisenhower decided that AAF and ground force budgets should be presented separately since that would "strengthen our position vis a vis the Navy, particularly its Air and Marine Corps plans." He also wanted air and ground force proposals to "parallel the Navy program, with service support for each and an indication of economies to be gained by common support of Air Ground and Navy." In this way, he hoped to expose the duplication and waste inherent in budgeting by service, strike a blow for unification, and perhaps convince the Navy to agree to joint planning.[29]

These hopes came to nothing. Budget negotiations between the services ended in frustration and deadlock. In the end the JCS simply bundled up the force level and budget requests produced by the individual services and sent them to the White House. The president would have to decide the size of the defense budget and how funds would be distributed. Before Truman made his final decision, Eisenhower reduced his request for ground forces by some 216,000 men and recommended a similar reduction in his estimate of AAF needs. Truman gave Eisenhower what he requested and cut the Navy's request by 27 percent.

On January 9, 1946, Eisenhower forwarded a memorandum to the other members of the JCS reminding them that in August the president had called for a "comprehensive plan" for the development of a postwar military establishment and that thus far nothing had been done. He also noted in this memorandum that costly duplications and overlap existed between the forces called for by War and Navy department planners. These, he pointed out, were the result of "separate interpretations by the services of their missions and roles" and that this problem would have to be dealt with before an overall strategic plan could be agreed upon. To resolve these difficulties he suggested that the problem be turned over to the Joint Strategic Survey Committee (the JSSC was the highest-level planning group in the JCS organization), which could clarify the missions of land, sea, and air forces, eliminate areas of duplication, describe the responsibilities of the War and Navy departments, and produce the integrated plan for the postwar military establishment that the president had requested.[30]

At first Admiral Nimitz and Admiral Leahy, who was at the time the titular chairman of the JCS, ignored Ike's memorandum, but they could not stall indefinitely. Eisenhower was, after all, calling on the JCS to respond to a long-standing presidential request. When Nimitz finally decided that he had no choice but to address this problem, he warned Eisenhower that there were bound to be issues about which the Army and Navy would not agree. He also pointed out that the services were still governed by policies described in *Joint Action of the Army and Navy*, the prewar policy statement that emphasized a high degree of independence for the separate branches and encouraged overlap. In plain English, he was saying that the Navy would not tolerate any attempt by the Army and the AAF to reduce to insignificance or do away with the Marine Corps or the Navy's air arm.[31]

For his part Eisenhower insisted that the services must be mutually interdependent and rejected the concepts sanctioned in *Joint Action of the Army and Navy* as outmoded doctrine. "Our problem," he said, "should be solved on the basis of what is best for national security; not by reference to documents, agreements and laws, many of which are either outmoded by modern developments or were instituted under emergency conditions." While denying that he intended the destruction of the Marine Corps, Eisenhower insisted that the Marines would have to be reduced in size as well as in the scope of their operations. He believed that the corps should be restricted to "small, readily available and lightly armed units, no larger than a regiment," and that its mission should be "to protect United States citizens ashore in foreign countries and to provide interior guard of naval ships and naval shore establishments." The Navy, he charged, had created what amounted to a duplicate army that should now be largely demobilized, leaving all future large-scale ground operations to the Army. Eisenhower offered similarly forthright though unacceptable proposals to the Navy with regard to the future of its air arm, which, he thought, should be confined to "ship, carrier, and water based aircraft" while the AAF assumed control of all land-based aircraft. He tried to resolve the question of which service was to control airborne antisubmarine operations by suggesting that the AAF assign land-based aircraft to the Navy for this purpose under the principle of unified command.[32]

In his long and barely civil response, Nimitz got to the heart of the dispute between the services when he remarked that the Navy could not accept as valid Eisenhower's "land, sea, and air principle of organization of the armed forces." He went on to charge point-blank that Eisenhower's purpose was to diminish the Navy by abolishing "an essential component of Naval Aviation which operates from coastal and island shore bases" and through the "elimination of the Marine Corps as an effective combat element." Nimitz even implied bad faith on Ike's part, charging that his proposals involved abandoning agreements "arrived at between the Army and the Navy from time to time over a period of more than twenty years and which have resulted in a responsibility for functions proven highly effective in World War II." The only thing Nimitz and Eisenhower were able to agree upon was that a further "exchange of papers on the subject of the missions of the land, naval, and air forces will serve no useful purpose."[33]

Eisenhower tended to dismiss Nimitz's fears regarding the intentions of the Army and the AAF as entirely unfounded. He claimed not to put any stock in the theory advanced by numerous naval officers that "some 'swallowing up' process would inevitably follow upon any closer unification of the services." He was personally certain, he wrote, "that no one wants it." If, however, "such a notion was alive somewhere," he continued, "I, for one, would battle it to the death. . . . One brother does not devour another; a guard on a football team is equally important with the tackle!"[34] Yet, while he vehemently denied any intention of destroying the Marines, his thinking regarding the future of the corps appeared to stop just short of that. Nor was Nimitz entirely off the mark in suspecting that the AAF sought to diminish the role of the Navy in the new postwar establishment. Many airmen, Jimmy Doolittle was one of the most outspoken, believed that the Navy was obsolete and that in the future national security would depend upon control of the air. Since funds were likely to be in short supply in peacetime, the Navy and the Army, too, would have to be relegated to subordinate roles while the lion's share of funding went to an independent air force.

Colonel W. Barton Leach was among the more calculating of those inside the Air Force to advocate this point of view. During the war and for several months thereafter, "Bart" Leach was attached to the Office of the Air Force Chief of Staff. In 1946 he returned to his position on the faculty of Harvard Law School but remained thereafter a frequent advisor to high-ranking Air Force officers. In a letter written early in 1946, he argued that achieving Air Force independence was only a first step toward guaranteeing that the Air Force would control the lion's share of the budget and have the capability to carry out its strategic mission. Once independent, he wrote, the Air Force should take dead aim at the battleship. The country, could not pay for both big planes as well as big ships. Therefore, if the Navy was allowed to build battleships, the Air Force was certain to be short changed, and in the next war the national security would depend on the Air Force. The Navy and Army would be reduced to virtual insignificance."[35]

Because the Navy would not willingly accept this diminished role, Leach wrote, it was essential that the Air Force establish public and legislative relations offices so that it might contend effectively with the entrenched power of the Navy. The Air Force had two interrelated responsibilities. The first was to prepare to carry out its strategic mission. The second was to begin at once a public relations program designed to convince Congress and the public to properly fund the air arm. This program should not be considered the product of narrow self-interest. On the contrary, "it was a public responsibility."[36]

Nor were AAF leaders in any doubt about the ultimate ambitions of the Navy. Leach believed that the admirals would soon realize that their "present weapons" were becoming obsolete. Their response, he predicted, would be to develop the Navy's own strategic bombing capabilities and compete with the Air Force for scarce budget dollars. The best way to prevent this, Leach argued, was to deny the Navy any role whatsoever in the operation of land-based aircraft. The future, he wrote, must belong to the Air Force.[37] Carl Spaatz, speaking before the Aviation Writers Association, put the same proposition this way: "The Unification fight resolves itself into one thing—whether the country is to have two Air Forces or one Air Force." He believed that the Navy intended to "develop air power under the Navy" and that "the fight is between those with entrenched organizational interest as against those [including himself] concerned with the security and defense of the U.S."[38]

In March 1946, with tensions between the services already running high, the situation was exacerbated by the impending publication of *The Case against the Admirals*, a book by Thomas B. Huie. A reporter, novelist, and former associate editor of *American Mercury Magazine*, Huie had served during the war as an officer in the Seabees. His book was a diatribe against all "ancient minded obstructionists," ground force generals and admirals alike, who failed to see that airpower had changed for all time the nature of warfare. Its focus was on the Navy's opposition to unification. In their blindness, Huie charged, the Navy brass had, prior to World War II, opposed the development of strategic air power, insisted on "the outmoded, wasteful, and inefficient dual organization" that existed when we entered the war, and obstructed efforts intended to create unified commands. Now, in the face of a clear need "for a single, progressive, economical and flexible organization for war," they were "shouting 'nothing has changed,' still putting command position before common sense." America, he wrote, "must demand a single, flexible, progressive war organization, supersensitive to scientific development, if we are to safeguard our nation in a restive world."[39]

Somehow Admiral Nimitz came into possession of galley proofs of Huie's book prior to its publication. He forwarded a brief synopsis of the work to Eisenhower hoping to enlist his help in an effort to block publication, since, he said, "the net result . . . will be harmful to both services and particularly unfortunate at this time when further evidence of disunity between the services can be used to our national disadvantage." Nimitz's appeal must have rung hollow to Eisenhower, considering all that had passed between them. In any event, he refused to become involved in an effort to kill the Huie book. He did, however, issue a stern warning to his subordinates, reminding them as he had often done in the past, that the War Department "does not approve of methods intended to discredit another service." In pursuing the objective of unification, he wrote, those under his command "must be objective, logical, and public minded." It was the job of the secretary and his aides to tell the Army's story to the public. "The job of the officer," he wrote "is not that of a political conniver!"[40] These were noble sentiments, but the fact is that low-down politics was the order of the day.

Ike's unwillingness to help block publication of *The Case against the Admirals* in no way deterred the Navy. Admiral Arthur Radford, the deputy chief of naval operations for air, first appealed directly to Huie to withdraw the manuscript. When he refused, the Navy's public relations division attempted to undermine Huie's credibility by warning potential reviewers that the book contained numerous serious factual errors, which in fact it did. At the same time, if the Washington rumor mill is to be trusted, the Navy put pressure on large book sellers not to stock the book.

While the Navy was working to destroy Huie's credibility, certain unnamed AAF officers provided money out of their own pockets to help promote his book. According to Demetrios Caraley, Army officers were also involved in this fracas. In *The Politics of Military Unification*, published in 1966, he claimed that officers "sent a copy" of *The Case against the Admirals* "to each congressman and congressman-elect under the guise that it came directly from the author, using letterhead paper that Huie had supplied for the purpose."[41]

The methods used by the Navy to undermine the effect of the Huie book, and the efforts of Army and AAF officers to promote it, brought neither side much credit. In his nightly news broadcast, commentator Eric Severeid observed that "the fight" between the services had "become more intense, more bitter than ever before." The whole issue of unification, "so extremely important to the nation, has been dragged down to a new, low level, and to a large degree is being conducted now by the methods and standards of cut-throat politics." It was, he thought, "a remarkable and disturbing spectacle." The "distrust and animosity" were so pervasive that it was "doubtful, at this late stage, if the firmest orders from service commanders or the commander in chief, can stop it." As Severeid saw it, the "one move that can put an end to" this vicious infighting "and resurrect the sense of common allegiance to the common authority, is action by Congress. No one knows whether they will decide for unification or against it; but what is required is a deci-sion—one way or the other."[42]

At the time Severeid made these remarks, President Truman was al-ready deeply involved in his own campaign to convince Congress to act. A colonel in the Army Reserve prior to the outbreak of World War II, the presi-dent had been a supporter of unification long before it became a national is-sue. During the war, while serving as the chairman of the Senate Special Committee to Investigate the National Defense Program, he gained inti-mate knowledge of just how wasteful and inefficient both industry and the armed forces were in the conduct of the war, knowledge that convinced him that unification was not just a good idea but a vital national interest. In 1944 he published an article in *Colliers Magazine* entitled "Our Armed Forces Must Be Unified" in which he detailed much that he had learned. In that same article he argued that the debacle at Pearl Harbor might not have oc-curred had the base been under unified command and that the disaster had come about at least in part because Army and Navy commanders there had not coordinated their activities. Truman was quite serious about this, telling White House counsel Clark Clifford "that if the Army and Navy had fought our enemies as hard as they fought each other, the war would have ended much earlier." "We must never fight another war the way we fought the other two." [43]

Clifford, a captain in the Naval Reserve, agreed with the president. Still, he did not hold out much hope for unification, which he later described as the president's "impossible dream." The Navy, with powerful friends in Congress, was certain to fight unification every inch of the way. That was especially the case since the president had already been identified in the minds of many, including Navy Secretary Forrestal, as "an Army man." A full month before Truman became directly involved in the unification de-bate, George Elsey, the president's assistant White House aide for naval af-fairs, informed Clifford that by and large ranking naval officers assumed that Truman "had developed prejudices against the Navy which cause him to disregard naval wishes and that he will force the Navy into a single department of defense which will be dominated by the Army and the Air Forces."[44]

Disregarding Clifford's fears as well as a warning from Postmaster General Robert Hannigan that he was involving himself in a political fight he might not be able to win, Truman sent a special message to Congress on December 20, 1945, that contained the outlines of a unification proposal that was similar in most respects to the Army's Collins Plan.[45]

The storm over the president's proposal broke early. "Uncle" Carl Vinson, the powerful chairman of the House Naval Affairs Committee, launched an immediate attack on Truman's proposal, telling reporters that "the very phraseology of the scheme smacks of the Germany of the Kaiser and of Hitler, of Japanese militarism." He even accused Truman of practicing "military power politics," that his real purpose was to "sink the Navy."[46] Georgia's powerful Senator Richard Russell, a man Truman deeply admired, was another prominent Democratic member of Congress who opposed the president's proposal. A less determined man might have been daunted by the formidable opposition that was forming, but Truman was not easily intimidated.

At the president's request Utah's Senator Elbert Thomas, chairman of the Senate Military Affairs Committee, drafted a unification proposal similar to the one Truman outlined in his December message to Congress. He then organized a subcommittee made up of himself, Senator Warren Austin of Vermont, and Alabama's Lister Hill. The subcommittee's job was to go over the draft and come up with a compromise proposal that would be acceptable to the Army, the Navy, and the AAF.

In an attempt to bring the warring parties together Thomas invited the Navy and War departments to each assign an officer to help draft a bill. Eisenhower and Secretary of War Patterson chose Major General Lauris Norstad, assistant chief for plans of the Air Staff, to represent the War Department. The Navy sent Admiral Radford. Very bright and totally opposed to both unification and the creation of an independent air force, Radford recalled his service on the committee without much pleasure. "I sat through hours of deliberation," he wrote, "with little or no opportunity to make constructive suggestions because the committee's collective mind was made up."[47] It was not quite as simple as that, nor as one sided. For four months the committee, aided by Radford, Norstad, Forrestal, Patterson, and Ferdinand Eberstadt sought a compromise solution.[48]

There was precious little chance of that. By early April 1946, it was clear that irreconcilable differences separated the Army and Navy. When the newspaper columnist, Joseph Alsop, contacted General Norstad about a piece he was writing on the unification controversy, Norstad remarked that "all discussions resolved themselves into a question of whether we were going to have a Single Department which we felt essential to achieve the principle of unification." "A Single Department under a Single Secretary," he told Alsop, "is clearly unacceptable to the Navy."[49]

The Thomas committee drafted nine separate versions of a unification bill in hopes of achieving a consensus, but without success. The Navy was having none of it. Finally, after three long months of debating the issues, Senator Thomas, General Norstad, and the other members of the subcommittee (save for Admiral Radford, who continued to oppose unification) met with the president at the White House, bringing with them a legislative proposal that was in many ways similar to the Army's unification plan. For an hour Truman and the subcommittee discussed the bill in detail. The president approved the proposal, promised his full support, and congratulated the subcommittee on a job well done. Subsequent to that meeting the Thomas bill cleared the committee and went to the full Senate.[50]

Not surprisingly, considering the effort that went into it, the bill did not include everything the War Department desired. Nevertheless, Eisenhower and Patterson both believed that it should receive unqualified support. If Army or AAF leaders began quibbling over details, the Navy was certain to argue that the War Department did not know what it wanted. Moreover, as Eisenhower pointed out, if attempts were made to change Senator Thomas's mind on certain issues, "there would be further delay of weeks," and any delay served the Navy's interest. There was no telling how long the public and the media would stay focused on the unification issue. It would be far better, he believed, to get the basic legislation on the books and "depend on later legislation or administrative procedures to get a few additions or subtractions." Aware that some officers had already entered objections or proposed changes to the bill, Eisenhower told a meeting of the War Council that he would "immediately stop officers from running up to Congress and talking gratuitously."[51]

Not long after the Thomas bill was sent to the Senate, Eisenhower was informed by a friendly member of Congress that "the Navy is going to have a friend on the Senate Naval Affairs Committee continue to delay passage of the bill in committee and on the floor." On April 30 that prediction came true when the Naval Affairs Committee, claiming jurisdiction over the Thomas bill on the ground that it involved naval matters, opened hearings. Using this friendly forum, the Navy launched a direct attack on the bill. In his testimony before the committee, Navy Secretary Forrestal pulled out all the stops, lambasting the proposal as a rehash of the Collins Plan while raising the dark specter of some future chief of staff using the vast powers that the War Department seemed willing to vest in him to create a military dictatorship. "I have deep misgivings about the danger of the concentration of such huge authority in the hands of one military man as S. 2044 entrusts to the Chief of Staff," he said. "By dominating the Secretary of Common Defense and the Joint Staff—as S. 2044 would permit him to do . . . he could mold military and perhaps national policy to suit his ends."[52]

Admiral Nimitz and a number of other high-ranking naval officers joined Forrestal in the attack. In his testimony General Alexander A. Vandegrift, commandant of the Marine Corps, went so far as to charge that the real purpose of those who advocated unification was to take control of the military out of civilian hands. He also stated in the baldest terms that "the enactment of S 2044" would "in all probability spell extinction for the Marine Corps," which, he said, "stood as a continuing affront to the War Department General Staff."[53]

When Vandegrift's testimony reached Eisenhower, who was at the time on an inspection tour in the Far East, he exploded in anger. It was a bald-faced lie to allege that the Army was attempting to take control of the military out of civilian hands. Every unification proposal, from Marshall's 1943 plan to the Thomas bill clearly maintained civilian control of the military through the president and a cabinet-level departmental secretary. The charge that the Army "General Staff," a euphemism that pointed directly to him as army chief of staff, was out to destroy the Marine Corps, was even more infuriating. Before the war the Marine Corps had been a force of about 25,000 men. The way Ike saw it the Navy had taken advantage of a wartime emergency to create a duplicate army that it was now unwilling to demobilize, even though it intruded on the Army's basic mission. How dare Vandegrift charge him with seeking to destroy the Marines when it was the Corps and the Navy that were at fault?

Eisenhower denounced the general's statement as "an attempt to confuse the issue by setting up a straw man." He "distorts and completely misrepresents the facts and gratuitously injects" into the discussion "extraneous and misleading matters." Some on Eisenhower's staff urged him to issue a public statement refuting Vandegrift's charges. For a time Eisenhower toyed with the idea of doing just that. In the end, however, he was unwilling to engage in a name-calling match with Vandegrift. Instead he decided to hold the high ground. Nor did he want any of his officers to go public. "[U]nder no circumstances," he wrote, "should the Army dignify such an attack by defending itself or disclaiming the motives charged by Vandegrift by resorting to profitless argument." At the same time, because that was the sort of thing politicians did, he urged staff members to recruit a friendly member of Congress to make a speech exonerating the Army.[54]

This byplay between Eisenhower and Vandegrift, while reflective of how bitter relations had become, was really beside the point. The fundamental fact was that by the end of the first week in May 1946, the Thomas bill was, to use an appropriate metaphor, sitting dead in the water. The administration and the Army were taking a political drubbing. It was not just Republican lawmakers who raised objections. Powerful Democrats, loyal to the Navy, were unwilling to support the proposal and the president's own secretary of the navy was publicly at odds with him.

Even so, the president had no intention of giving up the fight for unification. On the contrary, in early May, still hoping to come up with an acceptable proposal before Congress adjourned, he assigned Clark Clifford the seemingly thankless task of attempting to arrange a compromise between the services. Clifford was no doubt wondering where to begin when Admiral William B. Leahy told him that an agreement might be possible if the president was willing to make an initial concession. In his December 19 message, Truman had called for the creation of a chief of staff of the armed forces who would outrank the service chiefs and would serve as the principal military advisor to the president and the secretary of the new department. If the president abandoned that part of the plan, Leahy thought it possible that a settlement could be hammered out.

Clifford immediately went to work attempting to convince the Army and the AAF that the chief of staff's position was not "the crux of the matter," that the establishment of a single department was far more important.[55] Eisenhower, who was out of the country at the time, was not immediately consulted. On the evening of May 7, Clifford and Assistant Secretary of the Army for Air Stuart Symington had a long conference with General Norstad, the AAF representative who had participated in drafting the Thomas bill. Reluctantly, Norstad agreed that he would not allow "the Chief of Staff's position to stand in the way of the early attainment of unification." With Norstad and Secretary Patterson on board, Clifford then recommended that the president convene a conference at the White House that would include the secretaries of war and the navy, as well as a few key officers. At that meeting he could ascertain exactly what the areas of agreement and disagreement were, decide those issues, and, acting as commander in chief, "direct all services to support one position."[56]

Truman agreed to the meeting but was not yet prepared to force the issue. Instead, he opened the meeting by stating that his primary purpose was to end the "acrimonious inter-service disagreement" that was so damaging to the national interest. Then, in what had all the appearances of a staged performance, he announced that he had decided to drop his call for a single military chief of staff, which he now said "was too much along the lines of the 'man on horseback' philosophy." Patterson then told the president that while he did not entirely agree he was not going to "jump into the ditch and die for the idea."[57] With that obstacle out of the way Truman then instructed Patterson and Forrestal to draft a statement in which they identified areas of agreement and disagreement and submit it to him by May 31.[58]

The question then became whether Eisenhower and the Army would go along with the concession the president was offering to the Navy. Ike believed that ultimately a chief of staff would have to be appointed if the military establishment was ever to function efficiently, but he was ready to face facts. It was time, he told his deputy, General Thomas Troy Handy, to recognize "that the essentials . . . we are seeking" are "to establish the Air Force in its proper niche and to secure decisions rendered by a single authority." True unification, he now concluded, was not going to be won in a single campaign. Rather, he correctly foresaw that for "some years minor modifications will have to be sought from Congress in whatever bill may be passed."[59]

No doubt Truman hoped that Forrestal and Patterson would now find ways of resolving their differences without any further interference on his part. However, they remained deadlocked on the fundamentals—the future of the Marines, the Navy's air arm, an independent air force, and the need for a single department for defense. Clifford later recalled that when he brought this news to the Oval Office, the president "all but snorted in annoyance and contempt." He also decided that the moment had arrived to force a settlement.[60]

At a June 4 White House meeting, Truman heard all the arguments once again and announced that because the services were unable to resolve their differences "he would personally accept the responsibility for deciding the organization of the Armed Forces which was best for the United States and which the United States would support."[61] Eisenhower and Patterson immediately promised their support no matter what he decided. On the Navy side Nimitz offered a similar pledge. Though reluctant, Forrestal, who viewed the president as hopelessly prejudiced against the Navy's point of view, added his voice to those who promised to cooperate.[62]

On June 15, Truman wrote to Forrestal and Patterson. In this letter (copies of which went to chairmen of the key committees in the House and Senate) he pointedly thanked them for pledging to support him as he sought to compromise their dispute. He also detailed his decisions regarding four points that, he somewhat disingenuously argued, were still at issue. Truman announced that he was abandoning the idea of a single military chief of staff and took the Navy's position regarding the future of the Marine Corps, which would remain a relatively large fighting force of division-size ground units with its own tactical air units. On the other hand, he came down in favor of an independent air force, which would control all land-based planes regardless of function, and again asserted his commitment to a single military department headed by a cabinet-level secretary.[63]

As soon as Patterson received Truman's letter, he contacted Eisenhower suggesting that they acknowledge the president's letter and endorse his decision. In hopes of putting pressure on the Navy, he also thought that arrangements ought to be made with the White House to have the correspondence published. Eisenhower quickly agreed, no doubt hoping, as Patterson did, that Forrestal and Nimitz would be obliged to send a similar pledge.[64] When no letter was forthcoming from Forrestal, Truman called him to the White House. He wanted to know why.

Clark Clifford recalled that the meeting was anything but friendly. Forrestal, he wrote, entered the Oval Office "with tight lipped grimness, . . . accused Patterson and Eisenhower of using 'steam roller tactics,' and said he was totally opposed to the idea of a single Department of National Defense." Forrestal's diary entry tells a somewhat different story. He did accuse Eisenhower and Patterson of "steam roller tactics" and made it clear that he and Admiral Nimitz would insist on the right to oppose elements of any bill "that did not correspond with what the Navy viewed as its basic interests." He also warned the president that certain elements within the Navy were fanatical on the issue of control of land-based aircraft for use in anti-submarine warfare. He did not entirely close the door on a single department, telling the president that he would reluctantly support a proposal for a single secretary of national defense if that official had little or no real power. The essential point, he said, was that he must be "free to run his own Department without kibitzing from above." Finally, just as Clifford alleged, he did threaten to resign if his conditions were not met.[65]

Truman was probably tempted to let Forrestal go then and there, but that, Clifford later observed, "would have turned Forrestal into a martyr and doomed hope for military unification on any basis." So, he contended, the president began "a slow, patient, and skillful strategy designed to move Forrestal as far as possible without losing him." The way to deal with the Navy, he felt, was to negotiate with Forrestal. "It was the right strategy." [66] Along the way the president was, of course, required to make concessions, but Forrestal too gave ground. He agreed to the creation of an independent air force, something the Navy hierarchy still ardently opposed, and gave in on the creation of a single department headed by a secretary of common defense. How much power this new cabinet-level secretary would wield, however, remained unclear.[67]

While Truman negotiated with Forrestal, Clifford spent as much time as he could spare with Eisenhower, "trying to gauge his willingness to compromise." He was rewarded for his efforts when, at a dinner hosted by Assistant Secretary of War for Air Stuart Symington and his wife, Ike told the president's aide that "after all the difficulties he had encountered during World War II," he believed in unification "with all his heart." However, he recognized the "power and determination" of the Navy and would therefore accept a good deal less than he would like "in order to get the reform process started." [68]

In July, with the congressional session drawing rapidly to a close, President Truman announced that he had abandoned hope for the enactment of unification legislation during that session. Assuming that this marked the end of the fight, the Press Association wire service called the president's action "a prime victory for the Navy Department and its leaders."[69] "Hap" Arnold, writing from retirement in Northern California, could not have agreed more. He thought unification no longer a feasible option. Arnold based his thinking not only on the president's recent announcement, but also on the facts that a reorganized Congress would have David Walsh, a fierce Navy partisan and former chairman of the Senate Naval Affairs Committee, as the head of a new integrated Senate Armed Services Committee, and that Carl Vinson would head a similar committee in the House. At the same time, Arnold noted that there existed widespread support for an independent air force and urged his old friend, Carl Spaatz, who had taken over as air force chief of staff, to seriously consider seeking that option. Spaatz agreed that prospects for unification appeared grim. He also knew that the president had not yet given up the fight. Spaatz's strategy was to let the unification fight play itself out over the next several months. If, as he suspected, it proved impossible to get another bill out of committee, that would be the time to propose as a compromise a single department.[70]

A few weeks after this exchange of views between Arnold and Spaatz, Forrestal informed the president that at the next session of Congress he intended to introduce a unification bill that included only the few peripheral points already formally agreed upon in negotiations between himself and Patterson.[71] The secretary's announcement, which may well have been an attempt to back away from more important concessions offered in private talks between himself and Truman, prompted the president to call a meeting of all the players in this frustrating game for the following day. At that meeting Truman got things off to a fast start by announcing that he wanted an agreement soon and that everyone was to "let their hair down" and say what needed to be said. Once the terms of settlement had been agreed upon, he added, Admiral Leahy and Clifford would draft legislation that would then be submitted to Congress.[72]

Eisenhower and Patterson came to this conference aware that only a weak bill had any chance of gaining the Navy's support. Eisenhower had already admitted in conversations with Clifford that he believed the reform process was going to take years, during which time legislation would be periodically reviewed and changed. Patterson, therefore, opened the discussion on a conciliatory note, indicating his willingness to accept substantial limits on the powers of the new secretary of common defense, just as Forrestal had earlier required. However, Forrestal, terribly intense, did not seem to notice that he had just won an important concession. In what Clifford recalled as an irrational display of pique, he insisted that the secretary's functions "be strictly limited in scope, with no real authority over the services." He then once again warned the president that he would not support any bill "which did violence to my principles," and that if the administration produced such a bill he would resign.[73]

Truman, no doubt angered by Forrestal's repeated threats of resignation, nevertheless restrained himself. Clifford had warned him that something like this might happen and that it was important to keep Forrestal on board. So the president held his temper, remarking dryly that he "expected no such necessity need arise."[74]

Before proceeding further, Forrestal, intensely distrustful, wanted to spell out the duties of the secretary of common defense.[75] Eisenhower, however, convinced that this would only lead to further conflict, suggested that it might be a mistake to attempt this prior to the enactment of legislation establishing the office. Since all sides at least agreed that a single department would be created, why not leave the details to be worked out later?[76] In an attempt to calm Forrestal, who grew agitated at this suggestion, he added that he could not imagine "that the Navy need fear any actions following such legislation that would impair its ability to perform its mission."[77]

Clifford, witnessing this near disastrous meeting, thought he saw in Eisenhower's proposal, the work of a master conciliator. However, Forrestal saw only trickery and told the general point-blank "that the Navy did have deep apprehensions as to what would happen to it under such a plan as the War Department has proposed." He also told Ike that the Navy "did fear that the Marines would be subject to great restrictions and that the Navy would be denied the use of the means to carry out the missions which only it fully comprehended."[78]

That meeting ended with no resolution of the differences between the armed services. Bitter interservice wrangling continued for the remainder of the year with the Navy continuing to insist on firm assurances that the Marine Corps would have a major combat role and that the Navy could continue to operate long-range land-based aircraft.[79] The president had already conceded on the question of the Marine Corps. AAF leaders, fearing that the Navy had its own ambitions in the field of long-range strategic bombing, were unwilling to surrender the second point.[80]

Negotiations dragged on into January, 1947, at which time Eisenhower and Patterson decided to concede all remaining matters at issue. There were at least two good reasons for this. First, if a bill was not submitted soon to Congress there would be little chance of passage before 1948, far too late given the national security needs of the country as the cold war intensified. Second, Eisenhower was deeply concerned by the anger that prevailed on all sides. Had it been possible to achieve real unification, he might have been willing to continue the fight, but the compromise then being considered fell far short of that goal. Given the fact that the services found themselves in "a controversy of which the intensity seemed to be out of proportion to anything warranted," one that was "colored by fears, by prejudice, and in many instances by traditional jealousies," he thought that restoring good will would be "more conducive to efficient operations than is any mere organizational detail."[81]

On January 3, while riding back from a cabinet meeting, Patterson made exactly this point to Forrestal, expressing his concern over the intense feelings the unification fight had engendered. He thought that if "officers went down to testify in a mood of bitterness and hatred, they would do serious damage to the services and to national defense." To avoid that, he said, the Army was prepared to be "flexible" on the subjects of the Marines and the Navy's use of land-based aircraft. Forrestal was impressed with both the tone and substance of Patterson's remarks, noting in his diary that the conversation "was in an entirely different key and tenor than any talk I've ever had before with Patterson."[82]

Over the next few days Army and Navy representatives resolved their remaining differences and drafted a letter to be signed by the two service secretaries agreeing on terms of a legislative proposal. One of the last issues to be decided had to do with the roles and missions of the services. The Navy, still concerned about the future of the Marines and its air arm, would have preferred to see these spelled out in detail in the legislation. The Army and AAF believed, to quote Lauris Norstad, "that such action would freeze the military establishment in the mold of World War II, that it would dictate obsolescence in the Armed Forces *and that you can't possibly get agreement on the subject between the services anyway* [italics added]." Reluctantly, the Navy agreed that the roles and missions of the services would be loosely defined in an executive order to be drafted by service representatives and signed by the president immediately following enactment of the law. Unlike binding legislation, an executive order could be changed from time to time with relative ease.[83]

On January 15 Forrestal and Patterson announced that they had reached agreement on a legislative proposal.[84] The bill itself was forwarded to Congress on February 26, 1947. Borrowing heavily from the Navy's 1945 Eberstadt Plan, the bill created a National Military Establishment (NME) made up of three independent services headed by a single cabinet-level secretary of national defense. However, the new secretary had no administrative authority. Moreover, aside from three assistants, he had no staff and therefore lacked the capacity for independent analysis. He might, depending upon his political skills, be able to play the role of arbiter when conflicts arose among the services, but he was not to be a true policy maker. The bill also created the Council of National Defense, the National Security Resources Board, and the Central Intelligence Agency. The War Council, made up of the secretary of national defense, the service secretaries, and the service chiefs, would "concern itself with matters of broad policy" relating to the armed forces. The departments of the Army, Navy, and Air Force became subordinate units of the NME. They were to be administered by secretaries who did not have cabinet-level rank but who did sit on the National Security Council and who, along with members of the JCS, had the right to appeal over the head of the secretary of national defense to the president and Congress when they disagreed with the actions of the secretary. As for the JCS, that body remained unreformed. It would have no chairman and would be unable to arrive at decisions except by unanimous agreement.

Arriving at an agreement on the terms of the bill had been a nightmare. At length, having progressed this far, all sides agreed that nothing should be allowed to stand in the way of passage. The names of those witnesses who would be sent to testify before Congress were agreed upon in advance. To be certain that the testimony was uniformly supportive, it was also agreed that no one who spoke would propose any changes in the carefully crafted measure.[85]

Despite his own belief that the bill was terribly inadequate, Eisenhower testified on its behalf. However, he refused to hide his disappointment, making it clear that he had only abandoned his commitment to a single military chief of staff and what he conceived to be real unification because of the astonishing level of opposition the idea encountered. Nor was he prepared to state that he believed the plan then before Congress was going to produce positive results. In fact, he argued, time might finally demonstrate that a single chief of staff with decision-making authority was essential.[86] He further disturbed troubled minds when he remarked that the single most important aspect of the bill was that it placed the armed forces under a single civilian head.[87] Though he realized how powerless the new secretary of national defense would be, he looked to him to fill the role he had at first envisioned for a chief of staff. "[T]he broad powers of the secretary," he said, "will provide the one great element of a modern security structure which is markedly absent in our present organization. That is flexibility." The new secretary of national defense, he argued, would "constantly bring to our ever-changing problems, involving the three services, solutions applicable to the time and conditions. Without such single direction we tend to become compartmentalized into fixed forms and practices that always grow more rigid with time."[88]

The Navy's leaders had fought tenaciously to be certain that the new secretary's powers would be severely limited. They wanted a captive administrator, not one with broad powers. Now, Eisenhower raised the specter of control from above all over again. So, too, did Under Secretary of War Kenneth Royall, who also made a statement in favor of a strong secretary with the power to "allot functions to meet changing conditions" and "prescribe in the light of changing conditions the method of performing those functions and services which support them."[89]

The testimony given by Eisenhower and Royall reignited the fear on the part of some in the Navy that even the weak proposal then before Congress might provide the basis for an attack on the Navy's air arm and the Marines. Thus, when General Vandegrift, commandant of the Marine Corps, testified before the Senate Armed Services Committee, he violated an interservice agreement by proposing changes in the bill. The general urged Congress to protect the Marines by clearly describing in the legislation the roles and missions of the Marine Corps.[90]

"[F]urious at Vandegrift's insubordination," Clark Clifford telephoned Forrestal and demanded that he "rein in the Marines." Forrestal, angry himself, blamed Eisenhower and Royall, who, he said, had "reawakened the Navy's fears."[91] To make the point that threatening to tamper with the Marine Corps was political dynamite, Forrestal invited Clifford to meet with a number of influential senators including Leverett Saltonstall of Massachusetts, a leading Republican, Millard Tydings of Maryland, a Democrat and a firm supporter of the Army's position, and the Virginia Democrat Willis Robertson. At that luncheon meeting Clifford pointed out that what Vandegrift was demanding violated an agreement made earlier between Forrestal and Patterson. He did not get far before Saltonstall interrupted to remark: "The Marines occupy a unique and singular place in the hearts of the people." "Don't fool around with them." Tydings agreed. "This is not a matter of logic, but emotion," he said. "These are the boys who took Mount Suribachi. . . . The American people will never forget them or let them down." Clifford left that meeting convinced that "unless some additional concession" was "given to the Marines, the whole bill could blow up in our face." The bill was therefore amended to give the Marines as well as the Navy's aviators what they wanted. Their roles and missions were defined in considerable detail in the law.[92]

Shortly before final enactment of the National Security Act of 1947, Eisenhower confided to his diary his disgust with the so-called unification law. "The proposal for such a move aroused the most intensive campaign of special interest that I have seen in Washington," he wrote. "Some services were apparently so unsure of their value to the country that they insisted upon writing into the law a complete set of rules and specifications for their future organization and duties." "Such freezing of detail in an age that is witnessing the most rapid and significant scientific advances of all history, he went on, "is silly, even vicious." [93] Nor was Eisenhower at all optimistic about the future. He told his long-time friend, General Walter Bedell Smith, that because of "prejudice, lack of understanding, and out right self-seeking," he expected the military to go through a prolonged period of "doubt, indecision, and practical bewilderment." What made him angriest was the "particular character of . . . the opposition." "So many things," he thought, had been "placed above the welfare of the country."[94]

Real unification remained Eisenhower's ultimate hope. He predicted that the new organization would fail and hoped that "as changes are needed possibly even the supporters of special interests can be made to see the necessity." [95]

One can readily understand Eisenhower's feelings. Even beyond his losing battle against the Marines, he had many reasons to be displeased. First, he doubted that the new system of committees and councils created under the law would function any more efficiently than had the older wartime committees. Second, because the law preserved the autonomy of the services, competition rather than cooperation was likely to remain the rule. Third, the unreformed JCS system was inadequate to meet America's security needs in the postwar world. Finally, the Army had come out of this long struggle the big loser, for now it would have to compete for resources against not one but two glamour services, the Navy and the Air Force.

NOTES

1. *New York Times* (hereafter cited as *NYT*), 11 Dec. 1945.

2. R. P. to Spaatz, 14 Dec. 1945, Papers of General Carl Spaatz, Box 266, Manuscript Division, Library of Congress (hereafter cited as LC). See also Leach to Smith, Papers of General Lauris Norstad, Box 33, Eisenhower Library (hereafter cited as EL).

3. Eisenhower's memorandum to his staff, 10 Dec. 1945, in Alfred D. Chandler, Stephen E. Ambrose, Louis Galambos et al., eds., *The Eisenhower Papers*, 17 vols. (Baltimore: Johns Hopkins University Press, 1970–1996), 7: 609–16 (hereafter cited as *EP*). See also Eisenhower to Spaatz, 21 March 1947, ibid., 8:1617.

4. Royall to Manasco, 17 Jan. 1946, copy in Norstad Papers, Box 33, EL; see also Leach, memorandum for General Smith, 12 Jan. 1946, ibid.

5. Eisenhower to Nimitz, 24 Dec. 1945, *EP*, 7: 703 n. 1.

6. Quoted in Robert A. Divine, *Eisenhower and the Cold War* (New York: Oxford University Press, 1981), 3–7.

7. Eisenhower to Hazlett, 9 July and 27 Nov. 1945, in *Ike's Letters to a Friend*, ed., Robert Griffith (Lawrence: University of Kansas Press, 1980) 26, 30.

8. E. B. Potter, *Nimitz* (Annapolis: Naval Institute Press, 1976), 8–9.

9. Eisenhower to Hazlett, 25 Jan. 1946, *EP*, 7:786–87.

10. Eisenhower to Patterson, 28 Jan. 1946, ibid., 796–97n.

11. Ibid., 795.

12. Ibid.

13. Eisenhower to JCS, 17 Dec. 1945, ibid., 642; Eisenhower to Vandenberg, 13 Feb. 1946, ibid., 862–63; Handy to Patterson, 1 Aug. 1946, ibid., 863 n.; Eisenhower to Nimitz, 29 Dec. 1945, ibid., 696–99.

14. Eisenhower to Hazlett, 27 Nov. 1945, in Griffith, *Ike's Letters to a Friend*, 27–31; see also Eisenhower to General Henry S. Aurand, 26 Dec. 1945, *EP*, 7:681. Ike thought bringing academy cadets into intimate contact "such a fundamental requirement that whenever I have spoken on the subject I have tried to show that mere mechanical integration at the top is only a start toward the objectives we are seeking." See also Patterson to Brown, 20 Jan. 1947, Robert Patterson Papers, Record Group 107, Box 6, Modern Military Branch of the National Archives, College Park, MD (hereafter cited as NA). Patterson agreed with Eisenhower on the merit of exchange programs between West Point and Annapolis.

15. Eisenhower to Gary, 13 Jan. 1949, *EP*, 10:427.

16. Eisenhower to Nimitz, 30 Jan. 1947, ibid., 8:1467–68; Eisenhower to Taylor, 21 Aug. 1947, ibid., 9:1886–87.

17. Eisenhower to Eberstadt, 20 Sept. 1948, *EP*, 10:208–12 n. 27.

18. Eisenhower to Nimitz, 30 Jan. 1947, ibid., 8:1468.

19. Eisenhower to Maxwell Taylor, 21 Aug. 1947, ibid., 9:1886–88. When Taylor proved just as disinterested as Holloway in Eisenhower's ideas, he stamped Taylor's reply "File and forget!" but he never did. See ibid., 1888n.

20. Minutes of a meeting of the War Council, 19 Sept. 1946, Robert Patterson Papers, Box 43, LC. The Navy was not interested in a collaboration. See Eisenhower to Nimitz, 26 June 1946, *EP*, 7:1009.

21. Eisenhower to JCS, 31 Dec. 1945, *EP,* 7:707–708.

22. Vincent Davis, *Postwar Defense Policy and the United States Navy, 1943–1946* (Chapel Hill: University of North Carolina Press, 1965), 157; Michael Sherry, *Preparing for the Next War: American Plans for Postwar Defense, 1941–1945* (New Haven: Yale University Press, 1977), 93–94. Sherry makes it plain that the Navy more or less "arbitrarily" decided it could assume a budget of about $3 billion after the wartime emergency was over and crafted a budget to fit that figure.

23. For Budget Director Smith's views, see Smith to Manasco, 30 Jan. 945, in JCS 749/11, CCS 040, Box 20, NA. See also Sherry, *Preparing for the Next War*, 220; Davis, *Postwar Defense Policy and the United States Navy*, 15.

24. James F. Schnabel, *The History of the Joint Chiefs of Staff*, 6 vols. (Wilmington: Michael Glazier, Inc., 1979), 1:228.

25. *Time*, 3 Dec. 1945, 26–27.

26. Schnabel, *History of the Joint Chiefs of Staff,* 1:228.

27. Memorandum for the record, 12 Dec. 1945, American-British Conversations, 040 [2–Nov-43], Sec. 5 B, NA (hereafter cited as ABC 040).

28. Memorandum for the record, 26 Dec. 1945, ibid.

29. Ibid.; see also Eisenhower to General Henry H. Arnold, 24 Dec. 1945, *EP*, 7:679–80; Davis, *Postwar Defense Policy and the United States Navy*, 15.

30. Eisenhower's memorandum to the Joint Chiefs of Staff, 9 Jan. 1946, *EP*, 7:742–45.

31. Schnable, *The History of the Joint Chiefs of Staff*, 1:242.

32. Eisenhower's memorandum to the Joint Chiefs of Staff, 15 March 1946, *EP*, 7:927–32.

33. Nimitz to Eisenhower, 30 March 1946, J.C.S. 1478/12, Records of the Combined Chiefs of Staff, 370 [8–19–45], Sec. 4, and enclosure A, NA (hereafter cited as CCS 370)

34. Eisenhower to Hazlett, 27 Nov. 1945, in Giffith, *Ike's Letters to a Friend*, 28.

35. Leach to Smith, 29 Jan. 1946, Norstad Papers, Box 33, EL. Curiously, Leach ignored the significance of the aircraft carrier in this analysis. This, however, does not detract from his main point, which was that there would not be enough money to fund both a large Navy and a powerful strategic Air Force.

36. Leach memorandum for General Spaatz, 13 Dec. 1945, Spaatz Papers, Box 266, LC. For more Air Force statements regarding the obsolescence of the Navy see Davis, *Postwar Defense Policy and the United States Navy*, 147, 152–56.

37. Ibid.

38. Spaatz, remarks made by General Spaatz before Aviation Writers Association Dinner, 14 March 1946, Spaatz Papers, Box 266, LC. Just before the struggle over unification was settled in 1947, Forrestal denied that the Navy had any ambitions regarding the development of a strategic-bombing capability. See Walter Millis, ed., *The Forrestal Diaries* (New York: Viking Press, 1951), 223–24 (hereafter cited as Forrestal, *Diaries*).

39. William Bradford Huie, *The Case against the Admirals* (New York: E. P. Dutton and Co., 1946), 15.

40. Eisenhower to Hull and Collins, 9 March 1946, *EP, 7:909–10.*

41. Demetrios Caraley, *The Politics of Military Unification* (New York: Columbia University Press, 1966), 223; see also Symington to Forrestal, 15 March 1946, Norstad Papers, Box 33, EL. Forrestal queried Assistant Secretary of War for Air Stuart Symington about the possible involvement of AAF officers in supporting the Huie book. Symington told Forrestal that he had questioned almost everybody in the air staff and had been assured that no one in the AAF had contributed "advice or assistance in the writing of the book you mentioned." Symington, who was fiercely partisan, then remarked archly that an unnamed naval officer had only recently informed him of "the creation and functioning of an anti-unification organization, which we just can't believe true."

42. Eric Severeid, Transcript of News Analysis, 31 March 1946, in Spaatz Papers, Box 266, LC. For more on the Huie book, see also the *Chicago Daily News*, 24 Aug. 1946. A copy of this piece may be found in ibid.

43. Clark Clifford, with Richard Holbrook, *Counsel to the President: A Memoir* (New York: Random House, 1991), 146; for more on the Truman Committee, see David McCullough, *Truman* (New York: Simon and Schuster, 1992), 253–91; Harry S. Truman, "Our Armed Forces Must Be Unified," *Colliers Magazine*, 26 Aug. 1944, 16–17.

44. Elsey to Clifford, 23 Nov. 1945, Papers of George Elsey, Box 82, Harry S. Truman Library; see also Forrestal, *Diaries*, 118.

45. Truman, Special message to Congress, 19 Dec. 1945, *Public Papers of the Presidents: Harry S. Truman, 1945* (Washington, DC: GPO, 1962), 546–60; Forrestal, *Diaries*, 118–20.

46. *NYT*, 20 Dec. 1945.

47. Stephen Jurika, ed., *From Pearl Harbor to Vietnam: The Memoirs of Admiral Arthur Radford* (Stanford: Hoover Institution Press, 1980), 88–89.

48. For notes on the discussions between Patterson, Forrestal, and Eberstadt that took place at this time, see Eberstadt, Memorandum of discussions between Judge Patterson, Mr. Forrestal, and Myself, Patterson Papers, R. G. 107, Box 6,

NA; Minutes of War Council Meeting, 10 April 1946, Patterson Papers, Box 23, LC; Telephone conversation, Norstad and Patterson, 22 March and 2 May 1946, Norstad Papers, Box 31, EL.

49. Norstad, Memorandum for the record, 4 April 1946, memorandum of a telephone conversation between Norstad and Patterson, 2 May 1946, Norstad Papers, Box 31, EL. At that point in time it is very clear that the Navy was not interested in any plan that did not guarantee it a cabinet-level secretary with immediate access to the president.

50. Norstad, Memorandum for the record, 5 April 1946, ibid.

51. Minutes of a meeting of the War Council, 10 April 1946, Patterson Papers, Box 23, LC.

52. U.S. Congress, Senate Naval Affairs Committee, *Hearings: Unification of the Armed Forces,* 79th Cong., 2d sess., 44.

53. Ibid., 105–19; see also Norstad, Memorandum on Senate hearings, 4 May 1946, Norstad Papers, Box 31, EL.

54. Eisenhower to General Alexander D. Surles, 9 May 1946, *EP*, 7:1057–58.

55. He first convinced Stuart Symington and Norstad, the Air Force officer closest to the negotiations, to drop their insistence on a single, powerful chief of staff. See Memorandum for the record, 8 May 1946, Norstad Papers, Box 31, EL.

56. This quote is from the Norstad memo of May 8. Clifford may have used such words in his effort to convince Norstad to give up on his hopes for a powerful chief of staff, or this may simply have been Norstad interpreting Clifford's meaning. For the War Department's position on unification going into this meeting, see Memorandum, 10 May 1946, Patterson Papers, R. G. 107, Box 6, NA.

57. Norstad, Record of a meeting with the president, 13 May 1946, Norstad Papers, Box 31, EL; Forrestal, *Diaries,* 160–62; Caraley, *The Politics of Military Unification,* 136. It can hardly be doubted that Patterson had been consulted about the decision to abandon the idea of a chief of staff ahead of time.

58. Forrestal, *Diaries,* 161.

59. Eisenhower to General Thomas T. Handy, 15 May 1946, *EP*, 7:1061–62.

60. Clifford and Holbrook, *Counsel to the President,* 150.

61. Notes on conference at White House, 4 June 1946, Norstad Papers, Box 31, EL.

62. Forrestal, *Diaries,* 164–67; Norstad, Notes on a White House Conference, 4 June 1946, Norstad Papers, Box 31, EL.

63. Copies of this letter were also sent to the key committee chairmen in both houses.

64. Patterson's memo is quoted in Eisenhower to Handy, 10 May 1946, *EP*, 7:1064 n. 5.

65. Clifford and Holbrook, *Counsel to the President,* 150–51; Forrestal, *Diaries,* 168–70. Following this meeting Forrestal did forward to Truman a carefully guarded letter of support. See Forrestal to Truman, 24 June 1946, copy in Patterson Papers, R. G. 107, Box 6, NA.

66. Clifford and Holbrook, *Counsel to the President*, 151.

67. Forrestal to Truman, 24 June 1946, copy in Patterson Papers, R. G. 107, Box 6, NA.

68. Clifford and Holbrook, *Counsel to the President*, 152–53.

69. Press Association dispatch, 19 July 1946, in Spaatz Papers, Box 266, LC.

70. Spaatz to Arnold, 6 Aug. 1946, ibid.

71. Forrestal, *Diaries,* 203.

72. Ibid., 204.

73. Clifford and Holbrook, *Counsel to the President*, 153–54.

74. Forrestal, *Diaries*, 205.

75. Ibid.

76. Patterson to Symington, 17 Sept. 1946, Patterson Papers, R. G. 107, Box 5, NA. When, shortly after this meeting, Symington suggested that detailed planning should begin, Patterson rejected his advice. Like Eisenhower, he did not want to get into details, fearing that the more specific the planning, the more fiercely the Navy would resist reform. It would, he wrote, be a "better strategy for the War Department to press the case on only two or three points on a high level—a single department, three equal branches."

77. Ibid.

78. Forrestal, *Diaries*, 205.

79. Memorandum for the record, 21 and 7 Nov. 1946, Norstad Papers, Box 31, EL.

80. Forrestal, *Diaries*, 223–26.

81. U.S. Congress, House Committee on Expenditures in the Executive Department, *Hearings: National Security Act of 1947*, 80th Cong., 1st sess., 272.

82. Forrestal, *Diaries*, 228–29.

83. Norstad to Leach, 7 April 1947, Norstad Papers, Box 33, EL.

84. Forrestal and Patterson to Truman, 16 Jan. 1947, Patterson Papers, R. G. 107, Box 6, NA; see also *NYT*, 17 Jan. 1947.

85. Persons to Patterson, 5 March 1947, Patterson Papers, R. G. 107, Box 6, NA; Minutes of a War Council Meeting, 6 March 1947, Patterson Papers, Box 23, LC.

86. U.S. Congress, Senate Committee on the Armed Services, *Hearings, Unification of the Armed Forces,* 80th Cong., 1st sess., 99.

87. Ibid., 91.

88. Ibid.

89. U.S. Congress, Senate Committee on the Armed Services, *Hearings on the National Defense Establishment,* 80th Cong., 1st sess., 358.

90. Ibid., 411–32.

91. Clifford and Holbrook, *Counsel to the President*, 155.

92. Ibid., 156; as amended, the bill stipulated that [n]aval aviation shall consist of combat and service and training forces, and shall include land-based naval aviation, air transport essential for naval operations, all air weapons and air tech-

niques involved in the operations and activities of the United States Navy, and the entire remainder of the aeronautical organization of the United States Navy, together with the personnel necessary therefore." The bill also stated that the Marine Corps "shall be organized, trained, and equipped to provide fleet marine forces of combined arms, together with supporting air components, for service with the fleet in the seizure or defense of advanced naval bases and for the conduct of such land operations as may be essential to the prosecution of a naval campaign."

93. Ferrell, *Eisenhower Diaries*, 142.

94. Eisenhower to Ambassador Walter Bedell Smith, 18 April 1947, *EP*, 8:1648–49.

95. Ferrell, *Eisenhower Diaries*, 142.

3

"I Was Wrong, . . . I Cannot Make This Work. No One Can Make It Work."

General Eisenhower was no doubt stunned when, after Robert Patterson turned the job down, President Truman appointed James Forrestal to be the first secretary of national defense. No doubt, too, he wondered if it would be possible to work with a man who had only recently charged that he was part of a conspiracy to weaken the Navy and destroy the Marine Corps. In fact, however, as Ike came to realize, he and the new secretary had much in common. Though Forrestal preferred to call it "integration" rather than "unification," he too envisioned a security establishment made up of balanced land, sea, and air forces working closely together. He told Eisenhower and the other members of the War Council (precursor to the Armed Forces Policy Council) that he intended to administer the National Military Establishment not only "in accordance with the letter of the law, but with the spirit behind it which has as its eventual goal the achievement of a really integrated and thoroughly meshed military organization whose fundamental mission and objective is the security of the United States."[1]

Like Eisenhower, Forrestal also believed in the importance of interservice teamwork. The two did differ on one fundamental, however. Accustomed to life in the military, Eisenhower believed that cooperation could be required, that those who for one reason or another refused to act as part of the team should be disciplined and if necessary removed. Forrestal, on the other hand, believed that friction of any sort within an organization interfered with its efficient operation, that a "decision that leaves scars" will damage the working environment of an organization. Therefore, decisions should be arrived at gradually as a result of negotiations between interested parties. His attitude toward administration was summed up in the simple phrase, "evolution, not revolution."[2]

Eisenhower and Forrestal also agreed on the vital importance of establishing an overall strategic plan in the event of war with the Soviets.[3] In the midst of the cold war this was a matter of enormous consequence and should have been given a high priority. Unhappily they were unable to win the cooperation of either the Navy or the Air Force. Neither service would support any strategic concept that clashed with its own doctrines, or limited its ability to contest for the largest possible portion of a shrinking defense budget. And shrink it did. Between 1946 and 1947 the military budget fell from $45 billion to $14.4 billion. The result was a furious competition among the services that Air Force Secretary Stuart Symington likened to "throwing a piece of meat into the arena and letting 300 hungry tigers go after it."[4]

The Navy and Air Force were also involved in a bitter doctrinal dispute that in 1949 exploded onto the front pages of the newspapers in what came to be known as the "Revolt of the Admirals." The Air Force staked its claim to the lion's share of the defense budget on its ability to carry out a strategic-bombing campaign using long-range land-based bombers carrying atomic weapons. Thus, for example, a 1947 Air Force study that was leaked to the *New York Times* noted that the atomic bomb would give the offense a distinct advantage over the defense in any future war. The same study claimed preeminence for the Air Force among the services when it observed that "strategic bombardment . . . provides the single most important element of our military capabilities."[5]

The Navy did not dispute the view that air power and the atomic bomb were the twin keys to victory in a future global war. It did insist, however, that the Navy, not the Air Force, was best equipped to deliver nuclear weapons over enemy targets.

In the period immediately following World War II, the Navy underwent a major transformation. Admiral King and the other "battleship admirals" who wished to continue the old emphasis on powerful surface ships lost influence to other men who believed that in order to avoid being reduced to insignificance, the Navy would have to seek its future not on or under the waves, but in the air in competition with the Air Force. These advocates of naval air power sought a strategic bombing role for the Navy to be carried on from a new generation of large "super" aircraft carriers. In a secret memorandum, a portion of which unaccountably found its way into Drew Pearson's syndicated column, one of these men, Vice Admiral Daniel Gallery, argued that the Navy was the service "destined to deliver the atom bomb" and that "it is time right now for the Navy to start an aggressive campaign aimed at proving that the Navy can deliver the atom bomb more effectively than the Air Force can."[6] That was precisely what the Navy did. In public refutation of Air Force claims, Navy spokesmen argued that the Air Force's lumbering strategic bombers would fall easy prey to modern air defense systems, and were therefore unreliable for "delivering scarce and expensive atomic bombs." They insisted that smaller super-sonic jets deployed from supercarriers would be far more effective bomb delivery systems than long-range bombers.[7]

Within weeks of taking the oath of office as secretary of national defense, Forrestal realized that his position was untenable, that the Air Force and the Navy would never willingly accept a clear definition of their separate roles and missions, coordinate their activities, or agree upon a single, integrated defense budget. At one point in time, Eisenhower might have taken a certain grim satisfaction from the fact that Forrestal, the man most responsible for crafting the National Security Act, was unable to maintain discipline within his own household. However, by early 1948, as he prepared to leave the Pentagon for a new career as president of Columbia University, he experienced none of these feelings. It was depressing to bear witness to the constant squabbling between the Air Force and the Navy, and to realize that the members of the JCS, men he had known for decades, were unable to set their narrow parochial interests aside and deal with issues vital to the national security. It was equally upsetting to watch as the armed services lost the respect and public admiration they had earned at such a high price during World War II.

In February 1948, before leaving for New York and his new post, Eisenhower drafted a long valedictory message for Forrestal, a memorandum detailing his views on what needed to be done to end interservice rivalry and transform the secretary's office into an organization capable of managing the military. Aware that Forrestal was not yet ready to adopt the highly centralized management system he favored, Ike limited himself to proposals he thought the secretary would consider. First, he insisted that Forrestal could not go on handling every last detail of his office unaided. He needed at the very least a small staff of civilian and military advisors headed by a military man. Since Congress would not approve the appointment of a true chief of staff, he recommended that Forrestal choose for the post an officer who ranked below the members of the JCS. This "administrative assistant" could provide the briefings and independent professional advice the secretary needed.[8]

Ike had nothing good to say about the JCS as constituted. So long as each member continued to regard "himself merely as the special advocate or pleader of the service he represents," that body would never serve any useful purpose. If Forrestal could somehow convince the chiefs to approach problems from the proper perspective, the JCS could become an invaluable resource. Was this possible? Eisenhower believed it was. These men had reached "the pinnacle" of their careers and should be capable of viewing "every problem from its broad national viewpoint." It would be up to Forrestal to convince them of that. In like fashion, he encouraged the secretary to require the JCS to agree upon a clearly defined strategic concept. Only then would it be possible to define the roles, missions, force levels, and budgets for the various branches. Also, since he was certain that the Navy and Air Force would never come to an agreement on the relative merits of long-range bombers as opposed to aircraft carriers, it would be up to Forrestal to put his foot down and in the absence of agreement to decide "who is to do each job."[9]

Finally, because of "the importance of making the most out of the national security dollar," Ike urged Forrestal to do everything possible to end the wasteful duplication that was endemic to the military. The primary example of such waste, he argued, was the Marine Corps, which served as a duplicate army, one that had at its disposal its own air force. Nor did it make any sense for the Army to operate ocean transports. That ought to be the Navy's responsibility. Hospital services, transport facilities, storage, and numerous other functions ought to be consolidated. In order to eliminate the competition for scarce resources that drove costs up, procurement should be placed under the control of a single Army-Navy Munitions Board. Ike reminded Forrestal that the true purpose of the National Security Act had been to achieve "greater efficiency and economy through a maximum of interdependence among the services."[10] Whether that goal could be achieved would depend on the strength and determination of the secretary himself.

Forrestal took Eisenhower's comments to heart. With the cold war intensifying, the public relations war between the Navy and the Air Force going full tilt, and no sign that the services were capable of developing either a strategic plan or a budget, something had to be done. The management system he had done so much to create was failing. On February 21, he informed Ike that he was considering taking the members of the JCS on a retreat somewhere out of Washington where it would be possible to do some "sustained thinking."[11] A few days later, with the Communist coup in Czechoslovakia very much on his mind, he informed the JCS that he wanted them to develop a paper describing in detail the specific roles and missions each service would undertake in the event of war and have it on his desk by March 8. With that in hand, he told President Truman that he personally would decide these issues: "From the standpoint of budget considerations, the present world situation and public opinion, I think I cannot do anything else."[12] A few days later he made his plans public, telling reporters that he was taking the members of the JCS out of Washington so that they might thrash out the long-standing controversy over "who will do what with what." If the chiefs could not agree among themselves, he said, he would make the decisions for them.[13]

These were brave words. However, the fact of the matter was that Forrestal lacked the power to require the services to come to an accommodation. Instead, at a meeting held in Key West, Florida, he mediated a compromise between the Air Force and the Navy that gave the Air Force primary responsibility for carrying out strategic-bombing campaigns while recognizing the Navy's right to a secondary role in this field.[14] Though he put the best face possible on his effort, the fact is the Key West agreement resolved nothing. The Navy continued to pursue its ambition of playing a major role in strategic aerial warfare and persisted in an aggressive propaganda campaign designed to convince Congress and the public that the Air Force would not be able to perform as promised in the event of war with the Soviets. Meanwhile, in a nasty confrontation, recently retired Air Force Chief of Staff Carl Spaatz informed Forrestal that the Air Force did not agree with the decisions reached at Key West, that the real issue was whether the United States was to have one air force or two.[15]

A few months after Forrestal mediated the Key West agreement, the interservice dispute flared once again when the Air Force attempted to take control of the Armed Forces Special Weapons Project (AFSWP) and with it the nation's nuclear arsenal. In August 1948, Forrestal again stepped in, taking the JCS on a second retreat, this time to Newport, Rhode Island. The result was another relatively meaningless agreement. The Navy granted the Air Force temporary control of the AFSWP and the Air Force agreed that when planning strategic operations it would take the Navy's capabilities into account.

Forrestal matched his nearly futile attempts at resolving differences between the Air Force and the Navy with some equally unsuccessful moves designed to implement the changes Eisenhower had recommended in the way the NME did business.[16] He asked the members of the JCS to appoint a deputy to handle the day-to-day administration of the services so that they could spend more time in joint planning.[17] He looked for a way to enlarge the Joint Staff so that it would be truly able to fulfill its many functions. He even considered expanding the powers of Eisenhower's close friend, General Albert Gruenther, the director of the Joint Staff, so that in some ways he would become the "administrative assistant" Eisenhower had recommended. In fact, however, hamstrung by legislative restraints and the unwillingness of the services to cooperate, there was little he could do on his own to reform the department.[18]

By the summer of 1948 a frustrated Forrestal was ready to throw in the towel. At one of their regular breakfast meetings, he poured out his feelings to White House Chief Counsel Clark Clifford. Admitting that the management system he had fought so passionately to create was a hopeless abortion, he said: "I was wrong, . . . I cannot make this work. No one can make it work." An astonished Clifford assured Forrestal that he had done as much as was humanly possible, and urged him to discuss the matter with the president. Forrestal was not yet ready to make any hard and fast recommendations. Instead, in his own characteristically meticulous way he began to collect the views of those who would be most directly affected by change. He met with the service secretaries and held evening seminars at the Pentagon that included Eisenhower, Omar Bradley, and other high-ranking Army, Navy, and Air Force officers, as well as civilians with Pentagon experience. These meetings proved to be an eye-opening experience for Forrestal. The Navy leadership refused to consider any reforms whatsoever, while Army and Air Force officers proved cooperative. He later told Clifford that he had come to trust "some senior Army generals more than his former Navy colleagues." He mentioned Eisenhower and Bradley as men whose views he particularly valued.[19]

In a "Dear Jim" letter dated September 27, 1948, Eisenhower exploited his growing influence by urging Forrestal to press forward with reform. Negotiations to bring about an end to the Berlin blockade having failed, he found the international situation "completely depressing." He was, in fact, "beginning to think that" the Soviets "may push the rest of the world beyond endurance." The time had come, he thought, to prepare for a possible confrontation. The only bright spot in this otherwise gloomy picture, he believed, was that the critical international situation would make cooperation among the services easier to achieve. A sense of "common danger" and "urgency," he thought, would surely persuade the Navy and Air Force to resolve their differences.[20]

Forrestal, who met with President Truman in the Oval Office on October 5, was not so sure. He admitted to the president that the stand he had taken during the unification debate had been mistaken, and outlined some of the changes he thought necessary if the NME was to be strengthened.[21]

Although he did not agree with Eisenhower on every detail of what was shaping up as a major effort to revise the National Security Act, he adopted a number of ideas that Ike had been advocating for years. He wanted more power, particularly with regard to "budget procedures" and "legislation." He also wanted control over the public relations operations of the services, hoping in this way to discourage the Navy and Air Force from fighting their battles in the press. He asked for a larger staff including an undersecretary to handle routine matters. Most important, he wanted to reform the JCS by providing them with a strong chairman, and by separating the chiefs from their services so that they might focus their full attention on national rather than service interests.[22]

Truman, who had already been briefed on what to expect by Clifford, named Forrestal to head a group that would be responsible for developing possible amendments to the National Security Act. Others on the team included Forrestal's aide, Marx Leva, director of the Bureau of the Budget, Frank Pace, Jr., and Clifford.[23] Immediately after this Forrestal brought Eisenhower into the process, inviting him to Washington to "talk fundamentals: policy, budget and our whole military-diplomatic position." Ike also acted as an advisor to the committee, drafting the proposed amendments.[24]

Arriving in the capital on October 27, Eisenhower spent the next four days conferring with Forrestal, Army Secretary Kenneth Royall, and high-ranking Army and Air Force officers. In complete agreement with Forrestal on the threatening "state of world affairs" and the importance of "a united front on the part of the security establishment," Eisenhower spent his time in Washington preaching the gospel of unity to the service leaders. He left the capital thinking he had done some good. It was not long, however, before the conflict between the Navy and the Air Force erupted once again when Ferdinand Eberstadt, who chaired a subcommittee of the Hoover Commission considering possible changes in the National Security Act, opened hearings on whether naval aviation should be integrated into the Air Force, or vice versa.[25] Eberstadt made his own feelings known by at first inviting only the Navy's representatives to testify, thus providing them with another podium from which to attack the Air Force. Vice Admiral Arthur Radford was happy to oblige. In his statement this whip-smart, opinionated naval aviator fueled the already hot fires of interservice bitterness by attacking what he said was the Air Force claim that it could "quickly and completely" win a war against the Soviets with an all-out nuclear blitz. He also questioned the effectiveness of the Air Force's long-range bombers and insisted that by employing planes flying from carriers the Navy could drop more atomic bombs on an adversary's targets than could the Air Force.[26]

When testimony by Radford and other naval officers produced an angry protest from Secretary of the Air Force Stuart Symington, Eberstadt reacted by belatedly inviting Air Force officers to appear before his committee and by asking Eisenhower, a consultant to his commission, to take a position on the merger question. Ike refused to take sides, arguing that the real issue was interservice rivalry, a problem that could never be resolved until the roles and missions of each service were clearly defined and the services were required to limit themselves to fulfilling their true responsibilities.[27]

This latest flare-up in the ongoing interservice dispute prompted Eisenhower to become directly involved in efforts to restore harmony. On the same day that he wrote to Eberstadt, Ike informed Forrestal that if the administration needed him he was willing to help in any way he could. "I can scarcely think of any chore that I would refuse to do wherever people in responsible positions feel that I might be able to help," he wrote. "I know that you understand that you can call on me at any time for anything."[28] At the time Forrestal received this offer, the JCS was deadlocked and could come to no agreement on either the 1950 defense budget or a strategic plan in the event of another global war. He suggested to President Truman that Eisenhower might be just the man to bring order out of chaos. Ideally, he wanted to bring Ike to Washington to "preside over the Joint Chiefs," but if that proved impossible, bringing him back in an "informal" capacity would be "second best."[29] The president quickly agreed and on December 1 the three men held a preliminary conference at the White House. At a second meeting held nine days later, Eisenhower refused to become involved in efforts that had been on going for some time to develop the 1950 defense budget. However, he did agree that at the beginning of Truman's second administration, in January 1949, he would come to Washington to act as Forrestal's unofficial advisor.[30]

When Admiral William D. Leahy, the president's chief of staff and the sitting chairman of the JCS, unexpectedly retired, Forrestal offered Eisenhower the opportunity to sit with the Joint Chiefs as a sort of unofficial chairman.[31] Though originally opposed to a powerful military chief of staff, Forrestal had moved a long way toward Eisenhower's position on this question. Experience had convinced him that the JCS needed a strong leader who "would take precedence over all other military personnel" and would be the "principle military adviser to the Secretary of Defense and the President." Convincing Congress to agree to this was not going to be easy. Carl Vinson, the chairman of the House Armed Services Committee, was dead set against the creation of any such post. That was why it seemed important to bring in Eisenhower. "With Ike here for sixty days," he explained in a letter to a friendly congressman, "we can get the pattern set and prove its workability by pragmatic experience."[32] Forrestal also hoped that Eisenhower would be able to bring the JCS into agreement on a coherent military strategy and on a defense budget for 1951. If anyone was up to this job, he thought, it was Eisenhower. He was knowledgeable when it came to the problem of defending Europe and skilled at "identifying problems and bringing people together."[33]

Eisenhower put off a decision reagarding the offer to head the JCS until after he had an opportunity to assess the situation in Washington firsthand. In the interim he made frequent visits to the capital during which he advised Forrestal on a number of vital military issues and conferred with the committee that was then developing proposed amendments to the National Security Act.[34]

During this same period, Ike began thinking seriously about methods of transforming the JCS into an efficiently functioning institution. Majority rule was out of the question. The Navy would never go along.[35] In the end he concluded that the chiefs needed "a chairman at the very least . . . a fourth member who can divorce himself from his service background." In fact, he really thought, as he had all along, that "they needed a Chief of Staff."[36] He told W. Barton Leach, who was acting as an unofficial advisor to Air Force Secretary Stuart Symington, that he himself would be willing to take that job "on a permanent basis to straighten out this whole situation."[37]

Unhappily, as Eisenhower well knew, Congress would never sanction the creation of a powerful chief of staff. That being the case, he concluded that the president would have to seek legislation that would vastly expand the secretary's powers. There was no guarantee that Truman would risk another monumental fight such as the one that had characterized the first unification debate. Clearly, many questions remained to be answered.[38]

On January 20, 1949, Dwight and Mamie Eisenhower came to Washington for President Truman's inauguration. That night they attended the inaugural ball, and the next morning the general began his assignment as Forrestal's informal advisor by plunging into a round of meetings. A "week of struggle at the Pentagon" left him depressed and heartsick. The "bitterness" of the conflict between the Navy and the Air Force, he wrote, completely poisoned the atmosphere.[39]

Eisenhower was an Air Force partisan. There can be no question about that. Nevertheless, he recognized that the Air Force was partly responsible for the interservice dispute. Secretary of the Air Force Symington, Air Force Chief of Staff Hoyt Vandenberg, and others certainly made exaggerated claims for Air Force capabilities. Nor were they satisfied to negotiate for their share of the defense budget within the confines of the Defense Department. Instead, they did everything possible to capitalize on the general popularity of the Air Force in order to maximize their share of the budget. Moreover, Air Force leaders took every opportunity to embarrass the Navy. A particularly egregious example of this took place just after Eisenhower agreed to his temporary assignment in Washington. During joint maneuvers in North Pacific waters, a flight of B-29 bombers attached to the Alaskan Air Command caught a Navy carrier task force napping. The bombers flew directly over the task force at low level without being intercepted. The story was quickly leaked to the press along with photographs of the task force taken from the bombers flying overhead. "Wrecked Navy off Kodiak" blared a headline in the *New York Times*.[40]

The Navy cried foul. The Air Force units involved in this operation were under the command of the Joint Defense Force Commander, a naval officer who had "specifically forbade the release by subordinate commanders of matters touching upon the weaknesses or strengths of operating forces." In a letter to Eisenhower, Secretary of the Navy John Sullivan denounced the press release as striking "at the very heart of the principles of unification." It "is just such acts as this," he observed, "that generate the distrust on the part of one service toward another, which we are both trying to dispel."[41]

Eisenhower reacted immediately, asking General Gruenther, director of the Joint Staff, to issue orders designed to "prevent unsupervised unilateral release of any information regarding a joint exercise." It was clear, however, that orders such as these would do no good. The entire military establishment leaked like a sieve. It was hardly a secret that Forrestal wanted the services to stop taking potshots at one another. The only way to stop the leaks would be to take firm disciplinary action against those involved, but since numerous high-ranking officers were involved, that was literally impossible.[42]

Embarrassing the Navy was only one of the methods the Air Force used to make its case for increased funding. More commonly, it promoted itself through public stunts, grandstanding that was intended to capture headlines. One example of this was reported in the February 21, 1949, issue of *Time*. An XB-47 medium-range bomber set a new speed record of 607 mph on a flight from Muroc, California, to Andrews Air Force Base just outside Washington. The plane made the flight, according to *Time*, in order to be on hand for a private air show that the Air Force was staging for members of Congress who were then about to vote on the budget.[43] Another example of this sort of thing took place in March when the Lucky Lady II, a B-50 medium bomber specially equipped for in-flight refueling, completed a well-publicized nonstop around-the-world flight. At the conclusion of the flight, which in no way represented the real capabilities of America's aging fleet of B-29's and B-50's, Air Force General Curtis LeMay was quoted in the *New York Times* as saying, "It means" that, flying from bases inside the continental United States, the Air Force bombers could drop an atomic bomb "anyplace in the world that required" one. When asked, he also implied that the new in-flight refueling techniques could provide fighter escorts with the range to accompany bombers on long flights. Secretary of the Air Force Symington, who was equally enthusiastic about the flight, claimed that these techniques had transformed America's B-29's and B-50's into intercontinental bombers.[44]

This sort of game playing irritated Eisenhower. In the first place LeMay's interpretation of the significance of the B-50 flight came close to being an outright lie. Second, he was convinced that such forays into the press damaged the reputation of the services and gave clever journalists and politicians the opportunity to play them off one against the other to their mutual disadvantage. Therefore, even though Symington was at this time a friend and sometime bridge partner, and despite the fact that Eisenhower himself was quite friendly to Air Force ambitions, he sent what amounted to a kindly rebuke to the air force secretary.[45]

However much Air Force stunts annoyed Eisenhower, they were nothing compared with his anger at the Navy. Two days of briefings by naval personnel left him furious. There were, he conceded, "intelligent, enthusiastic and well informed people" at the Navy Department, but their main objective seemed to be "selling" rather than engaging in "critical analysis" to arrive at reasonable conclusions. Worse, considering Eisenhower's long-standing aversion to criticism of one service by another, the Navy's briefing officers made invidious comparisons between the Navy and the Marine Corps on the one hand and the other services. He was annoyed, too, that the Navy should attempt to convince him that the battleship *Missouri*, which he considered a museum piece, served "a highly useful national purpose!"[46]

More important, during these briefing sessions the Navy's leaders made it clear that they refused to accept "control of the seas" as their basic mission. Instead, he was distressed to realize, they viewed the Navy's fundamental purpose as the "projection of American Air power." To achieve their objectives, Eisenhower wrote, the powers that be in the Navy were "conducting a relentless propaganda campaign" that was "designed to delude Congress and the people into building up a useless & expensive Navy—thereby depriving the Air of what it needs."[47]

Eisenhower was especially irritated with Vice Admiral Arthur Radford, a fierce supporter of the Navy's air arm, who told him that the Air Force's big bombers would never be able to operate unescorted against modern air defenses. This, he insisted, was particularly true of the lumbering B-36, which he described as a "sitting duck." A fighter escort was essential to see bombers through to their targets, and only moveable or floating bases near targets could provide the fighters. Because of this, Radford argued, the bombing should be done by the Navy, using bombers flying from a new class of supercarriers. Radford's conclusion, Eisenhower noted curtly, was that "the Navy should have more money—the Air Force far less."[48]

For the sake of argument Eisenhower was willing to entertain the possibility that the Air Force was wrong, that big bombers might be more easily intercepted than had been thought. Perhaps all of the assumptions about the effectiveness of strategic air power were mistaken. That could be studied. However, if it was true that strategic bombers would have trouble reaching their targets, he failed to see how bombers flying from aircraft carriers would have any better chance of success since the carriers could not carry sufficient numbers of long-range fighters to protect them. If in fact the Navy was correct and the theories upon which aerial warfare was based had to be revised, then the huge cost of supercarriers would be no more justified than the cost of heavy bombers since the only purpose of such ships could be "bombing operations against land targets."[49]

During the two weeks following President Truman's inaugural, as he studied the problems he would encounter if he agreed to become the unofficial chairman of the JCS, Eisenhower became more convinced than ever that the president would have to take drastic action to end the interservice dispute. "Something has to snap," he wrote, "and so far as I'm concerned it will have to be the patience of the Pres. & Sec. Of Def. They are going to have to get tough! And I mean tough!" Eisenhower was not sure that Forrestal, at least, had any toughness left. The secretary was seriously depressed, blaming himself "for the unconscionable situation now existing." He even confessed to Ike that whereas once he had "accepted unequivocally and supported vigorously" the Navy "party line," those days were gone. He felt betrayed by his one-time friends, remarking that while he now had confidence in a large number of Army officers, he trusted practically none of the admirals. That gratified Eisenhower who realized that it "cost him a lot to come to such a conclusion."[50]

On February 9 Eisenhower went to the White House for an hour-long meeting with President Truman. He brought with him a series of proposals, including suggested amendments to the National Security Act, that were designed to get unification back "on the rails."[51] Something had to be done, he told the president, about the whole messy business of roles and missions. Some of the Navy's "assumed missions" had to be abolished in order to provide more funding for the Air Force. The Navy also had to be told in no uncertain terms that its responsibility was to establish control of the seas. Nor could Forrestal go on bearing total responsibility for everything that went on in his department. He needed a deputy to handle routine matters and a staff. Above all Congress had to be convinced to give the JCS a chairman.[52]

Ike was especially critical of the JCS, whose members were discouraged, preoccupied, and frequently unable to arrive at important decisions. Because there was no chairman to set an agenda, work regularly went undone. Often, members even failed to turn up for meetings. Some among them, he told the president, even appeared to be deliberately blocking the decision-making process at the JCS level and then going over Forrestal's head directly to Congress to get what they wanted.[53]

In a subsequent report John Ohly, one of Forrestal's three assistants, confirmed Eisenhower's judgment of the JCS as constituted. After reviewing the status of all their current projects, he concluded that the chiefs had some forty separate unresolved issues before them, including major questions such as the "Control and Direction of Strategic Atomic Operations," the 1950 defense budget, and the development of strategic war plans. It was clear, Ohly concluded, that given existing differences between the services, few of these issues would soon be resolved.[54]

Because Congress was certain to take its time enacting needed amendments to the National Security Act, Eisenhower urged the president to appoint an interim presidential chief of staff who would serve as Forrestal's principal military advisor. This individual would be responsible for making certain that issues were brought before the JCS in a timely fashion. That would keep the members from ignoring pressing issues, a pattern of behavior that had become characteristic. If the JCS continued to be incapable of arriving at decisions, the chief of staff should be empowered to advise the secretary of defense regarding the implications of a particular question so that he could make a final determination. Ike felt certain that if given a choice between making a decision themselves or allowing a chief of staff and the secretary to make it for them, the chiefs would be considerably more inclined to find areas of agreement.[55]

Eisenhower was aware that the major overhaul of the National Security Act he was proposing might reignite "the bitter interservice war" that preceded the passage of the original law. He therefore told the president that a legislative package such as the one he envisioned should not be sent to Congress until discipline had been reestablished inside the defense establishment. Truman would have to make it clear to everyone involved that they would have to choose between offering "positive, dynamic, unswerving support of recommended measures" and being removed. Whether or not the president decided to seek legislation, Eisenhower believed, he should put the services "on sharp notice" that he would insist upon total "respect for the decisions of the Secretary of Defense," that "appointments, assignments, and relief will be on the recommendation of the Secretary of Defense," that "the Joint Chiefs of Staff must, as his own body of military advisers, act decisively—and must place Joint Chiefs of Staff work in first priority, even if it demands one hundred percent of all their working time." Above all he believed that the chiefs must be brought to understand that "every Presidential decision is a command that must compel complete and loyal support." Individuals who refused to conform should be immediately reassigned. Once the president had made his position clear, Eisenhower continued, it would be up to Forrestal to "assert his authority so firmly that any defection brings *instant* action."[56]

Eisenhower was enormously pleased with the outcome of this meeting. The president was enthusiastic about everything he proposed and indicated that he had every intention of seeking changes in the National Security Act. He agreed to support the strongest possible Air Force, to discipline the Navy, and to seek an extra appropriation for the modernization of some of the Army's obsolete equipment. The two men agreed on another important point as well. Ike had long been convinced that the services could only plan efficiently for "the long haul" if they were provided each year with a consistent annual budget. He and Truman agreed on a figure of $15 billion annually, with $600 million of that to be used for the purchase and stockpiling of strategic materials.[57]

The only point of disagreement between Eisenhower and Truman came over the question of who would ride herd over the Joint Chiefs in the immediate future. Ike, who was not keen on undertaking the job himself, recommended Air Force General Joseph McNarney. The tough-minded McNarney had reorganized the War Department in 1942 and was a capable administrator. However, Truman wanted Eisenhower, not McNarney, and Ike reluctantly agreed.[58] After this, only one point troubled the general. Like Forrestal, Truman seemed to believe that he had "some miraculous power to make some of these warring elements lie down in peace together!!!!" He was by no means certain of that.[59]

Two days after his meeting with Eisenhower, Truman brought For-restal, the service secretaries, and the members of the JCS to the White House. With Eisenhower looking on, he gave them a presidential talking-to. He then issued a press release announcing that he had appointed Eisen-hower to be his principal military advisor and a consultant to Forrestal.[60] On March 5 he followed up with a special message to Congress recom-mending a series of amendments to the National Security Act that re-flected the thinking of Forrestal, Eisenhower, and the drafting team he had earlier appointed.[61]

Eisenhower began his new assignment with the JCS, hoping to use the budget process to advance the cause of unification. Earlier, while serving as army chief of staff, he had tried to convince his colleagues that if they would agree on a basic strategic concept, the tasks each service was to perform and the forces each required could be identified. It would then be possible to de-velop a defense budget based upon legitimate needs. He failed. A year and a half later, the same situation pertained. The United States was still without an agreed-upon plan of action in the event of war with the Soviets. This then became the first item on Ike's agenda for he remained convinced that if a clear strategic concept could be established, then the roles and missions of each service could be fixed and budgetary allocations decided upon ratio-nally.[62]

A few days after accepting his appointment, Eisenhower met with the JCS for the first time in his new role as their informal leader. At that meeting he made it clear that as far as the 1951 budget was concerned everything was on the table. He did not want the service chiefs coming to him with separate budget proposals. He did not want them to consider forces already in exis-tence when developing their thinking. His basic objective, as he explained later, was "to develop a peacetime military program and budgetary structure that would be related as closely as possible to an agreed strategic plan."[63]

Eisenhower seems to have been of two minds about whether he would get the cooperation he needed. He thought that the members of the JCS, Generals Omar Bradley and Hoyt Vandenberg as well as Admiral Louis Denfeld, recognized that they needed to work together in order to "regain and preserve the prestige that properly belongs to them." They also ap-peared to appreciate the danger of going to the press and Congress when-ever a decision came down that they opposed. They even seemed "ready & eager to begin again, from the very bottom, the study of our strategic posi-tion, in the effort to obtain the best possible layout of defense forces," given the limit on defense spending the president had established. At the same time, indeed in the same diary entry, he remarked that if they refused to cooperate, though "it would be repugnant—and out of character"—he would "quit and begin criticizing!" He would do this, he wrote, because it would "be the only way left to get action." Obviously, optimism had its limits.[64]

Eisenhower had only just begun working with the Joint Chiefs when there was a change at the top of the national defense establishment. By early 1949 it was apparent that Forrestal's "physical and mental condition was deteriorating rapidly."[65] On March 1, by which time the secretary was near a nervous collapse, President Truman forced him to resign effective April 1. He chose Louis Johnson, a West Virginia attorney and close political associate who had served as an assistant secretary of war in the Roosevelt administration, to replace him.

Although Eisenhower counted Forrestal a friend, he was not sorry to see him leave the Pentagon. Prior to the secretary's forced resignation, he had noted signs of his increasing mental problems. Forrestal suffered from insomnia, seemed incapable of making decisions, and was utterly paranoid with regard to certain members of the White House staff who, he repeatedly told Eisenhower, were "out to get him." Fearing that Forrestal was on his way to a nervous breakdown, Eisenhower and two of the secretary's closest aides, John Ohly and Marx Leva, tried to convince him to take some time off, to relax, but Forrestal refused. Ultimately, Eisenhower concluded that "the best thing for Jim's sake and the Defense Department was for him to resign."[66]

Louis Johnson, the new secretary of national defense, was a large man with equally large political ambitions. Former Secretary of War Harry H. Woodring, who had been Johnson's boss in the Roosevelt administration, admitted that Johnson was in many ways an able man, but added that he was "overambitious in the same way that some men are over sexed." Few who knew him doubted that he intended to use the Defense Department as a steppingstone to the 1952 Democratic presidential nomination. Bluff, arrogant, and often too quick to come to judgments, he was extremely adept at making enemies. Forrestal had been a conciliator, a judge, a negotiator. Johnson was determined to "knock heads" if necessary to bring the military establishment under control.[67]

The new secretary came to the Pentagon with his mind made up on certain fundamentals. He was a devotee of air power and strategic bombing. Indeed, during his previous stint at the War Department in the late 1930s, he had been a driving force behind the development of the B-17 Flying Fortress, the mainstay of the Army Air Force's assault on Nazi Germany in World War II. Also, Johnson was committed to advancing the cause of unification. According to President Truman's naval aide, Captain Robert L.

Dennison, he thought that anybody "who opposed unification was just beyond the pale."[68]

What one thought of Johnson depended in large part on how one approached these issues. The *New York Times* columnist, Hanson Baldwin, an
Annapolis graduate who consistently supported the Navy in its struggle
against unification, thought his appointment "disastrous," and remarked
that everything he did "was approached from a political point of view."[69]
Forrestal's naval aide, Captain Herbert Riley, who served in the Johnson
Pentagon for only a short while, recalled the experience vividly. Johnson
"wasn't a man you could argue with or to whom you could make a logical
presentation. Usually he would get up and walk out on you. Or, if he listened
he would throw you out of his office when you finished—without a word."[70]

Johnson's critics were many and vociferous, but he had his supporters as
well, including many holdovers from the Forrestal regime. When he first
heard of Johnson's appointment, Donald F. Carpenter, head of the Munitions Board, feared that he would fill the department with political cronies
more interested in advancing Johnson's political ambitions than the national security interests of the country. Carpenter was prepared to resign at
the first sign of this. Instead, he found in the new secretary a capable administrator who was gratifyingly loyal to his subordinates. "I never had as complete backing from a superior as I had from Louis Johnson," he said. Marx
Leva had a similar recollection, later observing that Johnson "gave us every
backing" and that "the relationship was fine." Wilfred J. McNeil, who had
been Forrestal's budgetary aide, described the first few months of Johnson's
tenure as a little "rough," but said that "in the last six months he turned out to
be a pretty good Secretary."[71]

Eisenhower too got on well with Johnson, whose opinions on air power,
the Navy, and unification were entirely compatible with his own. Though it
clearly depended on one's point of view, Ike insisted that Johnson was not
hostile to the Navy. He did, however, believe that since the Soviet Union had
no navy to speak of, and our ally Britain had the only other navy worthy of
the name, the current size of the American fleet was unjustified. On the
other hand, Ike added, Johnson had a healthy respect for the threat posed by
a large and growing Soviet submarine fleet, and was anxious to provide the
Navy with everything it needed to counter that threat and secure control of
the seas.[72]

Ike saw eye to eye with Johnson on another important score as well. He
had for some time been urging the president to knock some heads and save
money by enforcing cooperation among the services. One of his basic criticisms of Forrestal was that he had not been willing to get tough with the

services.[73] He was perfectly willing to admit that Johnson's "bull in a china shop" approach to administration lacked subtlety, but he believed Johnson was at least attempting to lead the military establishment in the right direction.[74] When, before leaving office, Forrestal expressed the fear that Johnson might be "too easy" on the services, Ike could hardly believe his ears. "Happily," he wrote, "I have no fear on this particular score." No, his only concern was "whether Johnson will have Forrestal's devoted & extraordinary sense of duty!"[75]

If Eisenhower was pleased with the Johnson appointment, the new secretary viewed the general as an indispensable member of his team. Indeed, Johnson told Ike that he had agreed to "take the job only if I stay on!"[76] It goes without saying that during their official relationship, Eisenhower had great influence with Johnson.

Eisenhower began to work with the JCS on a strategic plan in early March, during the last few weeks of Forrestal's tenure at the Defense Department. His first move was to provide the chiefs with a directive that was to guide their deliberations. The object of American strategy in the event of war would be to keep Western Europe out of Soviet hands. He drew a line on a map from the United Kingdom across Western Europe and the Mediterranean to Suez. Given a $15 billion annual budget, the chiefs were asked to develop a strategic plan to hold that line against the possibility of a Soviet advance westward. If that proved impossible, they were to plan to hold a bridgehead on the Continent and prepare a counteroffensive. If they could not hold any part of Europe with the forces available, they were to develop plans to keep the United Kingdom in allied hands as a staging area for a return to the Continent at the earliest possible moment. A secondary goal was to keep the western Mediterranean open. Finally, if possible U.S. and allied forces should attempt to hold a position in the Middle East. Included in the overall policy were a number of "musts." These included the defense of North and South America, Iceland, Greenland, Alaska, Okinawa, Japan, and communication routes between North America and the United Kingdom.[77]

Once they had agreed upon a firm goal and the strategy for achieving that goal, Eisenhower went on, the chiefs were to identify those forces that at a minimum would be necessary to carry out that strategy. He designated these forces as "red bricks," the basic building blocks of the military establishment. Eisenhower hoped that when costed out these forces would account for 80 percent of the total budget. He envisioned using the remaining 20 percent to add "blue" and "purple" bricks, forces that would be designed to achieve secondary goals.

Though Eisenhower's was an interesting idea, the Navy and Air Force refused to cooperate. At a March 2 meeting, Air Force Chief of Staff Hoyt Vandenberg insisted that the Air Force, which at the time had forty-eight groups, could not fulfill its mission unless it grew to more than seventy groups. For years Air Force leaders had been calling for a seventy-group Air Force. Vandenberg was simply using this number as the basis for bargaining, not thinking seriously about a joint strategic concept or the limitations all sides were required to accept given a clear budgetary ceiling. The Navy proved equally difficult to deal with. Fearing that it would result in a Navy much reduced in size, Admiral Denfeld and his deputy, Vice Admiral Arthur Struble, argued against Eisenhower's entire approach. They insisted that rather than start from scratch, strategic planning should be based on forces currently in existence. Eisenhower, of course, emphatically disagreed, and ended the discussion by curtly noting that "it was only straight military thinking to determine first the task, second the opposition that would be offered to the accomplishment of it, and third a determination of what would be necessary to overcome the opposition."[78]

By mid-March Eisenhower had grown angry. After a pair of particularly grueling meetings with the JCS, he wrote his old friend "Hap" Arnold: "I am so weary of this inter-service struggle for position, prestige and power that this morning I practically 'blew my top.' I would hate to have my doctor take my blood pressure at the moment." If that was a bad day, the next was worse. On March 15 the morning papers carried two stories leaked by Air Force partisans that were designed to strengthen the airmen's claim to a lion's share of the budget. One story, which contained classified information, defined the performance characteristics of the B-36 intercontinental bomber. A second story quoted a highly classified Air Force study on the ability of strategic bombers to penetrate Soviet air defenses.[79]

On reading these stories Eisenhower erupted in absolute fury. William Frye, deputy assistant secretary of defense for public relations, had never seen anything like it before. There they were, "Forrestal, Johnson, Eisenhower and Frye—with the General striding up and down the room asking rhetorical questions to the general effect were we living in a nest of traitors?" Frye spent the day in what he described as "a futile—a predestined futile—attempt to get some idea for Topside as to where the 'leak' had occurred."[80]

On March 19, after another frustrating meeting with the JCS, Eisenhower wrote despairingly in his diary that the "situation grows intolerable." Although only days before it had been the Air Force that had been the focus of his anger, on this day he was especially irritated with the Navy. Denfeld seemed a decent sort of fellow, but because he was retiring by nature, he allowed Struble to dominate the discussion. Ike despised Struble, who "infuriated everyone with his high, strident voice and apparent inability to see any point of view except his own" and who had "that trick in argument of questioning, or seeming to question the *motives* of his opponent."[81]

For two more days Eisenhower continued his round of meetings. As the deadlock continued, his frustration grew and his anger intensified until on March 21, just two days after making this last diary entry, he was struck down by what his doctor diagnosed as a serious case of gastroenteritis (a later diagnosis was ileitis). For five days he remained bedridden in his Washington hotel. On March 28 he fled Washington, flying first to the president's retreat at Key West, Florida, and then to Augusta, Georgia, for a convalescence that included plenty of rest, bridge, and golf.

While recuperating Eisenhower had time to reflect on the entire unhappy situation he had left behind in Washington. "The great difficulty," he thought, was the "tendency of each service" to judge its importance "in terms of the size of its current budget." As a result, the struggle over money went on "endlessly, in the Halls of Congress, in the public press, and in inter-service argument and conferences." The fact was, however, that in a democracy there would never be enough money to satisfy the armed services. Therefore, the "trick" was "to set an appropriate line between desirable strength and unbearable cost." The arguing had to stop. As professionals, the service chiefs should be concerned with "determining the general character of the defense establishment when needed" and reaching "conclusions as to the proper priorities in producing such defensive strength under limited budgets." Getting "everyone to approach these questions from the single viewpoint of the country's good . . . is truly difficult," he wrote. "Unless we find a solution to this problem quickly we are going to damage the country financially without adding to its defensive strength."[82]

When it became clear that Eisenhower would not be returning to Washington in the immediate future, the members of the JCS and their deputies flew to Augusta to continue their talks. The five days that Ike spent with the JCS in Georgia marked the beginning of more weeks of labor on the defense budget. The so-called red brick approach was an early casualty of this renewed effort. This planning principle had to be abandoned because the cost estimates made by the services to fund the force levels required came in at more than $16 billion. Ike then tried to go at the problem from the other end, asking the services to describe the forces they could provide while remaining within the president's established spending ceiling. Again he was thwarted, this time by inadequate analyses and incomplete information provided by the services.[83]

Though it was a frustrating business, Ike continued his efforts to develop some sort of reasonable defense budget and was in fact within $303 million of his goal when the roof fell in. With the economy in recession and federal revenues declining, the president decided that he could not support a defense budget of more than $13 billion.[84] The president's $2 billion reduction in projected defense spending was even worse than it appeared. The Army had not been able to modernize its equipment since the end of the war. Planes were wearing out and had to be replaced, and the cost of modern weapons had risen exponentially. During World War II, for example, a B-17 Flying Fortress cost $218,000. The new B-36 cost $3.6 million. A World War II P-51 fighter plane cost $54,000 while an advanced F-89 cost $855,000. Wilfred McNeil, the comptroller for the Defense Department, estimated that, because of increased costs, simply in order to retain the forces then in being the department would require $16.5 billion in 1951 and $17 billion in 1952.[85]

Although Eisenhower did not question the president's need to reduce spending, he complained to his diary about how difficult it was to plan when such things happened. "We absorb everything," he wrote, "rising costs . . . increased pay, stock piling—etc. etc." The services were "billions short of the sum total we would have had under the 15 b[illion] stable program." He was concerned for he believed that "the results would not show up until we get into serious trouble." The country, he thought, was in a way repeating the mistakes of the interwar years.[86]

On July 14 a depressed Eisenhower submitted his final budget proposal to Johnson along with a secret memorandum in which he made one key observation and two important recommendations. First, he noted that in the event of war with the Soviets the services would not have the capability to carry out their assigned tasks. A $13 billion defense budget would not provide the wherewithal the armed services required to carry out any sort of reasonable, overall strategic concept. As a result, "someone was going to have to suffer if we were going to retain respectable amounts of forces in those categories of greatest emergency value to us." He therefore suggested that Johnson withhold roughly $300 million and make the services bid for it. This tactic, he believed, would force them to "finally produce the facts and arguments that would show where the damage was greatest, so that he could allot this reserve at those particular places." He also suggested that, given the inadequacy of the proposed defense budget, the secretary should allocate an especially large sum to the Air Force for aircraft procurement.

The Air Force had a "known ability" to deliver atomic bombs. Because there was not enough money to adequately fund the needs of all the services, the bomb, and the ability of the Air Force to deliver it, would have to serve "as a deterrent to any potential aggressor who may be contemplating war as a solution to international problems."[87]

If July was a month of failure and despair for Eisenhower, August brought some good news. Congress had passed a series of important amendments to the National Security Act. Public Law 216, signed by the president on August 10, transformed the NME into the Department of Defense, a full-fledged "executive department." Under the law the secretary of defense was recognized as the president's principal military advisor, granted increased authority over the services, and provided with a deputy and three assistant secretaries, one of whom was to be the comptroller of the department. The Joint Staff was increased in size from 100 to 210 officers, and the Munitions Board was given a permanent chairman with the power to make decisions. Congress also mandated that the services should follow uniform budgetary and fiscal procedures that would be established and administered by the Office of the Secretary of Defense. The services, meanwhile, were downgraded from "executive" to "military" departments and the service secretaries were removed from the National Security Council.

Eisenhower, who had much to do with initiating these changes, was pleased. At the same time, however, he remained disappointed that Congress failed to endorse his thinking regarding certain key issues. First, the law limited the power of the secretary of defense by requiring that the services be "separately administered" by their respective secretaries. To protect the Marines and the Navy's air arm, the law also forbade the secretary from making any change in the combatant functions of the services. Moreover, while the legislators had established a chairman for the Joint Chiefs of Staff, his powers were sharply circumscribed. He was to serve as the "presiding officer" of the JCS, provide an agenda for meetings, assist the chiefs in carrying out their business promptly, and inform the secretary of defense regarding issues the JCS could not resolve. However, he had no real power. The JCS remained the principal military advisors to the National Security Council (NSC) and the secretary of defense. They also retained control over the Joint Staff, which meant that the secretary would still lack a staff of his own to which he could look for independent professional information and advice. As before, the JCS could take no action, establish no policy, unless all members were in agreement. Congress also stipulated that individual members of the JCS who disagreed with Defense Department policies could, after informing the secretary, take their views and complaints directly to Congress. In Eisenhower's judgment the 1949 amendments to the act were another step in the right direction, but it is certain that he believed much remained to be done.[88]

Following the enactment of the 1949 amendments to the National Security Act, Secretary Johnson offered Eisenhower the appointment as chairman of the JCS. Ike was not interested. He had just experienced what it meant to be a powerless chairman and had no desire to repeat the exercise. Moreover, he now knew that it was impossible to count on the consistent annual funding level that he thought essential. The fact that Johnson admitted to thinking in terms of a $10 billion budget level further discouraged him. In the end he recalled concluding: "You don't want me. I can't agree with this." Planning was impossible given the highly politicized, frustrating, haphazard process by which budgetary decisions were taken. So, he later wrote, "I cleaned up the loose ends of the assignment, and returned to Columbia, convinced that Washington would never see me again except as an occasional visitor."[89]

Eisenhower's recollections could lead one to believe that he had severed his ties with the Johnson Defense Department, but this was far from true. He continued to serve as an occasional advisor to Johnson and the newly installed chairman of the JCS, his old friend Omar Bradley. Moreover, he supported Johnson's efforts to reduce costs when those efforts did not interfere with the armed services' ability to carry out their basic responsibilities. Thus, he was anything but displeased when Johnson closed fifty-one military installations and ordered the dismissal of 135,000 civilian employees. In a "My Dear Louis" letter written in August he expressed real satisfaction on learning that "you have taken the bull by the horns in your drive for real economy." While he found it regrettable, he acknowledged that there appeared "to be no other way to force governmental agencies to get down to the bitter task of making every dollar go as far as it can in meeting essential costs."[90]

At the same time, he continued to believe that the administration's 1951 defense budget proposal was inadequate. Moreover, even though his name had become closely identified with the budget, he was not shy about saying so. In a speech given subsequent to leaving Washington, he criticized the Truman budget and warned that the United States "had already disarmed to the extent—in some directions beyond the extent—that I with deep concern for her present safety, could possibly advise." That speech prompted the Senate Appropriations Committee to ask Ike to present his views in person.[91] On March 29, 1950, he told the committee that he had always believed a budget of between $15 and $16 billion was needed and that the administration's plan bordered on the unwise. Specifically, he recommended as a minimum increased funding for the acquisition of aircraft, antisubmarine warfare, Alaskan defenses, and the modernization of some of the Army's obsolete equipment. When asked how much he would add to the budget, his estimate was at least $500 million.[92]

Eisenhower's criticism, coupled with salvos from the press, especially by Stuart and Joseph Alsop who in their syndicated column charged that the administration was presiding over the unilateral disarmament of the United States, convinced Johnson and Truman to propose a $350 million supplement to the budget. It is interesting to note that the proposed increases were specifically designed to respond to objections previously raised by Eisenhower. Two hundred million dollars would go for Air Force procurement with the Navy getting most of the rest for aircraft and improvements in antisubmarine warfare. The Army would also get funds for modernization. There was no need to do anything further about Alaskan defenses since that issue had been resolved after Ike left the Pentagon.[93]

Having bowed to his critics, Johnson anxiously sought a letter from Eisenhower endorsing the revised budget, and he got one. "So far as I can determine," Ike now cheerfully wrote, "your recommendations accord exactly with what I personally believe should now be done. I hope the Committee agrees with you in detail."[94]

Eisenhower was also more than an observer of the final blowup between the Air Force and the Navy over the relative merits of long-range bombers as opposed to carrier-borne aircraft. His role in this aspect of the saga began before he left the Pentagon while he was in Augusta recuperating from his ileitis attack. Johnson, who was then surveying the entire defense establishment, looking for ways of reducing spending, raised the issue of the supercarrier *United States* (the ship's keel had just been laid) while in Augusta conferring with Ike and the JCS. Five days later, having returned to Washington, he wrote Eisenhower requesting the chiefs' views on whether or not the ship ought to be built.[95] Johnson denied having "any preconceived notions" about the ship, but noted that while everyone on the civilian side, up to and including the president, had approved the project, the Joint Chiefs had not yet given their assent. A few days later Eisenhower forwarded a memorandum to the chiefs, asking that they consider the issue without waiting for his return to Washington. Not surprisingly they proved unable to achieve unanimity and instead forwarded three separate opinions to Johnson. In a long statement, Admiral Denfeld supported continuing with the construction of the ship. Vandenberg opposed it on the ground that it was designed to launch long-range bombers, an Air Force responsibility, and was therefore a redundancy. Army Chief of Staff Bradley supported Vandenberg.

When Johnson learned that the JCS had been unable to arrive at a decision, and that two of its members opposed building the ship, he telephoned Eisenhower seeking his views. Ike's thinking counted heavily with Johnson, who had demonstrated time and again how much he relied upon him. The general had never been particularly enthusiastic about the supercarrier, but earlier he had supported the construction of one such vessel for possible use as an "*interim or emergency weapon.*"[96] Despite these earlier views, Eisenhower now joined the opposition. With Eisenhower and a majority of the JCS opposed to the ship, Johnson went to the president and received permission to halt construction. It is important to note that Johnson had support for his decision not only from the president but from one of the Navy's longtime champions. Carl Vinson, the powerful chairman of the House Armed Services Committee, said: "We cannot afford the luxury of two strategic air forces. We cannot afford an experimental vessel that, even without its aircraft, costs as much as 60 B-36 long range bombers. We should reserve strategic air warfare to the Air Force." "It is simply a matter of the proper allocation of war missions between the Navy and Air Force. It is the business of the Air Force to use long-range bombers in time of war." [97]

In a letter written subsequent to these events, Eisenhower revealed what was running through his mind as he cast the last and certainly deciding vote on the future of the supercarrier. First, the Navy's argument that it could successfully perform bombing missions from such ships but that the Air Force could not achieve similar results using land-based bombers was unconvincing. If the Navy's claim that land-based planes could not penetrate Soviet air defenses was valid, he failed to see how planes from a carrier would fare any better. Second, given the fact that the ship's mission would be a redundancy, it was difficult to justify its $500 million price tag, not to mention the cost of developing and deploying specially designed aircraft "in an era when we are going to face smaller and smaller appropriations." Eisenhower was not against "experimentation, providing the nation could afford it." However, his recent budget-making efforts convinced him that it was necessary to draw a line "between the requirements of economy on one side, and hope for improvement in our defense establishment on the other."[98]

Johnson's decision notwithstanding, the Navy refused to give up on the supercarrier without a fight. OP-23, a highly secret research organization attached to the Office of the Deputy Chief of Naval Operations for Administration and headed by Captain Arleigh Burke, was soon at work on a public relations campaign designed to highlight the virtues of the carrier and the inadequacies of the Air Force's long-range B-36 bomber. In their enthusiasm, officers attached to this office went too far when they decided to help Cedrick R. Worth, a civilian employee of the Navy Department, develop a paper in which he claimed that both Louis Johnson and Secretary of the Air Force Symington were engaged in corrupt practices associated with the purchase of B-36 bombers from the plane's manufacturer, Consolidated Vultee. This document, which began to circulate anonymously in the spring of 1949, prompted Congress to intervene. On August 9 Carl Vinson's House Armed Services Committee held hearings that exonerated both Johnson and Symington of any wrongdoing.[99]

A second House Armed Services Committee hearing, which opened in October, was designed to set to rest questions about the B-36 bomber by investigating its strengths and weaknesses. During the hearings, overwrought witnesses for the Navy said many things, at least some of which they would later regret. In his testimony, Admiral Arthur Radford, who later became the foremost advocate of nuclear weapons in the Eisenhower administration, denounced the idea of "an atomic blitz" as deeply immoral. The mass extermination of millions of men, women, and children, he said, was utterly abhorrent to him. "I don't believe in mass killing of noncombatants," he said. It was not the American way of war. Admiral Radford also told the committee that he did not believe the threat of a full-scale airborne nuclear attack would be "an effective deterrent to a war, or that it [would] win a war." Radford went on to argue that even if one did accept the premise that atomic bombs could win wars, the B-36 was hardly the instrument to achieve that end since it was highly vulnerable to interceptor aircraft and could not attack targets with precision from high altitudes. The plane, he said, was "a billion dollar blunder," the "battleship of the air."[100]

One after another, high-ranking naval officers testified on the inadequacies of the B-36. On October 13, Chief of Naval Operations Admiral Louis Denfeld concluded a week of angry, headline-grabbing testimony by giving his complete support to the claims of the rebels who had preceded him. He told Congress that the Navy was being undermined by the other two services and that unification could not succeed until the Navy had a "full partnership." He denounced the B-36 and charged that the Air Force and the Army were involved in "a steady campaign to relegate the Navy to a convoy and antisubmarine service." Denfeld even challenged the testimony of Navy Secretary Francis P. Matthews, who had attempted to play down the significance of the controversy by claiming that the agitation against the B-36 was confined to a disaffected few. It was the entire Navy, Denfeld insisted, that was distressed, fearing that at the beginning of some future war it would not have the weapons it needed to do the job required. Denfeld also criticized Secretary Johnson for his refusal to properly fund the Navy and for acting arbitrarily in killing the supercarrier program.[101]

Watching these developments from his offices at Columbia University, Eisenhower was appalled. On October 14, his fifty-ninth birthday, he told his diary: "The bitter fight still goes on in Washington, with the Navy cursing the other services. The whole performance is humiliating—I've seriously considered resigning my commission, so that I could say what I *pleased* publicly." In fact, however, Eisenhower had no desire to participate in the demeaning display. Nor did he think Army and Air Force officers should respond to the Navy in kind. He felt so strongly about this that he telephoned his old friend, Omar Bradley, and told him just that. The fact that the Navy seemed intent on humiliating itself did not mean that the other services should follow suit. He thought the Defense Department ought to confine itself to a single dignified rebuttal. This, he believed, "would tend to point up and emphasize the difference between doing these things properly and doing them through the headlines."[102]

Eisenhower's views notwithstanding, as the Navy's attack gained momentum, Louis Johnson as well as Army and Air Force leaders felt a growing need for some high-powered support. General Albert Gruenther, a close and valued friend, sent Eisenhower a copy of Denfeld's statement along with a note indicating that he as well as others had more or less expected Radford and other aircraft carrier admirals to take the position they did. However, for the chief of naval operations to denounce the defense secretary and by implication the president himself was something else entirely. Gruenther explained that Army and Air Force men were "depressed" by the tone of Denfeld's remarks and looking for support. It was clear from the purport of his letter that Gruenther believed a response to the Navy's accusations was essential. Who was better positioned to deliver it than Eisenhower?[103]

Gruenther was not the only one urging Eisenhower to testify. Committee Chairman Carl Vinson invited him to Washington as did Louis Johnson, who telephoned urging him to come. The Navy's behavior, he said, was an attack on the president, the entire concept of civilian control of the military, and his own efforts to reduce defense spending. Stuart Symington too chimed in with a call of his own, urging Ike to appear. The admirals "really have gone below the belt this time," he said.[104]

Ultimately, Eisenhower did agree to testify, but when he did, it was to play a different and more personally acceptable role at the hearings. There was nothing in his testimony about the B-36 or the supercarrier. Instead his was a plea to "stop looking backward & cursing mistakes & those who've made them." He refused to take sides in the Air Force–Navy controversy, arguing that those involved were all patriotic Americans whose motives were above suspicion. He would not contribute to the divisiveness within the military establishment, telling the committee that in his view the current controversy was the result of a limited defense budget and the impossibility of working out a generally acceptable division of available funds.[105]

After the House Armed Services Committee wound up the B-36 investigation, Carl Vinson asked Eisenhower for an opinion regarding the conclusions that might be drawn from the affair. What should the committee recommend? In his reply to Vinson Eisenhower did not fail to take the Navy's leadership to task for some of its behavior. After all, he observed, "when men in uniform feel capable and qualified to defy orders of civilian superiors, we are coming dangerously close to violating that basic concept of American political life which makes the military organization completely subordinate to civilian authority." Yet Eisenhower refused to recommend punishment for those guilty of insubordination. Instead he explained away some of the more extreme behavior of certain naval officers as stemming from an honest difference of opinion coupled with their fear that the Navy would be outvoted by the other two services "in any tripartite councils."[106]

More concerned with the future, Eisenhower explained that he believed recent events demonstrated the need "for a different approach to security development" than had been the case. He believed the basic question was how to make unification work. As much as he believed in the importance of creating a powerful chief of staff, he thought that this was not the time for more legislative action. He feared that any such effort would result in "renewed arguments that could not fail to prolong and possibly even intensify the heat and rancor of the quarrel." In any event, the inadequacy of the law was only part of the problem. The way in which it had been administered had also been faulty. In Eisenhower's judgment there was plenty of blame to go around. The Defense Department was at fault for not exercising sufficient control over the officer corps. Congress, too, was at fault for allowing itself to be used as a forum by discontented representatives of the armed services.[107]

In this long message to Vinson, Eisenhower returned to a theme he had only touched upon during his public testimony. Recent experience had reaffirmed his long-held conviction that the budget held the key to harmony. Interservice bickering could be traced to the fact that by setting a spending ceiling, the Budget Bureau set in motion a competition for the lion's share of the defense dollar. That competition was especially intense because the sum allocated did not approximate what the services believed they required. Here Ike put his finger on a key issue, one that would plague his White House years as it had Truman's. However, he had no viable solution to offer.[108]

Eisenhower sent these observations to Vinson in January 1950. In that same month, acting on a recommendation from Secretary of State Dean Acheson, the president authorized an NSC study of the country's defense posture. The result was NSC 68/2, which called for a massive rearmament program. The president's reluctance to commit to such a spending program delayed the march toward rearmament for a time, but the outbreak of the Korean War ended the president's resistance. Military expansion then began in earnest. As for Eisenhower, before the end of the year he was back in uniform as commander of NATO forces in Europe. When next he addressed the question of unification and the reform of the military establishment it would be at another time and from another place, the White House.

NOTES

1. Steven L. Rearden, *The History of the Office of the Secretary of Defense: The Formative Years* (Washington, DC: Historical Office, Office of the Secretary of Defense, 1984), 36.

2. Robert G. Albion and Robert H. Connery, *Forrestal and the Navy* (New York: Columbia University Press, 1962), 31.

3. Eisenhower to the JCS, 10 Nov. 1947, in Alfred D. Chandler, Stephen E. Ambrose, Louis Galambos et al., eds., *The Eisenhower Papers,* 14 vols. (Baltimore: Johns Hopkins University Press, 1970–96), 9: 2052–53 (hereafter cited as *EP*). It was essential, Eisenhower argued, that such a plan "include missions, priority of missions, required strength of the military forces, the allocation of this strength to the Army, Navy and Air Force, deployment of forces, employment of forces by component, programmed development of military installations and bases, as well as policies on equipping and maintaining the military forces."

4. Quoted in E. B. Potter, *Admiral Arleigh Burke* (New York: Random House, 1990), 315.

5. *New York Times* (hereafter cited as *NYT*), 9 and 10 April 1947.

6. Paolo Coletta, *The U.S. Navy and Defense Unification, 1947–1956* (Newark, University of Delaware Press, 1984), 92. Using a wide array of primary sources, Coletta provides a very complete summary of the war between the Navy and the Air Force. See also Steven Rearden, *History of the Office of the Secretary of Defense,* 1:390.

7. *NYT*, 10 April 1947. For more on this see an address by Assistant Secretary of the Navy John N. Brown in *NYT*, 31 May 1947. See also General Hoyt

Vandenberg to Stuart Symington, 9 July 1947, Papers of Hoyt Vandenberg, Box 58, Manuscript Division of the Library of Congress (hereafter cited as LC).

8. Eisenhower to Forrestal, 7 Feb. 1948, *EP*, 9:2242–51.

9. Ibid.

10. Ibid.

11. Walter Millis, ed., *The Forrestal Diaries* (New York: Viking Press, 1951), 378 (hereafter cited as Forrestal, *Diaries*).

12. Ibid.

13. Forrestal, *Diaries*, 390; Douglas Kinnard, *The Secretary of Defense* (Lexington: University of Kentucky Press, 1980), 26–28.

14. Forrestal, *Diaries*, 392–93. The Key West agreement was unfortunately one of those compromises each side could interpret to serve its own purposes. While the Navy agreed not to develop a separate strategic air force, the Air Force agreed that the Navy might develop such weapons that it deemed essential to its mission and that in carrying out that mission naval aircraft would "have the right to attack inland targets." The Air Force also recognized "the right and need for the Navy to participate in an all-out air campaign."

15. Forrestal, *Diaries*, 389–90.

16. CRESAP, McCORMICK, and PAGET to Forrestal, 6 May 1948, R. G. 330, Records of the Office of the Secretary of Defense [D 70–1–50] (hereafter cited as OS/D), Modern Military Branch, National Archives (hereafter cited as NA).

17. The members of the JCS refused to comply.

18. Ohly to McNeill, 19 May 1948, *The Joint Staff—Limitation on its Size*, OS/D [D 70–1–50], NA; Ohly to Forrestal, 3 June 1948, *Reorganization of the Joint Chiefs of Staff*, ibid.; Ohly to Forrestal, 18 Oct. 1948, *Proposed Additional Duties for the Director of the Joint Staff*, ibid.; Gruenther to Forrestal, 19 Oct. 1948, ibid.

19. Clark Clifford, with Richard Holbrook, *Counsel to the President: A Memoir* (New York: Random House, 1991), 160.

20. Eisenhower to Forrestal, 27 Sept. 1948, *EP*, 10:230–34.

21. Clifford and Holbrook, *Counsel to the President*, 160–61; Forrestal, *Diaries*, 497–98.

22. Forrestal, *Diaries*, 539–40.

23. For the recommendations made by this committee, see Forrestal, Pace, and Clifford to Truman, 10 Feb. 1949, OS/D, CD [12–1–8], NA.

24. Forrestal, *Diaries*, 500.

25. This fairly amazing idea was offered by Army Secretary Kenneth Royall who believed that given existing law the Navy and Air Force could never be made to cooperate. Royall thought that the issue ought to be put directly to Congress and a decision taken. Of course, Royall, a staunch supporter of unification, believed the logical approach would be to put all aviation under the control of the

Air Force, and he probably never dreamed anyone would seriously consider the alternative.

26. Quoted in Paolo Coletta, *The U.S. Navy and Defense Unification, 1947–1953* (Newark: University of Delaware Press), 105–106.

27. Eberstadt to Eisenhower, 1 Nov. 1948, Eisenhower's Pre-presidential Papers, Box 37, EL; Eisenhower to Eberstadt, 4 Nov. 1948, *EP*, 10:280–83. For the reform recommendations Eisenhower made to the Eberstadt Commission, see Eisenhower to Eberstadt, 20 Sept. 1948, ibid., 204–12.

28. Eisenhower to Forrestal, 4 Nov. 1948, ibid., 283.

29. Forrestal to Truman, 9 Nov. 1948, OS/D clas.-numeric File, CD [5–1–25], NA.

30. Eberstadt to Eisenhower, 7 Dec. 1948, Eisenhower's Pre-presidential Papers, Box 37, EL. Eberstadt wrote to Eisenhower urging him to help Forrestal, who, he said, had done an extraordinary job in a difficult situation. At this point, Eberstadt believed, his greatest need was for wise and loyal advisors.

31. Eisenhower to Forrestal, 4 Nov. 1948, *EP*, 10:283 n. 3.

32. Forrestal, *Diaries*, 540.

33. Ibid.

34. Eisenhower to Marx Leva, 11 Dec. 1948, 14 Jan. 1949, *EP*, 10:358–60, 432–34; Alice C. Cole et al., eds., *The Department of Defense: Documents on Establishment and Organization, 1944–1978* (Washington, DC: Office of the Secretary of Defense, Historical Office, 1978); Forrestal, *Diaries*, 540. Forrestal called for the establishment of an undersecretary of defense, the elimination of the presidential chief of staff's position, establishment of a chairman for the JCS, expansion of the Joint Staff, and dropping the service secretaries from the National Security Council.

35. Robert A. Ferrell, ed., *The Eisenhower Diaries* (New York: Norton, 1981), 152, 156 (hereafter cited as Ferrell, *Eisenhower Diaries*).

36. Leach to Vandenberg, 5 Jan. 1949, Vandenberg Papers, Box 43, Manuscript Division, Library of Congress (hereafter cited as LC).

37. Ibid.

38. Ferrell, *Eisenhower Diaries*, 151.

39. Eisenhower, diary entry, 27 Jan. 1949, *EP*, 10:448–51.

40. *NYT*, 13 Feb. 1949.

41. Sullivan to Symington, 15 Feb. 1949, CCS 354.2, Central Numeric File [9–29–48], Sec. 1, NA; Laler to Gruenther, 17 Feb. 1949, ibid.

42. Eisenhower to Gruenther, 16 Feb. 1949, ibid.; Laler to Gruenther, 17 Feb. 1949, ibid.

43. *Time*, 21 Feb. 1949, 22.

44. *NYT*, 3 March 1949.

45. Eisenhower to Symington, 7 March 1949, *EP*, 10:533–34.

46. Eisenhower, diary entries, 27 Jan., 2 Feb. 1949, *EP*, 10:448–51, 461–62. Later, Eisenhower insisted that all battleships be mothballed.

47. Ibid. Not long before Eisenhower took up his new responsibilities, the Navy established a special group known as OP-23. Its job was to develop position papers in support of the Navy's ambitions. For more on OP-23, see Potter, *Admiral Arleigh Burke*, 317–19; Coletta, *The Navy and Unification*, 115, 181.

48. Eisenhower, diary entries, 27 Jan., 2 Feb. 1949, *EP*, 10:448–51, 461–62.

49. Ibid.

50. Ibid.

51. Notes used during a conference with the president, 9 Feb. 1949, Eisenhower's Pre-presidential Papers, Box 116, EL.

52. Ibid.

53. Ibid.

54. Ohly to Forrestal, "Status of Major JCS Projects," 19 July 1948, OS/D [12–1–16], NA; see also memo on "split" views of the JCS, Wedemeyer to Bradley, 28 July 1949, Central Numeric File [12–1–9], ibid.

55. Eisenhower to Forrestal, 4 Feb. 1949, *EP*, 10:469.

56. Notes used during a conference with the president, 9 Feb. 1949, Eisenhower's Pre-presidential Papers, Box 116, EL.

57. One day after his conference with Eisenhower, Truman received the recommendations of the legislative drafting committee that he had empowered to propose amendments to the National Security Act. See Forrestal, Pace, and Clifford to Truman, 10 Feb. 1949, copy in Eisenhower's Pre-presidential Papers, Box 116, EL.

58. Eisenhower diary entry, 9 Feb. 1949, *EP*, 10:482–84.

59. Ibid.

60. *NYT*, 12 Feb. 1949; *Time*, 21 Feb. 1949, 22; see also Vinson to Forrestal, OS/D, Central Numeric File, [D 34–6–47], NA.

61. *Public Papers of the Presidents: Harry S. Truman, 1949* (Washington, DC: GPO, 1964), 163–66.

62. Ferrell, *Eisenhower Diaries*, 150.

63. Eisenhower to Louis Johnson, 14 July 1949, CCS 370 [8–19–45], Sec. 18, NA. Eisenhower may have called this meeting in response to a memorandum from Chief of Naval Operations Admiral Louis Denfeld that proposed a status quo budget based on forces in being and budget levels established for 1950. See JCS 1800/31, 8 Feb. 1949, CCS 370 [8–19–45], Sec. 18, NA.

64. Eisenhower, diary entries, 19 Feb., and 19 March 1949, *EP*, 10:497–98, 545–47.

65. Ibid.

66. Ibid.

67. Marquis Childs, "The Battle of the Pentagon," *Harper's*, Aug. 1949, 52.

68. Coletta, *The Navy and Unification*, 127.

69. Ibid.

70. Ibid., 133.

71. Rearden, *History of the Office of the Secretary of Defense*, 1:50.

72. Eisenhower to Hazlett, 12 Aug. 1949, in Griffith, ed., *Ike's Letters to a Friend* (Lawrence: University of Kansas Press, 1981), 59.

73. Eisenhower, *At Ease: Stories I Tell My Friends* (Garden City: Doubleday, 1967), 332.

74. Eisenhower to Hazlett, 12 Aug. 1949, in Griffith, *Ike's Letters to a Friend*, 59.

75. Eisenhower, diary entry, 19 March 1949, *EP*, 10:545–47.

76. Ibid.

77. Eisenhower to the JCS, 3 March 1949, CCS 370 [8–19–45], Sec. 14, NA.

78. Memo for General Gruenther, 2 March 1949, ibid.

79. *Washington Post*, 15 March 1949.

80. Rearden, *A History of the Office of the Secretary of Defense*, 1:81.

81. Eisenhower, diary entry, 19 March 1949, *EP*, 10:545–47.

82. Eisenhower to Hazlett, 27 April 1949, in Griffith, *Ike's Letters to a Friend*, 54–55.

83. Denfeld to the JCS, 3 May 1949, CCS 370 [8–19–45], Sec. 15, NA. In this memo Denfeld demonstrated that "red brick" planning would result in the total elimination of the Navy's air arm and marine aviation, a 45 percent reduction in the fleet marine force, and a 50 percent reduction in the cruiser force. For a detailed description of Eisenhower's efforts to produce a budget, see Kenneth W. Condit, *History of the Joint Chiefs of Staff, 1947–1949* (Wilmington: Michael Glazier Inc., 1979), 2:257–81.

84. Budget Director Pace's statement in "Discussion Following Budget Presentation," 21 Oct. 1949, CCS 370 (8–15–49), Sec. 20, NA.

85. McNeil to Johnson, 11 May 1949, O/SD, Clas. Numeric File, CD [5–1–46], NA.

86. Eisenhower, diary entry, 4 June 1949, *EP*, 10:606–607.

87. Eisenhower to Johnson, 14 July 1949, *EP*, 10:699–704. Eisenhower continued to work on the 1951 budget for another month, submitting his final thinking to Omar Bradley, the new chairman of the JCS, in late August. See Eisenhower to Johnson, ibid., 735–36.

88. Alice C. Cole et al., *The Department of Defense*, 81–105.

89. Eisenhower, *At Ease: Stories I Tell My Friends*, 355.

90. Eisenhower to Johnson, 26 Aug. 1949, *EP*, 10:735.

91. *NYT*, 30 March 1950.

92. Ibid.

93. Ibid., 5 and 27 April 1950.

94. Eisenhower to Johnson, 25 April 1950, *EP*, 11:1082.

95. At the time only the ship's keel had been laid. The Navy believed it was being discriminated against because it found the money to begin construction of the ship by abandoning other projects in its budget. With the permission of Secretary Forrestal, the Air Force had recently made a similar adjustment in order to add to its B-36 strength.

96. Eisenhower to Forrestal, 21 Dec. 1948, *EP*, 10:381.

97. Coletta, *The Navy and Unification*, 103.

98. Eisenhower to Hazlett, 12 Aug. 1949, in Griffith, *Ike's Letters to a Friend*, 58.

99. For more on the activities of OP-23, see Potter, *Admiral Arleigh Burke*, 316–30.

100. It is worth noting, considering Radford's stated opposition to using nuclear weapons against civilian populations, that only a short while later, as chairman of the JCS from 1953 to 1957, he was the Eisenhower administration's most outspoken advocate of the use of nuclear weapons.

101. Rearden, *History of the Office of the Secretary of Defense*, 1:415–21; Condit, *History of the Joint Chiefs of Staff*, 2:338–50.

102. Eisenhower to Royall, 10 Oct. 1949, *EP*, 10:775 n. 5.

103. Eisenhower, diary entry, 14 Oct. 1949, ibid., 778–79 n. 2.

104. Eisenhower to Royall, 10 Oct. 1949, ibid., 775 n. 6.

105. House Committee on the Armed Services, *Hearings: Investigation of the B-36 Bomber Program*, 81st Cong., 1st Sess., 562–66; *NYT*, 21 Oct. 1949; Ferrell, *Eisenhower Diaries*, 164.

106. Eisenhower to Vinson, 3 Jan. 1950, *EP*, 11:889–904.

107. Ibid.

108. Ibid.

4

"A Hydra-headed Monster"

In the brief five-year period between 1945 and 1950, Eisenhower saw re-peated in microcosm one of the more depressing aspects of the history of the American military establishment. First came rapid demobilization and budget cuts that ate into the sinew and bone of the armed services. "We 'ab-sorb' everything," he complained in 1949, "rising costs . . . increased pay, stockpiling, etc. etc." It was peacetime and neither Congress nor the public seemed to care. Even President Truman, whom Ike credited with a concern for military preparedness, could not be counted upon to propose consistent, adequate support. "We are repeating our own history of decades," he wrote, "we just don't believe we ever will get into a real jam."[1] Then came the Ko-rean War with its vast and hurried rearmament program. The Navy got its Forrestal class of supercarriers, the Air Force, growing rapidly, was sched-uled to expand to 143 wings by 1954, and the Army expanded to a full twenty divisions. It was the "feast" side of a "feast or famine" cycle that had been repeated many times before in American military history, and Eisen-hower, back in uniform as commander of NATO forces in Europe, was not pleased. It seemed clear to him that the Truman administration had failed to address the basic problem of protecting the integrity of the economy while providing for the national security.

In early 1951 after years of being courted by Republican leaders, Ike at last decided to run for the presidency. He had many reasons for abandoning his lifelong horror of politics. Not the least of these was his opposition to the vast military spending programs undertaken by the Truman administration. In his judgment Washington was spending wildly without giving enough consideration to the need for, or effectiveness of, the weapons it was acquiring. These expenditures along with some of a political nature, he wrote, were driving the country "straight toward inflation of an uncontrollable character."

Eisenhower thought that every weapons development program should be thoroughly evaluated to be certain it was needed and that the services were not duplicating one another's efforts. The armed services themselves ought to be "ruthlessly pulled apart and examined in order to get down to the country's requirements." A complete study of "the economics of national security" seemed essential. "If we don't have the objective, industry-government-professional examination that will show us where and how to proceed in this armament business," he wrote, "we will go broke and still have inefficient defenses."[2]

Ike was "astonished" that "Stu" Symington, Defense Secretary "Bob" Lovett, and Air Force Secretary Thomas Finletter, men he regarded as "conservative and cautious," could sanction such wild spending. The only justification for such a program was "an immediate prospect of war." He was convinced that a war with the Soviet Union was no more likely than it had been two or three years before when the administration was spending a virtual pittance on defense. Of course, the United States needed to be strong, but strength should be measured in economic and moral as well as military terms. He thought that "any person who doesn't clearly understand that national security and national solvency are mutually dependent, and that permanent maintenance of a crushing weight of military power would eventually create dictatorship, should not be entrusted with any kind of responsibility in our country."[3]

Because Truman had followed a "guns and butter policy" that allowed inflationary forces to take root in the economy, Eisenhower believed the nation faced difficult choices. Congress could declare a national emergency and empower the president to implement wide-ranging economic controls, but these might well have to remain in place until the cold war was resolved. That would destroy America's free economy as well as individual liberty and result in "a new conception of the relation of the individual to the state—a conception that would change in revolutionary fashion the kind of government under which we live." It would be tragic, he thought, if in the name of preserving liberty we adopted practices that led to its destruction. A better option was to avoid the need for economic controls by flattening "the military production curve so as to minimize the effect of military production upon our economy." "[W]e should," he thought, "figure out our strength objectives and push toward them steadily," while "having in mind that we must retain a strong and solvent economy."[4]

Eisenhower believed that in moments of crisis when Congress proved willing to spend lavishly on defense, service leaders, conditioned by years of scarcity, exaggerated threats to the nation's security. The result had often been unnecessary congressional appropriations, veto fights, and disagreements among the services that degenerated into "public brawls." The time had come, he thought, to put an end to this expensive and unseemly business.[5] Each service should be provided with only those resources required to fulfill a set of clearly defined responsibilities. The alternative was for each of the three services to duplicate one another's efforts at enormous cost. "We cannot pretend to do everything in every field all the time," he warned.[6] For Eisenhower, the key to ending interservice rivalry and wasteful spending was, as it had been for many years, the unification of the armed services.

Ike renewed his call for the reform of the military establishment at a time when a number of influential observers were making similar appeals. Early in 1952, former Secretary of the Air Force Stuart Symington released a scathing condemnation of inefficiency inside the Pentagon that made the front page of the *New York Times*. Symington claimed that current Pentagon practices produced incalculable "waste in men, money and time." He was especially critical of the JCS, which, he said, needed a major overhaul. The 1949 amendments to the National Security Act had given the JCS a chairman, but left him powerless. This, Symington argued, was absurd. Every successful business enterprise had a chief executive officer who was ultimately responsible for the welfare of his company. In like fashion the military needed a chief of staff with decision-making powers. It only made sense to give "authority to the best man available in order that he can direct agreed policy."[7]

In a series of speeches and magazine articles completed between September 1952 and February 1953, Vannevar Bush, a long-time supporter of unification who was justly famous for his role in the development of the atomic bomb, delivered a crushing critique of the current military organization. He pointed out that the chain of command as defined in existing legislation was a hopeless muddle, that the chairman of the JCS lacked real authority and could not resolve disagreements among the chiefs, that the members of the JCS and Joint Staff often found themselves deeply conflicted when service loyalties and the national interest could not be reconciled, and that in general the services were not responding creatively to the impact science was having on weapons development. In an article in *Colliers Magazine* entitled "What's Wrong at the Pentagon?" he warned that "the organization under which our military planning is being done is faulty, that the planning itself is defective, and that the nation, therefore, is in serious danger."[8] In an essay published several weeks after Eisenhower won the presidency, Harold H. Martin, well known for his writings on military affairs, endorsed the Bush critique, adding that "if Eisenhower is to find a bold new approach to the problem of national survival, he must begin by overhauling the ponderous and creaking Defense Department machinery." Otherwise, Martin continued, "interservice rivalry can never be controlled—certainly not with the JCS set up as it is."[9]

Eisenhower's most important ally in the struggle to achieve further reforms was Robert A. Lovett, the outgoing secretary of defense. "Bob" Lovett's career bore a striking resemblance to that of his close friend, James Forrestal. When the United States entered World War I, Lovett, like Forrestal, became a naval aviator. After the war, he too went into banking, working in international finance with Brown Brothers, Harriman and Co. Lovett continued his work as an international banker until 1940 when, again like Forrestal, he joined the Roosevelt administration. Forrestal became assistant secretary of the navy; Lovett served as assistant secretary of the army for air.

During the war Lovett and General George C. Marshall developed a close working relationship and became fast friends. In 1947 when Marshall took over the State Department, he brought Lovett along as his deputy. Three years later, after agreeing to replace Louis Johnson in the Defense Department, he brought Lovett back to Washington once again, this time as his deputy at the Pentagon. Lovett, a man who shunned the spotlight and had absolutely no political ambitions, was not enthusiastic about returning to Washington. However, as he once wryly noted, there were three people in the world he could never refuse, his wife Adéle, the president, and George Marshall.[10]

The team of Marshall and Lovett was held together by more than friendship and mutual respect. They were philosophically akin, sharing many views to which Eisenhower also subscribed. Marshall, of course, had not changed his opinion regarding the vital importance of unification. Lovett agreed. Moreover, they both believed that military needs should be measured against the economic well-being of the country as a whole. In emergency situations such as the Korean War, the military required extraordinary support. Under ordinary conditions they believed in adequate, consistent funding, nothing more. Thus, Lovett once remarked in words that might have come directly from Eisenhower: "We seem to have had only two throttle positions in the past, wide open when we are at war—and tight shut when there is no shooting. We have to work out a system that will give us a cruising speed. When you have to drive some distance, a good cruising speed is the fastest, safest way to get there." On another occasion he said: "The country . . . has to make up its mind to keep steadily on this project of strength and must not indulge in those excessive swings from an armed state to impotency. They are very costly and extremely dangerous. Less money annually, but steadily, can accomplish much more than huge sums today and nothing tomorrow—and the over-all cost will be much, much less."[11]

When Marshall retired in September 1951, Lovett replaced him as secretary of defense, remaining in office until the end of President Truman's administration. During this period of astonishing growth in the military establishment, Lovett had to deal with the same sort of problems that had plagued his predecessors—a JCS organization that frequently deadlocked, interservice rivalry, disagreement over priorities in achieving expanded force levels, and of course an entirely unrealistic attitude on the part of the services toward budget making. Preparing the defense budget for the 1952 fiscal year was a case in point. Lovett was dumbfounded when the services submitted proposals amounting to "an astounding" $104 billion. Blessed with a fine sense of humor, the secretary, who described these proposals as "letters to Santa Claus," settled down to the difficult business of transforming a wish list into something realistic. In the end he produced a budget of $60.4 billion. Though less than 60 percent of what the services claimed they required, the budget stands to this day as the largest peacetime military budget on record both in terms of real dollars and as a percentage of the gross national product.[12]

Lovett had a similar experience while working on the 1953 budget. This tussle with the military, however, was resolved when the president stepped in. At a December 28, 1951, meeting of the National Security Council, Truman warned that over-spending on the military could ruin the economy and give Moscow "the fruits of a hot war victory without having to fight it." He established a limit of $60 billion for all military and military-assistance spending for the coming fiscal year. The JCS warned that this funding level posed a serious threat to national security. Lovett and Truman remained adamant, sending Congress a $52.1 billion budget proposal. Congress, even less inclined to support the military, cut more than 9 percent from that figure.[13]

In the summer of 1952 Lovett instructed Assistant Secretary of Defense Charles Coolidge to report on the progress being made in moving toward real service unification. The Coolidge study became the basis of a long, informal letter that Lovett sent to the president detailing his concerns. In this letter Lovett noted that "unification," properly viewed, was an evolutionary process and that "much remains to be done in order to provide a more efficient and economical form of national security."[14]

The secretary proposed a number of changes that were much in keeping with views long held by Eisenhower. First, he insisted that the powers of the secretary of defense needed further strengthening. All doubts that the secretary was the president's deputy in the area of national security affairs with authority over the service secretaries should be erased. This was essential because the service secretaries had on too many occasions used a clause in the existing law that stipulated that the services should be "separately administered" to undermine Lovett's policies and programs. Next, Lovett took aim at two semi-independent agencies, the Munitions Board and the Research and Development Board, both of which, he thought, should be abolished, their functions transferred to the Office of the Secretary of Defense.[15]

Then, very carefully, the secretary came to the central point of his letter, the future of the JCS. Lovett recognized, of course, that "the proper set-up of the Joint Chiefs of Staff is the most difficult and delicate one in the field of our national defense structure." At the same time, he noted that as presently constituted the JCS system was not functioning efficiently. The chiefs liked to argue that for the most part they acted in harmony, that very few "split papers" were forwarded to the secretary, and this was true.[16] However, it was an open secret that there were dozens of issues, many of them important, that the chiefs simply refused to address because they knew in advance that they would not be able to agree on a recommendation and did not wish to trumpet their failures to a broader public. It was also well understood that many issues were decided not on the basis of what was in the national interest but as a result of political logrolling among the chiefs.

Lovett complained that he had not always received sound military advice from the chiefs. The problem, as he saw it, was that they were currently assigned to play two often conflicting roles. Each was the head of his service and as such deeply concerned with protecting its interests. At the same time the chiefs were the principal military advisors to the secretary and the president. In that role they were asked to think and act in terms of the national interest. When these two interests collided, as they frequently did, each chief characteristically thought of his service first. The same was even more true of the members of the Joint Staff.[17]

Lovett offered two possible solutions to the problem of reforming the JCS and providing the secretary and the president with military advice based on national and not parochial service interests. One approach would be to create a new combined staff made up of ex-service chiefs at the end of their careers who might not be so completely beholden to their individual services. They would be aided by staff officers who would also be separated from their services and whose future professional advancement would not be dependent on the services. Such a group, Lovett thought, might be "beyond the range of partisan-service ambitions."

Aware that he was proposing what amounted to a "general staff" that would probably be unacceptable to Congress, Lovett offered an alternative that he thought might be more politically feasible. Members of the JCS should be relieved of responsibility for the day-to-day administration of their services and be required to focus their attention exclusively on joint planning and global strategy. If they were not separated from the services they commanded, he asked, how could they support any action that they deemed detrimental to their service? If they could not do that, how could they even begin to think in terms of the national rather than their own service's interest?[18]

In his long letter Lovett made two other recommendations of consequence. First, he argued that the chairman's power should be enhanced so that he might play a more decisive role in guiding JCS deliberations. He also suggested that if the secretary was to be a truly independent executive, he should have his own permanent staff of military as well as civilian advisors. To ensure that he would get sound advice he recommended that for purposes of career advancement the military officers serving on this staff should be made independent of their particular branch of the service.[19] In a final damning condemnation of the existing disorder, Lovett wrote that the country should no longer "maintain a Department of Defense organization which, in several parts, would require drastic reorganization to fight a war." The "contradictions and straddles" of the National Security Act, he said, should no longer be tolerated.[20]

Lovett's letter to the president was dated November 18, 1952, the same day on which Eisenhower, now president-elect, met at the White House with Truman and other key members of the outgoing administration. That meeting did not go well. The wounds of the recent political campaign remained raw and painful to the incoming president.[21] However, Eisenhower's hostility toward Truman did not extend to Lovett, who he had known and respected for many years. Following that frosty encounter in the Oval Office, Eisenhower and the defense secretary went to the Pentagon for a briefing with the JCS and private talks. It is probable that at this meeting they agreed that Lovett's letter should be published. In any event it was leaked to the press and became the first salvo in Eisenhower's effort to advance the cause of military reform. On January 2, 1953, the *New York Times* carried the essence of Lovett's letter as a front-page story with this lead: "Lovett Criticizes Defense Machine as Weak in Crisis." A few days later the Pentagon released the entire letter to the press. Then, in its January 19 issue, one day before Eisenhower took the oath of office, *Time* published a synopsis of Lovett's arguments in a long report of its own.[22]

The growing public awareness that there were serious problems at the Pentagon placed President Eisenhower in a strong position to pursue change. The first item on his agenda was to find a secretary of defense with enough experience managing large organizations to handle the job. "We have tried two investment bankers, a lawyer, and a soldier—and we are not yet unified," he wrote. He wanted an industrialist, "a man who is used to knocking heads together and who is not easily fooled."[23] The leaders of his transition team, Lucius Clay and Herbert Brownell, recommended Charles E. "Engine Charlie" Wilson, head of the General Motors Corporation, for the position. An engineer and "production man," Wilson had the sort of managerial experience Ike was looking for. Though he would subsequently change his opinion of Wilson, Eisenhower was at first unreservedly enthusiastic. If anyone could bring administrative order to the Pentagon, he believed it was a tough-minded businessman like Wilson.[24]

On January 29, 1953, nine days after taking the oath of office, Eisenhower took the first actual step toward reforming the military when he signed an executive order establishing the President's Advisory Committee on Government Organization. The committee, chaired by New York's Nelson Rockefeller, had as its other members the president's brother, Milton Eisenhower, president of Johns Hopkins University, and Dr. Arthur Flemming, director of the Office of Defense Mobilization.[25]

Three weeks after this, Secretary of Defense Wilson appropriated Rockefeller's committee for use as the nucleus of a larger group that he created to make recommendations for reforming the Pentagon. This group, also headed by Rockefeller, included Robert Lovett, David Sarnoff, president of the Radio Corporation of America, Vannevar Bush, and Omar Bradley, chairman of the Joint Chiefs of Staff. Later, Admiral Chester Nimitz, U.S.N. ret., General Carl Spaatz, U.S.A.F. ret., and General George C. Marshall, U.S.A. ret., were added to the committee as special consultants. All of these men supported the principle of service unification.[26]

The ten members of the Rockefeller committee held their first meeting in mid-February and met regularly three times each week until they had produced a finished report. They heard from twenty-two witnesses, including the members of the JCS, retired military officers, former service secretaries, and civilian officials of the Defense Department, as well as civilian employees who had experience dealing with the organizational problems of the department. The opinions expressed ranged from one extreme to the other. Thomas K. Finletter, who had just retired as secretary of the air force, called for a return to the intent of the 1947 law, which emphasized a high degree of independence for the services rather than centralized control of service activities. He also believed that the service secretaries ought to rank above the deputy secretary of defense and have their cabinet rank restored. At the other extreme stood Air Force Chief of Staff Hoyt Vandenberg, who called for an organization that looked and sounded very much like the Army's original plan for the unification of the services. Vandenberg recommended a "Chief of Staff of the Armed Services who would participate in the deliberations of the JCS but would have, "subject to the authority of the President and the Secretary of Defense, power of decision."[27] He also insisted that something had to be done about the duplication and waste that was endemic within the military establishment. At present, he noted: "The service chiefs have found themselves in disagreement not merely over the resources required to carry out defined responsibilities, but further over fundamental questions of what the respective responsibilities are, what service is to perform a given mission and which or how many of the services require resources for its performance." He argued for "a drastic clarification of the present roles and missions of the services."[28]

In framing its proposals the Rockefeller committee avoided extremes. No one on the committee seriously believed that returning to the days of James Forrestal and "the Revolt of the Admirals," as Finletter seemed to advise, would resolve anything. At the same time the committee members refused to endorse the extreme views advocated by Vandenberg, which, they believed, would only fuel the flames of interservice discord and would in any event encounter fierce opposition on Capitol Hill. Instead, following a course of action advocated by Robert Lovett, who supported an evolutionary approach, it sent to the secretary of defense a set of reform proposals that moved in the direction of unification while avoiding that dreaded word. Wilson approved these recommendations and sent them on to the White

House where they formed the basis of what emerged as Reorganization Plan Number Six.

A central object of the plan was to strengthen the power and authority of the secretary of defense while reducing the influence of the service secretaries. To accomplish this, Plan Six called for bringing the Munitions Board, the Research and Development Board, and a variety of other agencies on which the services had representatives under the direct control of the secretary of defense, who would be given six additional assistant secretaries to handle the workload.[29] Plan Six also provided the secretary with a general counsel who would hold a rank equivalent to that of an assistant secretary. A primary responsibility of the general counsel was to assert the defense secretary's power and authority over the various departments and agencies he administered.

The reorganization plan was also designed to enhance the power of the chairman of the JCS while reducing the power and influence of the service chiefs. This was to be accomplished in two ways. First, the chairman and the secretary, not the JCS, would control appointments to and manage the Joint Staff, which was to be expanded from 100 to 210 officers. The object of this change, as Eisenhower frankly admitted, was to separate members of the Joint Staff from their services and redirect their loyalties in the hope that they would then "center their entire effort on national planning" and show less concern for the special interests of their respective services.[30] Not incidentally, Plan Six also gave the secretary of defense access to the military staff that had been specifically denied to him under the original National Security Act. Through the Joint Staff he would, at least theoretically, have at his disposal the disinterested military advice the JCS had on too many occasions in the past failed to provide.

Eisenhower justified his attempt to strip the JCS of much of its power and authority on the ground that this would free the chiefs from routine responsibilities so that they might concentrate on matters of truly national concern. However, there can be little doubt that his underlying purpose was to enhance the power of the chairman and the secretary, who, through their new powers, would be in a position to heavily influence strategic planning and if necessary actually make independent decisions.

The proposed changes in the roles and responsibilities of the chairman and members of the JCS were important, to be sure, but in Eisenhower's mind, the most important aspect of Plan Six was that it placed great power in the hands of the secretary of defense. Charles Wilson would, he thought, be the first secretary who actually had the power to run the Defense Department. That, he said, was "more important than any of the [other] changes."[31]

Once White House draftsmen had distilled the essence of the Rockefeller committee report into six brief sections, it became the job of Eisenhower's special legislative assistant, Bryce Harlow, to decide how to proceed.
Congress had just voted to extend the Reorganization Act of 1949, which
granted the president the power to reorganize executive departments without having to go through the entire legislative process. Under the law,
though, it was necessary to submit reorganization plans to Congress. They
would automatically go into effect unless within sixty days a majority of the
full membership of either house voted against the changes. Nor could Congress amend reorganization proposals. The law required a straight up or
down vote.

Harlow had to decide whether to seek legislative sanction for the proposed changes or try and push reform through under the Reorganization
Act. The problem was that Plan Six went far beyond mere reorganization
and could very well be viewed as requiring legislative action. If the administration tried to push it through under terms of the Reorganization Act, "the
Armed Services crowd," by which Harlow meant Senator Richard Russell,
"Uncle" Carl Vinson, the majority whip in the House, Les Arends of Illinois, the new Republican chairman of the House Armed Services Committee, Dewey Short of Missouri, and the chairman of the Senate Armed
Services Committee, Senator Leverett Saltonstall, might feel aggrieved.
These congressmen and senators, and others too, claimed a proprietary interest in national security affairs. On the other hand, he worried that if the
administration tried a legislative approach opponents on the House Armed
Services Committee might "kill the entire thing." Worse, they might take
the opportunity to amend parts of the original National Security Act that
were unrelated to the plan or establish "prohibitions against certain of [the]
Rockefeller recommendations" so that in the future it would be more difficult to make needed changes. The best approach, Harlow finally concluded,
was to seek the support of Saltonstall, Arends, and other Republican leaders
and put Plan Six forward under terms of the Reorganization Act.[32]

Once it had been presented to Congress, Plan Six produced criticism
from the predictable places. Ferdinand Eberstadt warned that the "trend is
clearly toward the creation of a supreme military chief of staff with a general staff" while Thomas Finletter attacked it as a step toward the "German
General Staff idea" and "a single military force." [33] Nor did the plan receive
high marks from those in the media who had earlier opposed unification.
While the *New York Times* columnist Hanson Baldwin described the president's plan as "neither drastic nor revolutionary," he nevertheless warned
that an expanded Defense Department was likely to become a "Hydra-

headed monster." The ten assistant secretaries, each with their own assistants, would constitute individual constellations of power that would, he thought, interfere with each other and with the operations of the various military departments, leaving the country worse off than before. Baldwin was even more vehement in condemning the proposed reform of the JCS, which, he argued, put far too much power in the hands of the chairman. He predicted that the plan was certain to provoke "much angry discussion in Congress."[34]

In a series of articles that appeared in the *Washington Evening Star*, conservative columnist David Lawrence was even more vehement. He considered the entire process by which a president could make law without going to Congress unconstitutional. It was up to the legislative branch, he wrote, not the president "to write the laws needed to regulate the armed forces." Like Baldwin, Lawrence too was particularly disturbed by those aspects of the plan relating to the chairman and the JCS. He thought that with these new powers some future chairman could "if he chooses, make himself . . . the most powerful single military chief the United States ever had." Clearly, he believed, this so-called reorganization plan was intended to take the country another step in the direction of the "German General Staff concept." Nor was Lawrence impressed by the president's claim that he was freeing the JCS to work on issues of national importance. To Lawrence this looked "more like a plan to relegate them to the background so that a chairman of the Joint Chiefs may take over the main job of furnishing military advice to the President and the Secretary of Defense." Warning against the threat of "military absolutism," Lawrence urged Congress to kill the reform proposal. If the legislators did not act, he warned, "the die will have been cast toward the single military chief concept."[35]

The reorganization plan also ran into trouble in the House of Representatives. Congressman Les Arends, the majority whip, at first indicated to "Jerry" Persons, Eisenhower's representative on the Hill, that he might not be able to offer his support. The most influential newspaper in Arends's district, *The Daily Pantagraph*, which was owned by Adlai Stevenson, was a fierce opponent of reorganization. Ike tried to calm Arends's jittery nerves during one of his regular meetings with Republican legislative leaders. Arends would not be pacified until he had in hand a letter from the president stating that the plan would not lead the country in the direction of a single chief of staff for all the armed forces, did not represent a step toward a "Prussian General Staff system," and would not diminish the role of the service chiefs, and that the services would continue to be "separately administered."[36]

Clare Hoffman, the Republican chairman of the House Committee on Government Operations, which would vote on the plan before it went to the full House, opposed it both as a violation of the Constitution and because of the extraordinary powers it appeared to vest in the chairman of the JCS. A "man on horseback" was "on the road, and riding fast," he warned. Even though he would have to go up against his own president, the first Republican to sit in the White House in twenty years, Hoffman set out to kill those aspects of the plan that strengthened the power of the chairman and weakened the JCS.[37] He cobbled together a two-vote bipartisan committee majority and managed to pass a resolution recommending adoption of Plan Six minus those sections of the bill that strengthened the chairman and weakened the JCS. When the House Rules Committee refused to allow that proposal to be debated on the House floor, Hoffman, still commanding a majority of his committee, then managed to pass a resolution offered by California's Robert Condon rejecting in its entirety the Reorganization Plan. This tactic meant that there would at least be a full debate on the floor of the House, which took place over a ten-hour period on June 26 and June 27. Finally, after what was in some ways an embarrassing debate for the administration, the Condon resolution was defeated by a vote of 108 to 235. Three days later, on July 1, Plan Six went into effect.[38]

During the same period of time that the Rockefeller Committee was working on its plan to reorganize the military establishment, a fierce debate between the president's civilian and military advisors over the 1954 budget reinforced Eisenhower's commitment to reform. This experience also provided him with another reason, beyond the insistent demands of the Taft wing of the Republican party, for wanting to see some new faces on the JCS.

The Truman budget proposal for 1954, left behind for Eisenhower's consideration, called for $78.6 billion in total spending with $46.3 billion of that earmarked for the military. This program, the Bureau of the Budget estimated, would produce a deficit of $9.9 billion. Because Eisenhower was committed both politically and philosophically to cutting taxes and balancing the federal budget, it was certain that spending would be reduced. It was equally clear that the lion's share of the reductions would have to come from the military side of the budget.

Eisenhower may have assumed that the cuts would come relatively easily. If so, he soon found that making reductions would be more difficult than he had imagined. Indeed, the first national security issue to come before him, a growing need to defend the country against a possible Soviet nuclear attack, put upward pressure on the budget.

Just before leaving office, President Truman approved NSC 141, a study done under the auspices of Robert Lovett, Secretary of State Dean Acheson, and Director of Mutual Security W. Averell Harriman. This study painted a grim picture of the world situation. The Chinese and North Koreans seemed less likely than ever to settle the Korean War; the war in Indochina had become "more precarious" for the French; and efforts at developing a European army were being blocked by France's refusal to approve the treaty establishing the European Defense Community. Finally, and most ominously, the paper noted that Moscow was developing the capability to launch a surprise nuclear attack against the United States. Given the current state of continental defenses, the report continued, anywhere from 65 to 85 percent "of the atomic bombs launched by the U.S.S.R. could be delivered on target in the United States." This, NSC 141 continued, "would represent a blow of critical proportions." To deal with these problems the paper recommended that the military force levels called for under NSC 68/2 be achieved as quickly as possible and that additional resources be allocated for a civil defense program that would include shelters, an early warning radar system, and sufficient interceptor aircraft to provide a defense in depth against such an attack. The report also recommended increases in economic and military aid to America's allies.

The importance of initiating both continental and civil defense programs was further emphasized by two other studies waiting for the new president. The East River report, the work of a group of civilian scientists and engineers from Cal Tech and MIT, warned that a mere thirty atomic bombs dropped on carefully selected industrial targets in the United States could produce 25,000,000 casualties, more if the attack came during the day when people were at work. Like NSC 141, this report urged the creation of a sophisticated system of continental defenses. The last report, done by the Panel of Consultants on Disarmament, warned that the United States had been paying far too much attention to building its own nuclear arsenal, and too little attention to Soviet activities in the same field. Once the Soviet Union had developed enough nuclear weapons to devastate the United States, the consultants pointed out, it made no difference how many nuclear weapons the United States had. Like others who studied this problem, the panel concluded that "there is every reason to proceed with greatly intensified efforts of continental defense."[39]

In commenting on these three documents, Carlton Savage, an old hand at the State Department and a member of the Policy Planning Staff, argued that defensive measures should be undertaken as a "matter of great urgency." This seemed especially valid when one looked forward in time to the "Soviet development of the Hydrogen bomb and of inter-continental guided missiles." An experienced diplomat, Savage realized that as long as the United States remained vulnerable to a devastating attack, "our choice of action in the conduct of foreign relations is drastically narrowed and our ability to act with vigor and decisiveness gravely reduced."[40]

Eisenhower took these warnings seriously, telling the members of the revamped and expanded National Security Council that NSC 141 should be viewed as "a legacy from three important members of the previous adminis-tration who had no personal interest in having its proposals adopted." This did not mean, however, that defense budgets should be increased. On the contrary, the problem as he saw it remained as before, "to figure out a pre-paredness program that will give us a respectable position without bank-rupting the nation."[41]

The holdover members of the JCS were no help in solving Eisenhower's problem. On the contrary, they supported funding continental defense, which they deemed essential, but warned that funding for established pro-grams could not be reduced without endangering national security. In NSC 142, the chiefs also held that U.S. forces were stretched to the limit and would be unable to cope with any new crisis that might develop, as for ex-ample in Indochina where the French were encountering serious difficulties in their war with the Viet Minh. The clear implication of the chiefs' report was that the country should spend more, not less, on national security.[42]

On the other side of what quickly developed into a great divide inside the administration stood Secretary of the Treasury George Humphrey. A midwestern businessman, Humphrey was in some ways much like Eisen-hower. He was warm and modest, with an easy charm that made him ex-tremely likeable. In one significant way, however, the two men were very different. Eisenhower sought a balance between the economic and national security needs of the country. Humphrey, on the other hand, was a fanatic on the subject of reducing government expenditures and balancing the federal budget. He complained that those who drafted NSC 141 had not costed out what appeared to him to be some extremely expensive programs that, if im-plemented, were certain to add to the national debt and create grave prob-lems for the economy. The federal government, Humphrey insisted, would have to reduce its spending, which was "already over the limit." [43]

Humphrey's ally in the skirmishing over NSC 141 was Joseph Dodge, a former Detroit banker whom Eisenhower had appointed to the key post of budget director. Like Humphrey, Dodge believed that the administration's first priority should be to produce a balanced budget as soon as humanly possible. Since defense expenditures made up approximately 70 percent of all government spending, he too insisted that major cuts, not increases, in the defense establishment were essential.

Eisenhower, who had hoped that his civilian and military advisors would work together as a team in the search for solutions to the administration's fiscal problems, instead found himself presiding over a dog fight. The Humphrey-Dodge coalition won the battle over NSC 141 when Dodge informed the president that even without the expenditures called for in that document, unless something was done to control spending, deficits would grow and there would be no chance of balancing the federal budget before 1958. Dodge's budget and income estimates forced Eisenhower to make a choice, which he did. NSC 141 was heard from no more. This did not mean, however, that the question of continental defense simply disappeared. On the contrary, as Soviet capabilities grew, it came to play an increasingly important role in security planning and was a constant source of anxiety as well as an added strain on the budget.[44]

The rejection of the proposals made in NSC 141 still left Eisenhower with a budget badly out of balance. Dodge took a dual approach to the problem. At a minimum, he believed the administration should try to achieve a cash neutral budget for the coming fiscal year by cutting $6.6 billion from the Truman proposal. In this way the administration would at least be able to avoid adding to existing inflationary pressures. The budget director calculated that $1.6 billion could be squeezed from the nondefense side of the budget. It would be up to "Charlie" Wilson to extract the remaining $5 billion from the Pentagon's budget. Looking ahead, Dodge calculated that because a number of temporary taxes were scheduled to expire within the coming year, even greater reductions, again coming largely from the Pentagon, would be called for in the future. On February 12, at an executive officers meeting of the Budget Bureau, Dodge passed these thoughts on to his staff. Five days later they were relayed to Wilfred McNeil, the comptroller at the Defense Department, and through him to Secretary Wilson. [45]

On March 4 Dodge presented the president and the NSC with a second option, a more extreme plan that promised a balanced budget in 1955, but also called for cuts over two years of $22.8 billion, only $2 billion of which would come from nondefense-related programs. The rest would come from the armed services and from the Mutual Security Program, which helped fund allied rearmament efforts.[46]

Dodge's second option was enthusiastically supported by Humphrey, who insisted that the "money and resources required by the great security programs" that the Truman administration had developed "could not be borne by the United States unless we adopted essentially totalitarian methods."[47] Needless to say, the JCS did not share Humphrey's enthusiasm. Appearing before the NSC as a group, the chiefs strongly opposed Dodge's proposal. They detailed the extraordinary force reductions that it would require and predicted dire consequences if it was implemented.[48]

Eisenhower recognized that Dodge was going too far too fast and would not support this extreme proposal. He was therefore forced to admit that while a balanced budget should remain a goal of his administration, it was not within reach in the immediate future. At the same time, he was disappointed with the JCS presentation, remarking tartly after they had finished that the NSC might well be advised to commission a study "as to whether national bankruptcy or national destruction would get us first." Convinced that waste and duplication were endemic in the military, he told Charles Wilson that he wanted to know how much of the defense budget was made up of "overhead and administration" and what was the cost of "the actual units produced?" How much duplication of effort was to be found? Were there "avoidable costs?" Eisenhower guessed there were and cited as an example the Navy's new Forrestal class of aircraft carriers, which he frankly considered a waste of money.[49]

Wilson went immediately on the defensive, telling the president that when he accepted his appointment "he had no illusions as to the magnitude of his job as Secretary of Defense," but, he continued, "he was bound to say that the closer he got to it the bigger it looked." Eisenhower agreed that Wilson had a difficult assignment but insisted that he was determined "to get the right answer on these problems.[50] When Wilson warned that achieving the kind of cuts needed to approach a balanced budget while at the same time guaranteeing national security was not going to be easy, the president wondered derisively whether the presidential yacht *Williamsburg* might be in "jeopardy" and for the moment let the matter drop. Wilson was on notice. He had to come up with some answers.[51]

If Eisenhower was displeased with Wilson's performance, he was also deeply disappointed in the attitude displayed by members of the JCS. Their "stand pat" attitude, their refusal to aid in the search for that middle ground between the needs of the security establishment and the national economy, led him to cut them out of the final budget-planning process for 1954. From that point on, he relied on the advice of Wilson, his other civilian advisors, a group of seven outside consultants (conservative businessmen for the most part, dubbed by the press the "Wise Men"), and his own judgment in developing the budget.[52]

On March 31 the NSC met in an all-day session to finally decide the budget question. At this meeting the "Wise Men" took an extreme position.

Like Humphrey, they argued that the rearmament program begun in 1950 had resulted in serious negative consequences for the civilian economy. Dillon Anderson, speaking for the entire group, contended: "We have bitten off more than we can chew." The rearmament program, he said, had been "excessive" and had resulted in an enormous amount of waste. The roles and missions of the three services, he thought, should be clarified since there was much duplication there. Moreover, in the future the administration should rely more heavily on its nuclear strength, reduce the size of the armed services, and spend less on research and development as well as foreign military aid. The "Wise Men" thought that enormous cuts in defense spending were possible and that a balanced budget was within the president's reach. They urged him to go after it.

Eisenhower, who had been disappointed by the unwillingness of the JCS to identify methods of saving money, now showed considerable concern over the slash-and-burn enthusiasm displayed by the outside consultants, who seemed all too willing to reduce the security programs to unacceptably low levels in order to balance the federal budget. The United States could not abandon programs undertaken over the preceding few years without courting disaster. In the end Ike decided that the sane approach was to adopt a middle course in which the administration reduced spending and moved in the direction of a balanced budget while at the same time it continued to provide economic aid to its allies and maintained adequate military strength.

Toward the end of the March 31 meeting, Defense Secretary Wilson took the floor to present his ideas on the budget, ideas he and the president had almost certainly agreed upon beforehand. Wilson began by offering his "best guess" regarding possibilities for cost savings if the administration attempted to achieve the readiness levels called for in NSC 135/3 (the most recent update of NSC 68) by 1956. Assuming that scenario, Wilson said, the government would have to spend $45 billion annually for the next three years and $40 billion thereafter to maintain that same level of readiness. It might be possible, he said, to cut as much as $1 billion from the budget in overhead costs and duplication. Even this cut was based on the assumption that the Rockefeller committee, which at this time had not yet finished its work, would come up with a money-saving reorganization plan. Most of the $1 billion, he conceded, "would be saved from reductions in personnel."[53]

Since the costs of this approach were unacceptable, Wilson saw no alternative but to cut back and stretch out a variety of programs. Instead of even attempting to be prepared for general war by 1956 or any other specific date, Wilson proposed working on the "assumption of a 'Floating D-day,' " an idea Eisenhower had advanced during the campaign. By planning for the "long haul," he would be able to recommend a cut of $5 billion from the Truman budget for a total defense budget of $36 billion. Further reductions would come in succeeding years until in 1957 an annual figure of $33 billion had been achieved.[54] In making his presentation, Wilson pointed out that his plan had one significant short-term political advantage for the administration. Given funds already appropriated and in the system, it would not result in any reduction in actual strength over the next two fiscal years. He admitted, however, that the country would be "less well off in the third and subsequent years." Aware that Humphrey and Dodge envisioned greater cuts, Wilson also warned that any reductions below those he recommended would be damaging both politically and from a psychological point of view for they would certainly lead some to conclude "that the United States was abandoning a serious defense effort for itself and its allies." Wilson's proposal was enthusiastically seconded by the president and immediately approved by the NSC.[55]

A month later, one day before Ike submitted his budget to Congress, the NSC approved NSC 149/2, the first national security policy directive of the new administration. This paper, which described the impact the 1954 budget would have on the armed services, called for a force reduction of 250,000 officers and enlisted personnel. Because of exigencies connected with the Korean War, the Army would have its budget slightly enhanced. The Navy's budget, on the other hand, would be somewhat reduced. The Air Force would be the big loser, sustaining a cut of $5.1 billion. Whereas Truman had called for an Air Force of 143 wings by the end of 1956, the Eisenhower budget funded somewhere between 105 and 115 wings, ten of which would not be equipped with first-line aircraft. Moreover, even this force level might not be achieved until the end of 1957.[56]

Eisenhower did not send his 1954 budget proposal to Congress until April 30, the same day on which he submitted Reorganization Plan Six. However, Charles Wilson's announcement at a March press conference that large-scale defense cuts were coming set off a flurry of comment in the press. Because of what it termed "20 years of extravagant and fantastic Pentagon bungling," *Time* thought that, as Eisenhower claimed, "it may indeed be possible to get more strength for less money." The magazine was confident that to have his way Ike would have to use all "the weight of his military knowledge and prestige against a phalanx of Pentagon brass." Suddenly, *Time* observed, military men were buttonholing reporters, volunteering their opinions. One high-ranking naval officer warned that "Wilson is fiddling with our national security." An Air Force general remarked angrily,

"[Y]ou can't make across the board cuts without hurting the whole armed services." The respected author, columnist, and war correspondent, Anne O'Hare McCormick, struck a similar note in an article written at the time. The new Soviet leadership was just then making overtures to the West, calling for a reduction in tensions, and Western Europe appeared to be responding. McCormick, who doubted Moscow's sincerity, excoriated the administration for even considering defense cutbacks. "At a moment when Europe's inclination to relax has received such encouragement from Moscow," she wrote, "the talk of slow downs and cut backs reported from Washington is the height of folly. More, it is dangerous and irresponsible beyond belief."[57]

The debate over the budget moved into high gear after Eisenhower submitted his proposal to Congress. Congressional Democrats teamed with Air Force leaders in alliance against the administration proposal. Stuart Symington, now the junior senator from Missouri, led an attack that for a time virtually silenced the Republicans. In March he charged that defense cuts were not only unwarranted but dangerous. In April, while speaking before the American Society of Newspaper Editors, he claimed that Eisenhower was sacrificing security in the interest of a balanced budget. The United States, he insisted, was "growing weaker each day in relative military strength against Russia." Later, during an appearance on "Meet the Press," Symington charged that within a year the Soviets would have the capability of launching a nuclear attack on the United States that would destroy one-third of the country's industrial base and kill at least 13,000,000 Americans. Eisenhower, he said, was following a perilous course in reducing air power at the very time Russian air strength was on the increase. In a speech before the Reserve Officers Association, ex-President Truman, who supported Symington's charges, warned against "cutting corners on our national security." Eisenhower and Secretary of Defense Wilson were, he claimed, "letting their pocketbooks obscure their vision." "There can be no doctrine more dangerous than the notion that we cannot afford to defend ourselves."[58]

Attacks by Symington, Truman, and other important Democrats, which were given wide coverage in the press and on television, paralyzed the Republican leadership in Congress, which, while it certainly wanted fiscal restraint, did not want to be seen as "weak on defense." Ike, on the other hand, was furious and in no mood to surrender to pressure from the Democrats and the Air Force. He told Republican legislative leaders who gathered regularly at the White House that they should not believe those Air Force leaders who said they could not carry out their responsibilities if they did not get 143 wings. "I'm damn tired of Air Force sales programs," he said. "In 1946 they argued that if we can have seventy groups, we'll guarantee security for ever and ever and ever. Now they have a trick figure of 141 [*sic*]. They sell it. Then you have to abide by it or you're treasonous." He told the legislators that he simply would "not tolerate having anyone in Defense who wants to sell the idea of a larger and larger force in being, because that results in too much obsolescence and waste."[59]

On May 19, when a Senate Appropriations subcommittee opened hearings on the 1954 defense budget, the Eisenhower administration was on the defensive and getting little or no help from Republicans in Congress. Nor did Secretary of Defense Wilson's appearance before the committee improve the situation. Following his ill-prepared presentation, Wilson came under intense pressure from Republican Senator Margaret Chase Smith of Maine, who battered him with embarrassing questions. Were the cuts being proposed the result of fiscal or strategic considerations? Did the secretary think that the recent Soviet "peace offensive" meant that there was now less danger of aggression? What did the CIA think about this? In 1951 the JCS stated, and the administration as well as Congress agreed, that a 143-wing air force was the absolute minimum required to protect national security. "How had Soviet strength changed since that time so that we can reduce our Air Force?" Most tellingly, she asked, what did the members of the JCS have to say about the cuts and what part did they play in developing the recommendations then before Congress? Wilson fumbled and Chase fumed. At length she produced a list of thirty-two questions that she wanted answered, she acidly remarked, by someone "capable of answering them." According to *Time*, Wilson had totally failed to sell the subcommittee on the administration's budget cuts. His presentation had been so weak, in fact, that some believed $2 billion of the original $5 billion cut would be restored by the administration.[60]

Eisenhower had instructed Wilson to assert his authority in the Pentagon. He was particularly insistent that the military and naval brass keep their opinions regarding the budget to themselves. However, keeping the military under control was no insignificant task. In fact Air Force officers seemed willing to express their views to anyone with time to listen. Thus, Sam Yorty, a Democratic congressman from the Los Angeles area, home to a large segment of the aircraft industry, had no problem convincing General Robert E. A. Eaton, Air Force Director of Legislative Liaison on Capitol Hill, to go on the record. Eaton told Yorty that the 143-wing air force was "the absolute minimum to gain adequate national security" and challenged a claim Wilson had made during the recent hearings that a 120-wing force would be in place before June 1955. Eaton was certain that given the 1954 budget it would be the middle of 1956 before the Air Force would achieve that level. Even then, he went on, the Air Force would be short of equipment and manpower. Also, contracts already let would have to be dropped, creating the danger "that large segments of the aircraft industry would be cut so sharply that they could not adequately respond to later aircraft orders." Yorty gave Eaton's statement to the press, attacked Wilson as a "defeatist," and called for his resignation while warning that "the dollars he worships will not shoot down attacking enemy planes."[61]

Three days of testimony before the Senate Appropriations subcommittee by Hoyt Vandenberg, the outgoing air force chief of staff, added to Eisenhower's difficulties. Vandenberg was in an absolute fury. He had originally hoped to see a 155-wing air force in place by the end of 1954 but had settled for a goal of 143 wings in order to win the support of a united JCS. Now, with a force in being of just 98 wings, he was being asked to accept a "floating target" for 1956 or 1957 of 120 wings.

Vandenberg began his testimony with a prepared statement in which he argued that while the Eisenhower budget called for cuts, Moscow was adding "thousands" of Mig-15 fighter aircraft to its inventories as well as a new pure jet nuclear-capable light bomber, the IL-28, which would be able to attack troop concentrations, military bases, and supply depots throughout Europe. Given this growing Soviet strength, he argued, the 143-wing air force, which provided "only for tasks that are absolutely indispensable," was essential.

In his testimony Vandenberg made a point of observing that Defense Secretary Wilson had never advanced a sound strategic reason for abandoning the 143-wing goal. Nor could he since there had been no alteration in Soviet policy in recent years and Russian air strength had been on the increase. The Air Force, he told the senators, approved neither the 120-wing plan nor other aspects of the proposed budget that, he noted, also called for cuts in base construction, personnel, appropriations, force levels, expenditures, and "a heavy reduction in funds for research and development." The Eisenhower administration, he charged, was trying to foist off on the country a "second best" Air Force.[62]

Vandenberg also explained that the JCS had not participated in the preparation of the budget. Indeed, he had not seen it until May 7, when he immediately objected to it both orally and in writing. On the day following, he told the committee, the entire JCS warned Secretary Wilson against reducing force goals below already established levels. Indeed, he continued, the JCS had been on record since March, warning him that to reduce the Air

Force goal of 143 wings would increase the danger to national security "beyond the dictates of national prudence."[63]

Vandenberg found a good deal of support for his assault on the administration's defense budget in the press where criticism of the budget cuts became common fare. Former Secretary of the Air Force Thomas K. Finletter denounced the budget as a product of "ground soldier thinking." In his regular *Newsweek* column, General Carl Spaatz, former air force chief of staff and an old friend of Eisenhower's, joined the melee, remarking that the budget did "not provide for the kind of Air Force we need or a broad enough defense production base." "We all want economy," he wrote, "but not at the expense of security." In a follow-up column Spaatz warned that in the nuclear age survival would depend on having "the strongest Air Force in the world, confronted as we are by an aggressor, the U.S.S.R." It was "unthinkable," he wrote, "that the strongest nation in the world cannot afford to pay the price of its survival." The syndicated columnist Ernest K. Lindley did not think it was surprising that the Air Force was up in arms since the recommended cuts had not been made on military grounds but as a result of "fiscal considerations." According to Lindley, the administration had found much less waste and duplication than it expected. It had no place to reduce expenditures but defense, and therefore it decided to stretch out its procurement practices and cut back on force goals. That, Lindley explained, was why Wilson was in such difficulty in Congress and why he was getting so little help from his Republican friends there. *Time* reported that even Secretary of the Air Force Harold Talbott at first appeared disinclined to support the budget. According to the story, Ike confronted Talbott at a White House bridge party, saying: "I understand you're not supporting the budget." Talbott, reportedly "shaken by the steely presidential voice," got on the team.[64]

For a time it appeared that the Air Force and its allies had Eisenhower on the run, but the administration fought back effectively. General Jerry Persons, Ike's "man" on Capitol Hill, worked long hours keeping Republican congressmen on the right side of the issue. Then too, Defense Secretary Wilson made a return visit to the Senate Appropriations subcommittee. This time he gave a well-prepared defense of his budget proposals, and reminded Congress that there was something more than a budget at issue here, that under the Constitution the "authority, direction and control" of the military was supposed to be in civilian hands, and that the Air Force was challenging that principle. Perhaps most important, unlike his earlier appearances before Congress, this time Wilson, who had a bad case of foot-in-mouth disease, managed not to offend anybody.

Also, by this time Eisenhower himself had weighed in. Relying on his military reputation, he made a direct radio appeal for popular support. He defended his budget as an attempt to bring to an end "the indefinite continuance of a needlessly high rate of federal spending" as well as "any pennywise, pound foolish policy that could, through lack of needed strength, cripple the cause of freedom." The Soviets, he warned, "hoped to force upon America and the free world an unbearable security burden leading to economic disaster." He was determined to head that off. At the same time he noted that even given the $5.2 billion cut he was proposing, 60 cents out of every dollar spent on defense would still go either to the Navy's air arm or the Air Force, and that the Air Force would have at its disposal "more than 40% of all defense funds spent in 1954."[65]

Up to that point the Republicans in Congress had been at best timid supporters of the president's budget cuts. After Eisenhower's radio address, however, Les Arends, the Republican whip in the House, came out strongly in support of the budget. He reminded his colleagues that "this Air Force drive for a larger budget . . . is an annual event. It used to be accompanied by air shows, remarkable high speed or long distance flights, and suddenly discovered enemy threats to our nation." He went on to warn that in "planning an over-all defense program for our country's security all military extremisms must be resolved." In case anyone in the House had forgotten, Arends reminded them that "this is the great duty and responsibility of the President," who "by the very nature and background of his experience . . . is better equipped than any member of the Joint Chiefs of Staff, individually or collectively, to decide just how much of what . . . we need for our security." Arends left the well of the House to enthusiastic applause. The "Air Battle," as *Newsweek* dubbed this first great debate of the Eisenhower years, was over.[66]

For Eisenhower a more important test was yet to come. By July, Reorganization Plan Number Six was in place, strengthening immeasurably the powers of the Office of the Secretary of Defense and the chairman of the JCS, while reducing the power of the individual services. Moreover, Eisenhower had replaced the old members of the JCS with a new set of men who, he hoped, would play an important and constructive role as he pursued "security with solvency."

NOTES

1. Robert A. Ferrell, ed., *The Eisenhower Diaries* (New York: Norton, 1981), 159.

2. Ibid.

3. Quoted in Steven Ambrose, *Eisenhower: Soldier, General of the Army, President-Elect, 1890–1952* (New York: Simon and Schuster, 1983), 513.

4. Eisenhower to Baruch, 30 June 1952, and 10 March 1953, Whitman File, Administration Series, Box 5, the Eisenhower Library (hereafter cited as EL). In 1949, when Eisenhower proposed to President Truman that the military should have a consistent annual budget of $15 billion, he was making the same point. Later in Eisenhower's administration this same argument underlay the entire New Look policy and was described as planning for "the long haul."

5. Ibid.; *New York Times (hereafter cited as NYT)*, 17 Sept. 1952.

6. Ibid.

7. *NYT*, 18 Jan. 1952.

8. Vannevar Bush, "What's Wrong with the Pentagon?" *Colliers*, 27 Dec. 1952, 31–34. See also Bush speeches of 26 Sept. and 11 Oct. 1952 and 12 Feb. 1953 in CCS 040, Defense Department, Central Decimal File, (11–4–42), BP. Pt. 5, Box 8, Modern Military Branch, National Archives (hereafter cited as NA).

9. Harold H. Martin, "The Toughest Job Facing Ike," *Saturday Evening Post*, 14 March 1953, 31, 137–40.

10. E. B. Lockett, "Leave It to Lovett," *Colliers*, 30 June 1951, 31, 70–73.

11. Ibid.; see also Doris M. Condit, *The History of the Office of the Secretary of Defense* (Washington, DC: History Office, Office of the Secretary of Defense, 1988), 2:245–302.

12. Condit, *History of the Office,* 2:243–260. Considering the size of the defense budgets between 1951 and 1954 some may have difficulty accepting the idea that Lovett and Eisenhower shared certain basic assumptions about spending. It is important to note that Lovett, too, was planning for the "long haul." He assumed that after the services had reached full strength, as described in NSC 68/2, spending would be throttled back to approximately $40 billion annually or about $7 billion more than Eisenhower was hoping for.

13. Ibid.

14. "Mr. Collidge's Memorandum for Secretary Lovett," September 1952, CCS 040, Records of the Office of the Secretary of Defense (hereafter cited as OS/D), Central Decimal File (11–4–43), Box 8, National Archives (hereafter cited as NA); see also Collidge, memorandum for the record, 5 June 1952, CCS 040, OS/D, Office of the Administrative Secretary, AF-D; Robert Kent to John G. Adams, 4 June 1952, and Collidge to Gen. Carter, 9 May 1952, ibid.; Lovett to Truman, 18 Nov. 1952, in Alice Cole et al., eds., *The Department of Defense: Documents on Establishment and Organization, 1944–1978* (Washington, DC: Office of the Secretary of Defense, Historical Office, 1978), 115–26.

15. Lovett to Truman, 18 Nov. 1952, in Cole et al., *The Department of Defense,* 115–26.

16. Ibid.

17. Ibid.

18. Ibid.

19. Ibid. There was close cooperation between Lovett, his staff, the JCS, and members of the incoming administration. See Lovett to Truman, 3 Jan. 1953, CCS 040, (11–2–43), Sec. 9, Box 20, NA. The JCS instructed its Joint Strategic Survey Committee to study and report on the Lovett letter. The result was JCS 1977/7, a long report completed on March 18, 1953. In it the JSSC approved Lovett's plan to place the Munitions and Research and Development boards in the Office of the Secretary of Defense but took exception to most of his other proposals. Ibid., BP Pt. 5.

20. Lovett to Truman, 18 Nov. 1952, in Cole et al., *The Department of Defense,* 115–26.

21. Harry S. Truman, *The Memoirs of Harry S. Truman: Years of Trial and Hope* (Garden City: Doubleday, 1955), 521; Robert J. Donovan, *The Presidency of Harry S. Truman: Tumultuous Years* (New York: Norton, 1982), 403.

22. *NYT,* 2 and 7 Jan. 1953; *Time,* 19 Jan. 1953, 14–15.

23. Eisenhower to Gruenther, 26 Nov. 1952, Whitman File, Administration Series, Box 16, EL.

24. E. Bruce Geelhoed, *Charles E. Wilson and the Controversy at the Pentagon* (Detroit: Wayne State University Press, 1979), 34–37.

25. James Desmond, *Nelson Rockefeller, a Political Biography* (New York: Macmillan, 1964), 138.

26. The Sarnoff Commission on Manpower Utilization in the Armed Services released its report on February 17, 1953. On March 4, Sarnoff sent Wilson a copy along with a summary of the commission's findings. Sarnoff to Wilson, 4 March 1953, CCS 040 (11–4–43), OS/D, Central Decimal Files, 1954–56, JCS, BP, Pt. 5, Box 8, NA. The report recommended that at a minimum 500,000 civilian and military personnel be eliminated from Pentagon employ. It also called for a reduction of $5 billion in the Defense Department's budget.

27. Vandenberg's memorandum for the Committee on Defense Organization, 3 April 1953, Vandenberg Papers, Box 85, Manuscript Division, Library of Congress (hereafter cited as LC).

28. Ibid. Wilson provided Rockefeller with a seven-page description of the administrative arrangement he wanted. See Wilson to Rockefeller, 26 Feb. 1953, Whitman File, Administration Series, Box 40, EL.

29. The Rockefeller Committee Report and Plan Six may be found in Cole et al., *The Department of Defense,* 128–43, 157–59.

30. *Public Papers of the Presidents: Dwight D. Eisenhower, 1953* (Washington, DC: GPO, 1960), 225–37.

31. *Newsweek,* 11 May 1953, 27–28. For more on the 1953 reorganization, see John C. Ries, *The Management of Defense: The Organization and Control of the U.S. Armed Forces* (Baltimore: Johns Hopkins University Press, 1964),

152–71; Paul Y. Hammond, *Organizing for Defense* (Princeton: Princeton University Press, 1961).

32. Harlow, memorandum on defense reorganization, n.d., the Bryce Harlow Papers, Box 19, EL.

33. *NYT*, 12 May, and 18 June 1953.

34. Ibid., 3 May 1953.

35. *Washington Evening Star*, 1, 4, and 14 May 1953; *U.S. News and World Report*, 8 May 1953.

36. Eisenhower to Aspen, 25 May 1953, White House Central Files, Office Files, Box 23, EL.

37. For the administration's strategy in dealing with Hoffman, see Acting General Counsel John G. Adams to Deputy Secretary of Defense Roger Kyes, 10 June 1953, CCS 040 "D," Office of the Administrative Secretary, Box 730, NA. See also Harlow memorandum, 17 June 1953, "Purpose and Application of Sections 1 (c) and (d) of Reorganization Plan No. 6 of 1953, Harlow Papers, Box 19, EL.

38. R. Earl McClendon, *Changes in Organization for National Defense, 1949–1953* (Maxwell Air Force Base, Montgomery, Alabama: Air University Press: 1956), 54–62.

39. Report to the NSC, 19 Jan 1953, in Department of State, *Foreign Relations of the United States, 1952–1954* (Washington, DC: GPO, 1984), 2:209–22 (hereafter cited as *FRUS*); Memorandum by Carlton Savage, 10 Feb. 1953, ibid., 231–34; see also Fred Kaplan, *The Wizards of Armageddon* (1983; reprint, Stanford: Stanford University Press, 1991), 126.

40. Savage memorandum, 10 Feb. 1963, *FRUS*, 1952–1954, 2:231–34.

41. NSC discussion, 11 Feb. 1953, *FRUS, 1952–1954*, 2:236.

42. NSC discussion, 19 Feb. 1953, Whitman File, NSC Series, Box 4, EL; see also JCS 2101/84, 12 Jan. 1953, CCS 381 (1–31–50), Box 57, and JCS 2101/92, 12 Feb. 1953, ibid., Box 58, NA.

43. NSC discussion, 11 Feb. 1953, *FRUS, 1952–1954*, 2:236–37.

44. Paul Nitze and Carlton Savage, memorandum on continental defense, 6 May 1953, *FRUS, 1952–1954*, 2:318–23.

45. Hyde to McNeil, 17 Feb. 1953, CCS 040, Defense Department, Central Files, Office of the Administrative Secretary, A-C, Box 729, NA; NSC Discussion, 13 Feb. 1953, Whitman File, NSC Series, Box 4, EL.; Dodge to Eisenhower, 25 Feb. 1953, ibid., Administration Series, Box 12, EL.

46. NSC discussion, 4 March 1953, Whitman File, NSC Series, Box 4, EL.

47. NSC Discussion, 25 March 1953, *FRUS,1952–1954,* 2:262.

48. Ibid., 258–63.

49. Ibid.

50. Ibid., NSC discussion, 26 Feb. 1953, Whitman File, NSC Series, Box 4, EL.

51. NSC Discussion, 25 March 1953, *FRUS, 1952–1954*, 2:258–63. As though to make a point, subsequent to this meeting Eisenhower ordered the *Williamsburg* decommissioned. See Eisenhower to Wilson, 8 April 1953, Diary Series, Box 3, EL.

52. A list of twenty-eight possible outside advisors was presented to the NSC for its consideration at the February 25 NSC meeting. See Whitman File, Administration Series, Box 10, EL. Those selected to serve included Dillon Anderson, at the time a Texas attorney, James B. Black, president of the Pacific Gas and Electric Co., John Cowles, publisher, Eugene Holman, president of Standard Oil of N.J., Deane W. Malott of Cornell University, Charles A. Thomas, president of Monsanto Chemical Co., and Howard Bruce, a financier. See Memorandum of NSC meeting, 26 Feb. 1953, Whitman File, NSC Series, Box 4, EL.

53. NSC Discussion, 31 March 1953, *FRUS, 1952–1954*, 2:265. It should be noted that the figures Wilson presented were exactly those of the Truman administration's planners.

54. Ibid., 286–87.

55. Ibid. See also "Proposed Military Program," n.d., Whitman File, Administration Series, Box 40, EL.

56. NSC 149, in *FRUS, 1952–1954*, 2:307–15; Robert J. Watson, *A History of the Joint Chiefs of Staff* (Wilmington: Michael Glazier, Inc., 1979), 5:9, 61–62.

57. *Time*, 20 April 1953, 25.

58. *NYT*, 16 and 17 June, 23 July, and 8 and 15 Sept. 1953; *Newsweek*, 6 July 1953, 20.

59. Legislative Leadership meeting, 12 May 1953, Supplementary Notes, Whitman File, Diary Series, Box 7, EL.

60. U.S. Congress, Senate Subcommittee on Appropriations, *Hearings on Defense Appropriations for 1954*, 83rd Cong., 1st sess., 572–78; *Time*, 1 June 1953, 16.

61. *NYT*, 23 May, 2 June 1953; *Newsweek*, 1 June 1953, 20.

62. U.S. Congress, Senate, Subcommittee on Appropriations, *Hearings on Defense Appropriations for 1954*, 83rd Cong., 1st sess., 218–57. See also Garlock to Wilson, 26 May 1953, Whitman File, Administration Series, Box 1, EL. This top secret document, developed from figures provided by the Air Force itself, indicates that Vandenberg was wrong about the comparative strength of the United States and the Soviet Union. According to the Air Force, in 1954 the United States was outproducing the Soviets in jet aircraft as well as jet engines and had greater capacity to increase production. These numbers did not take into consideration the air strength of the NATO allies which was considerable.

63. Ibid.; for more on Vandenberg's testimony see the *NYT*, 4, 5, 16, and 17 June 1953.

64. *Newsweek*, 1 June 1953, 26; *Time*, 15 June 1953, 25.

65. Cole et al., *The Department of Defense*, 149–57.

66. Roger W. Jones to Eisenhower, 30 June 1954, Reports to the President on Pending Legislation, Box 25, EL. When Congress completed its work on the budget it had reduced proposed new obligational authority for defense, exclusive of mutual security funds, by $1.7 billion to $28.8 billion.

5

"This Concept Is a Crystalized and Clarified Statement of This Administration's Understanding of Our National Security since World War II."

Eisenhower's experiences during the first half of 1953 left him in no doubt that a new, less costly military strategy would have to be developed if he was to achieve an acceptable level of security at a cost the economy could bear. Nor did he doubt that this could be done. The 1953 Pentagon reorganization, which went into effect on July 1, provided Secretary of Defense Wilson with the power to encourage the growth of a more unified military establishment less given to waste and overlap. It also limited the ability of the separate services to resist change, strengthened the power of the chairman of the JCS, and in theory at least, focused the attentions of the members of the JCS on issues of national interest and away from the narrow, parochial, service-oriented concerns that had previously occupied so much of their time. He was, therefore, optimistic that a reconstituted JCS, guided by a revised national security policy that emphasized the importance of striking a balance between economic and security needs, would be able to produce an appropriate proposal.

Unhappily, Eisenhower soon learned that the strategic concept he envisioned would be more difficult to achieve than he had at first imagined. In the end, when it became clear that nothing less would do, he acted unilaterally and decisively, requiring Wilson and the JCS to come up with a strategy based on reduced force levels and arbitrarily established budgetary limits.

Admiral Arthur Radford was an unlikely candidate to succeed Omar Bradley as chairman of the Joint Chiefs of Staff. He had been a fierce opponent of unification during the political battles leading up to enactment of the National Security Act and had been at the center of the "Revolt of the Admirals" in 1949. Whereas Eisenhower had at that time been a staunch defender of the Air Force in general and the B-36 bomber program in particular, Radford had publicly denounced the plane as "a billion dollar blunder" and had repeatedly questioned the ability of the Air Force to carry out an effective strategic bombing campaign in the event of a war with the Soviet Union. By the end of 1952, however, Radford had changed many of his opinions. Fortuitous circumstance gave him the opportunity to explain these changes at length and in person to Eisenhower.

During the 1952 political campaign Eisenhower promised that if elected he would go to Korea as a first step toward ending the war there. Immediately following the election, the Defense Department began planning the trip. It seemed clear that General Bradley, the chairman of the JCS, should go along as a member of the party, but Robert Lovett thought that in order to avoid interservice bickering, a naval officer should go too. He suggested Radford, who, he told Ike, had a solid understanding of supply and logistical problems for the entire Pacific region.[1]

When Eisenhower's plane landed at Iwo Jima on its way to Korea, Radford was there waiting. The admiral remained with Ike throughout his stay in Korea and sailed part of the way back with his party on board the *U.S.S. Helena*. During this time, according to White House aide Sherman Adams, Radford told Eisenhower that "he had been wrong in 1947 in disapproving of a unified command" and that he "had come to share Eisenhower's belief that nuclear weapons and the need for close co-ordination of land, sea and air forces in a nuclear war required the removal of the old barriers between the services."[2] Radford also took the opportunity to discuss some ideas of his own that must have been of considerable interest to a president seeking methods of reducing federal spending. Radford argued that America's ground forces, stationed in far-flung bases across Europe and Asia, were overextended and would certainly be ineffective should another major war break out. Therefore, the logical thing to do was to emphasize America's nuclear striking power and to rely on indigenous ground forces as a first line of defense against local aggression. American ground forces should be redeployed to the United States where they would be reorganized to form a smaller, highly mobile strategic reserve that could come to the aid of allies in the event of war.[3]

Eisenhower was impressed. He told Charles Wilson, who was considering Radford for the post of chairman of the JCS, that although the admiral had behaved badly during the "Revolt of the Admirals," he nevertheless believed that, if appointed, Radford would serve with "patriotism, loyalty, and dedication." The decision was of course up to Wilson, but the secretary knew in advance that Eisenhower, who of course had more experience in these matters than he did, would approve a Radford nomination.[4]

Wilson and Radford left the presidential party at Wake Island and flew directly to Hawaii where Wilson remained for a time as Radford's guest. Wilson was impressed with the admiral. He was bright, articulate, a commanding presence—and his views on defense matters were clearly in sync with those of the commander in chief. Moreover, Radford had a well-earned reputation as a supporter of an assertive Asian policy. That made him more than acceptable to the Taft wing of the Republican party, which had been agitating for new and different personnel on the JCS.[5]

Before leaving for Washington Wilson asked Radford if he would be interested in becoming chairman of the JCS. Radford responded positively and the waiting began. In February, having heard nothing, he returned to Washington and paid what he described in his memoirs as "a courtesy call" at the White House. Still, no offer arrived. Unaware that the president had decided to wait until May before naming his new team, Radford fretted. His chances, he thought, were slim. The Air Force would probably oppose him because of the role he had played in the B-36 controversy. He also guessed that he had not convinced Ike that he really had changed his mind about unification and air power. Radford was mistaken. On May 10 he was told that he could expect his telephone to start ringing off its hook in two days when the White House would announce that he was to be the new chairman of the JCS.[6]

Immediately following the announcement of Radford's appointment, a number of newspaper reports indicated that the Air Force was not at all happy with Eisenhower's choice. To counteract these stories, and perhaps to eliminate possible opposition to his nomination in Congress, Ike asked Radford to announce publicly that once confirmed his "exclusive identification with the Navy would end" and "that he would from that time forth be the champion of all the services."[7] During his confirmation hearings before the Senate Armed Services Committee, Radford did just that, telling Stuart Symington that he would not be a Navy partisan, would do his best "not to favor any particular service," and would "try to call my shots as impartially as I can." He also told the senator that given the technological revolution that had taken place since the war, he would "probably modify" the views on unification he had expressed between 1946 and 1949, and came out four-square for a powerful strategic air arm.[8] The committee and the full Senate approved Radford's appointment without incident.

The other members of Eisenhower's newly appointed JCS included Army Chief of Staff General Matthew B. Ridgway, Admiral Robert B. Carney, chief of naval operations, and General Nathan F. Twining, chief of staff of the Air Force. On paper the group looked nearly perfect to Eisenhower. All of its members had experience in Europe as well as Asia and might therefore be expected to adopt the broad global perspective on defense matters the president desired. Moreover, each member had also served as the head of a unified command, an experience that Ike hoped would lead them to think in the interest of the combined military establishment and the nation as a whole, not in terms of a narrow service interest.[9]

In the spring of 1953 the president approved two major revisions to the basic national security policy that were of particular importance to Radford and his colleagues. Beyond provisions already discussed, NSC 149/2 stated that the preservation of a "sound, strong" American economy was "vital" to the "survival of the free world." Because continued and unchecked deficit spending would "eventually destroy that economy," it was essential that the national government reduce spending and move toward a balanced budget. Toward that end, the paper stated, the United States would abandon the Truman policy under which the United States was to be fully prepared for global war by 1956 or 1957.[10] Instead, the military program would be regularly reviewed and modified on the basis of "periodic recommendations from the Joint Chiefs of Staff whose judgments were to be made on the basis of changing tactical, strategic and *economic* considerations" [italics added]." To be certain that defense dollars were used efficiently, NSC 149/2 further stipulated that the roles and missions of the services should be reviewed with an eye toward eliminating redundancy and waste.[11]

On June 10 Eisenhower approved still another revision of the security policy. NSC 153/1 stated that "the basic problem facing the United States" was to strike a balance between "the need to defend the country against the Soviet threat and the need for a healthy economy." Because the increased emphasis on the importance of a "sound fiscal policy" inevitably involved "assuming increased risks in relation to the Soviet threat," the document concluded, the situation required a "more careful balance and improved efficiency in the various national security programs." That in a nutshell was the objective of Eisenhower's policy. It would be up to his civilian and military advisors, working together, to arrive at a resolution to this problem.[12]

When Admiral Radford reported for his new assignment early in July 1953, Charles Wilson handed him a memorandum from the president that asked for a complete reevaluation of the entire national security posture of the United States. Eisenhower wanted the chiefs to critically evaluate existing "strategic concepts" and plans for their implementation, the roles and missions of the services, the composition and readiness of existing forces, the impact of new (nuclear) weapons on strategy, and current military assistance programs. He asked for the chiefs' personal views, "having in mind the elimination of overlapping in operations and administration, and the urgent need for a really austere basis in military preparations and operations." He most emphatically did not want a staff-produced study that, he no doubt understood, would differ little if at all from what the old JCS would have produced. While he did not set any particular spending limit in this order to the JCS, he specifically directed their attention to those aspects of NSC 149/2 and 153/1 that emphasized the importance of reduced spending and a balanced budget as vital national security considerations.[13]

Ike was calling for a break with the past, one that would "provide a fresh view as to the best balance and most effective use and deployment of our armed forces, under existing circumstances." What he wanted, he concluded, was "interim guidance" to aid the National Security Council "in developing policies for the most effective employment of available national resources to insure the defense of our country for the long pull which may lie ahead."[14]

Before they began their weeks of study, Radford and the chiefs met with Eisenhower at the White House. In a crisp half-hour meeting he reiterated points made in the memorandum delivered earlier to Radford. He made it absolutely clear that he wanted a new strategic concept that would result in smaller forces and reduced military spending. As the meeting broke up Ike asked each man in turn whether there was any reason that he could not perform this task. They all assured him that they had no such problems.[15]

Radford and his colleagues spent several weeks prior to being officially sworn in holding joint meetings, working independently, and traveling to military bases and other installations both here and abroad.[16] They found agreements difficult to achieve except on one issue. The president and the secretary of defense had both instructed the chiefs to study existing service roles and missions with an eye toward eliminating overlap and waste.

This was an extremely sensitive issue involving the future of the Marines, the Navy's air arm, the National Guard, and the Reserves, to mention only some of the organizations that might be affected by a serious attempt to eliminate waste and overlap. Rather than enter this tangled thicket where each service had much to lose, the new members of the JCS sidestepped the issue by endorsing the status quo. They claimed that the 1948 Key West agreement provided the services with sufficient guidance regarding roles and missions.

Eisenhower viewed a careful study of the roles and missions of the separate branches as one of the keys to improving service efficiency. He had repeatedly emphasized this during the campaign, in his inaugural address, and at his July meeting with the chiefs. It is therefore difficult to explain why, given the importance Ike placed on eliminating waste and duplication, he let the chiefs get away with this and in so doing lost an opportunity early in his first administration to address issues that had concerned him for a very long time.[17]

When it came to developing a new and less costly military strategy for the United States, the new members of the JCS made no headway. Radford was displeased. It seemed clear to him that Eisenhower's call for solvency meant that an emphasis should be placed on land-based and naval air power as well as nuclear fire power "and that the other services, Army, Navy, and Marines, would have to adjust to organizations that could be fleshed out rapidly in case of emergency." Such an approach, he thought, would allow the Defense Department to reduce the size of the military establishment, cut spending, and satisfy the president's need for defense at a lower cost.[18]

However, Radford had problems convincing General Ridgway and Admiral Carney to go along with his ideas. By early August he was in a fairly desperate frame of mind. Finally, he borrowed the yacht *Sequoia* from the secretary of the navy, invited his colleagues aboard for an extended trip on the Potomac, and set sail, hoping that the four of them, isolated from interfering aides, telephones, and other earthly distractions, might agree on something. During the next several days, pushed and prodded by Radford, the group produced a paper that was largely of the admiral's design.

The report began by asserting that postwar U.S. military policy had been sound and that as long as the current strategy remained unchanged any across-the-board reduction in spending would necessarily result in decreased military effectiveness. It went on, however, to point out that even given current spending levels, the nation's military capabilities were bound to deteriorate as new needs developed. The most pressing of these, the paper noted, was for a system of continental air defenses that might cost as much as $20 billion. The Soviet Union's expanding nuclear capability also made it imperative that the United States expand its own "ability to retaliate swiftly" if attacked. Current spending levels were inadequate to meet these growing needs and at the same time fulfill existing global military commitments.

The paper also noted that World War II and the Korean War had more or less used up the pool of trained reserves, especially those with specialized skills. The military draft would produce an answer to part of this problem. However, it was unlikely that given its present size the military would be able to fully meet its growing need for trained specialists. Assuming this to be the case, the paper contended that America's military forces were bound to grow smaller and would, as a result, become less able to meet existing commitments. Obviously, the paper concluded, it was necessary to alter the existing strategy. On these points there was no disagreement, the country was "overextended" with problems that current policy and spending levels could not address.[19]

Given the above, as well as the requirement imposed by the president that spending be reduced, the paper proposed a new strategy that emphasized continental defense "and the capability for delivering swift and powerful retaliatory blows." Other "peripheral military commitments" would no longer have "first claim on our resources." American forces then stationed in Europe, Japan, and Korea should be redeployed back to the United States. America's allies would be called upon to develop the conventional forces needed to meet Communist aggression. If attacked they would be supported by U.S. naval and air power and by American ground forces, which would be formed into a highly mobile strategic force capable of moving quickly to their support.

Although the paper noted that a major redeployment of this sort would be expensive and that the administration could not expect immediate savings from the move, in the long run costs would be cut in two ways. First, it would be less expensive to maintain American military personnel in the United States than to keep them on foreign soil. Second, once the redeployment had been completed and allied forces put in place, it would also be possible to reduce the size of ground forces. It was clear from what the paper advocated that the Army would bear the brunt of reductions and that the United States would in the future rely more heavily on strategic air power and nuclear weapons to deter aggression or if necessary to fight an all-out war. In that regard the paper urged the president to "formulate a clear, positive policy with respect to the use of atomic weapons, and . . . announce it publicly."[20]

It is important to understand that this JCS paper did not constitute a set of firm recommendations. On the contrary, the emphasis that it placed on air power and nuclear weapons did not sit well with either General Ridgway or

Admiral Carney, who also had serious doubts about the wisdom of with-drawing American forces from their overseas bases. In fact they wondered if this aspect of the proposed cure might be worse than the disease the president was attempting to treat. The presence of American forces overseas stood as a guarantee that Washington was committed to defend its allies. The psychological impact of withdrawing these forces could be disastrous. If the United States did redeploy and reduce its forces as the paper suggested, might it not appear as though the administration was adopting the Fortress America concept advocated by former President Hoover and Senator Taft? How would the NATO allies respond to this drastic change in American policy? Would they view this as a return to isolation by the new Republican administration? The United States had consistently pressed its European friends to expand their own defense efforts, and they had done so but at considerable cost to the health of their economies. Might they not be tempted to slow down and stretch out their own efforts if the United States was doing the same thing? Or, would NATO simply collapse, opening Western Europe to Soviet expansion?

For all these reasons the paper was not presented to the president as the hard-and-fast recommendation of the new members of the JCS. Instead the ideas incorporated in the paper represented the only option the chiefs could envision that would satisfy Eisenhower's insistence on fiscal restraint. It would be up to the president and the National Security Council to decide whether the ideas incorporated in the paper merited serious consideration.[21]

The president was on vacation in Denver when Radford submitted the results of the JCS study to Charles Wilson. Impressed, the secretary of defense urged Radford to fly west and explain his ideas to the president in person. Radford wasted no time, flying to Denver immediately. Eisenhower read the document over several times, complimented Radford on his work, and indicated that he would take the proposal to the NSC as soon as he returned.[22] As things turned out, the NSC held its first discussion of the JCS paper on August 27, before Eisenhower returned to the capital. At that meeting things took an interesting turn. The paper presented the redeployment concept as a tentative idea to be approached with extreme caution, not as an official policy recommendation. Yet Admiral Radford used his not inconsiderable rhetorical and debater's skills to sell the idea to the council. He was, of course, enthusiastically supported by Treasury Secretary Humphrey, who called the paper "terrific . . . the most important thing that had happened in this country since January 20." Acting Secretary of Defense Roger Kyes agreed, calling the paper a "historic event." Radford was also supported by Nathan Twining, who, realizing that the Air Force had much to gain by endorsing ideas incorporated in the paper, said that he agreed with "everything that Admiral Radford had stated." Twining went further, claiming that even if there had been no budget problem, his views as well as those of his colleagues would have remained the same.[23]

Just how Twining could have arrived at that conclusion is something of a mystery since only a few moments before both Admiral Carney and General Ridgway had raised serious objections to the tenor of the discussion. Carney urged the NSC members to keep in mind the fact "that certain conditions had been imposed on the Chiefs in the preparation of this study, particularly budgetary limitations." It was because of these, he said, that the report's authors "could discern only one course of action which would concurrently safeguard the national security and meet the budgetary limitation." Carney himself thought the implications of the paper so extreme that "upon closer examination" they might prove "unacceptable."[24]

Army Chief of Staff Ridgway joined Carney in his dissent, reminding the group that the report was not an official recommendation by the JCS but a call for a careful examination of the concepts it contained. He went on to state that he personally would not support the withdrawal of American forces from their overseas bases. "Securing adequate protection of the vitals of the American continent," he said, "did not mean that you abandoned Europe." If NATO "got any inkling of the content of this new concept," he said, "rightly or wrongly, the NATO powers would almost certainly construe it as an abandonment, and the consequences would be terrifying."[25]

Ridgway was supported by Secretary of State John Foster Dulles, who warned: "If the United States undertook the redeployment proposed it would be viewed by our allies as a sign either that we believed the danger of war had diminished or that we were returning to isolation." Under either circumstance what would become of NATO? Would the allies continue on the road to rearmament agreed to at the 1952 Lisbon Conference? The altered policy recommended in the paper, he thought, "could result in a grave disaster" unless the State Department had sufficient time to make the allies aware that the United States had not abandoned them but was simply concentrating its forces for a more effective defense. Even so Dulles was not sanguine. "If we do not succeed in selling this interpretation of the proposed redeployment," he said, "we can anticipate that the governments and peoples of the free world will dismiss our proposed new policy as simply camouflaged isolation."[26]

Surprisingly, little time was spent on the nuclear question during this discussion. However, Vice President Richard Nixon, who chaired the meeting in Eisenhower's absence, did ask for some clarification regarding this issue. Radford responded that the chiefs wanted a clear policy supporting the use of such weapons. It made no sense, he argued, to spend large sums developing and deploying nuclear weapons while "holding back on their use . . . because of public opinion." He thought it "high time" to clarify "our position on the use of such weapons if indeed we proposed to use them." Curiously, since the discussion never got beyond the subject of a general war to consider lesser conflicts, Radford's answer seemed to satisfy the members of the council who immediately returned to what they considered the most significant aspect of the paper, the redeployment proposal. On that issue all agreed that the council would defer to the secretary of state whose responsibility it would be to assess the foreign policy implications of the withdrawal of American forces from overseas bases.[27]

Shortly after the NSC completed its first discussion of these questions, Robert Cutler, Eisenhower's special assistant for national security affairs, flew to Denver to brief Eisenhower on the meeting. The president was ecstatic for it appeared that the JCS had come up with the answer to his dilemma. He was, in fact, so enthusiastic that he insisted on adding the following to the final record of action on the meeting: "This concept [redeployment and the development of indigenous forces] is a crystallized and clarified statement of this Administration's understanding of our national security objectives since World War II." Eisenhower then began pacing the room while Cutler sat transcribing his thoughts. Stationing American troops in Europe had always been a "stop gap measure" designed to build the confidence and strengthen the morale of our friends overseas, he said. Our purpose had been to provide them with security and some breathing space during which they would develop the strength to "hold vital areas with indigenous troops until American help could arrive." From the beginning, he argued, the real purpose of our national policy had been to protect the United States from surprise attack, foster the development of "highly mobile" U.S. forces capable of coming to the aid of threatened allies, and develop mobilization plans that would allow us "to marshal our entire strength" in defense of ourselves and our allies. The chiefs' paper met all of these criteria. Ironically, Eisenhower, who seemed to be completely taken by the proposal, was insistent on one point only. After repeatedly observing to Cutler that the JCS had not developed a "new" concept, he said it should never be referred to as such. It was, he insisted, a "reaffirmation and clarification of what he had always understood."[28]

John Foster Dulles left the August 27 meeting of the National Security Council a worried man. He was convinced that under existing circumstances the redeployment of American forces back to the United States would have disastrous consequences. However, Radford was a persuasive man who was selling an idea that appealed to the president. Worse, Deputy Defense Secretary Roger Kyes's performance at the conference suggested that he had Defense Department support as well as that of Humphrey and others who placed a balanced budget first on the country's long list of national security concerns. An experienced diplomat and a first-rate attorney, Dulles knew that if he were to undercut this redeployment proposal he would have to offer his boss an appealing alternative.

After planning strategy with Robert Bowie, director of the Policy Planning Staff, and Douglas MacArthur II, counselor of the Department of State, Dulles flew to Denver for a meeting with Eisenhower at the Summer White House. A memorandum that he prepared for the meeting summarized the arguments he used at this conference and the many problems he foresaw should the United States decide on an early withdrawal of American troops from bases abroad.

Dulles took the position that the chiefs' observations regarding the weakness of America's current strategic position were sound. He agreed that there was a need for more spending on continental defense, the development of nuclear and thermonuclear weapons, and guided missiles. Nor did he dispute the view that a balanced budget was an important objective. He also agreed that American forces could not be stationed abroad indefinitely. The presence of U.S. troops and their dependents in Japan had already created problems that were bound to intensify as time passed. Similarly, as Moscow's nuclear reach expanded, allies who had once happily provided the United States with bases for Strategic Air Command bombers were becoming less willing to harbor such installations, viewing them more as "lightning rods" than "umbrellas." Obviously, Dulles admitted, sooner or later the troops would have to be brought home.[29]

Still, Dulles argued, the current international situation was not conducive to the large-scale redeployment of American forces that the JCS paper proposed. He pointed out that "the NATO concept" of collective security was losing its credibility among our friends. The alliance had been forged on the basis of America's nuclear supremacy, but in recent years the Soviets had been moving ahead in the nuclear field. Only weeks before they had exploded their first thermonuclear device. They were also hard at work on the development of guided missiles. One result of this was that as American vulnerability to a Soviet nuclear strike grew, our credibility as the defender of Western Europe diminished. The allies had become increasingly fearful that "we might stay out if Europe were attacked first." NATO was also being weakened by the member nations' continuing economic problems and the current Soviet "peace offensive," which invited them to let their guard down.[30]

Dulles told Eisenhower that under current conditions the redeployment of American forces back to the continental United States "would probably be interpreted abroad as final proof of an isolationist trend and the adoption of the 'Fortress America' concept." He doubted that "any eloquence or reasoning on our part would prevent disintegration and deterioration of our position, with our growing isolation through the reaction of our present allies." Under these conditions, Dulles argued, troop redeployment might not produce real economies. At present the United States benefited from being able to draw on "a common fund" for "community security." If NATO collapsed we would be forced to adopt a costly "go-it-alone military policy." Moreover, he warned, "the balance of world power, military and economic, would doubtless shift rapidly to our great disadvantage."[31]

If a major redeployment of American forces was not sound policy at the moment, Dulles asked, what could be done? He suggested as an alternative that Eisenhower consider some sort of "spectacular effort to relax world tensions on a global basis." Success would allow "mutual withdrawal of Red Army forces and of U.S. forces abroad." This in turn would make possible the "[s]tabilization of NATO forces and of prospective German forces at a level compatible with budgetary relief." It would also allow for the establishment of the strategic reserve called for in the JCS paper.[32]

The meeting between Dulles and Eisenhower went on for several hours. In the end the president agreed that "any withdrawal that seemed to imply a change in basic intent would cause real turmoil abroad." He would not, therefore, consider the redeployment of American forces until such time as the allies understood and accepted the premise that Washington had in no way altered its commitment to the defense of its friends. It would be Dulles's responsibility to convince them of this. Eisenhower was also in "emphatic agreement" with Dulles "that renewed efforts should be made to relax world tensions." He told Dulles that such an initiative ought to be taken in the near future.[33]

Given Dulles's views on the ambitions and purposes of the Soviet leadership, it is highly doubtful that he believed dramatic initiatives would have much effect on Moscow. He had achieved his own personal objective, however. He now reported to the NSC that the president believed "the action to accomplish the redeployment suggested by the Joint Chiefs, unless very carefully handled, could result in a gradual attrition of our whole security position overseas." Such a policy could convince our friends that we were reverting to isolation, weaken the ties that bound us to our friends, and "endanger our SAC bases." It was clear, therefore, that "the task must be handled in such a way as to avoid such erroneous interpretation." And that might take a very long while indeed.[34]

Any doubt that Dulles had made the case against the redeployment of America's foreign-based forces was erased during discussions held to iron out differences over certain key aspects of NSC 162/2, the first bottom-up reevaluation of America's national security posture since 1950 when President Truman had approved NSC 68/2. During the debate George Humphrey made an impassioned appeal in favor of redeployment, arguing that unless Washington was prepared to initiate a "thorough-going revision of our whole military strategy," there was no point in developing a new national security policy.[35]

Eisenhower liked Humphrey. At the same time, he recognized that he was a man whose vision did not extend much beyond his home state of Ohio. He was an old-fashioned midwestern businessman lacking in international perspective. Ike warned Humphrey that "if the Communists succeeded in gaining control of Europe," which he believed they could do if the United States withdrew its forces, "the world balance of power would be hopelessly upset against us." Should that happen Humphrey's own worst nightmare would come true, for shut up in the Western Hemisphere and lacking the collective support of allies, the United States would be forced to spend countless extra billions on its own defenses. Having thus tried to make Humphrey see the short-sighted error of his ways, Ike concluded that "[i]t was and would continue to be a sine qua non of American policy that Western Europe should not become communist." Therefore, anxious though he was to see the Europeans do more on behalf of their own defense, "we simply could not abandon what we had begun in Europe." Redeployment would have to wait for better times. [36]

During these same discussions Eisenhower also had his way with regard to another major aspect of the August JCS paper, nuclear weapons policy. Radford and the JCS wanted a clear and forthright statement from the administration indicating that the United States considered nuclear weapons to be conventional in nature and would employ them as such. Moreover, because so large a part of America's nuclear striking power was deployed at overseas air bases, they also believed that the United States should insist upon the right to use these weapons without the approval of the host countries.[37]

Treasury Secretary Humphrey agreed. Only the use of nuclear weapons "on a broad scale," he said, "could really change the program of the Defense Department and cut the costs of the military budget." In like fashion, Defense Secretary Wilson insisted that the current lack of definition regarding when or where nuclear lightning would strike made planning difficult. The Defense Department had to know, he insisted, "whether or not to plan for the use of these weapons. Do we intend to use weapons on which we are spending such great sums, or do we not?" Secretary of State Dulles, too, thought a more clearly defined policy was important, and took the occasion to restate the view he had expressed often in the past that "somehow or other we must manage to remove the taboo from the use of these weapons."

Despite these pressures, Eisenhower remained unmoved. He made it abundantly clear that no public statement such as the JCS proposed would be forthcoming. In fact he thought "nothing would so upset the whole world as an announcement at this time by the United States of a decision to use these weapons." Moreover, he said, unless the host countries were willing to negotiate prior agreements on the use of the nuclear weapons stored on their territory, they would continue to hold a veto power over their use. After forcefully reminding the JCS and the other members of the council that he would make "the ultimate decision" as to when and where nuclear weapons would be used, he assured them that if national security required it he "would certainly use them." In the meanwhile, for planning purposes, he said the JCS could assume the use of nuclear weapons in a general war. They should not, however, "plan to make use of these weapons in minor affairs."[38] Thus, at his insistence, NSC 162/2 stated only that in the event of war "the United States will consider nuclear weapons to be as available for use as other munitions." It did not state when, or under what circumstances, they would be used.

Of the several ideas originally advanced in the August JCS paper, only one found its way into NSC 162/2. The United States was to maintain a "strong military posture, with emphasis on the capability of inflicting massive retaliatory damage by offensive striking power."[39]

To Radford and the other members of the JCS, the security policy outlined in this latest national security policy statement looked like a warmed-over version of past policies and could not be viewed as forming the basis of the new, less costly strategic concept the president said he was seeking. The administration's failure to produce a new strategic doctrine that all sides could agree upon inevitably led to another round of struggle between Eisenhower's civilian and military advisors as they considered the 1955 federal budget. The Treasury Department and the Budget Bureau considered another round of budget cuts imperative. Budget Director Dodge estimated an $8.7 billion budget deficit and a $6.2 billion cash deficit for the 1955 fiscal year. Meanwhile, with $81 billion in bills coming due and not enough money in the till, George Humphrey was forced to ask Congress to raise the federal debt limit to $290 billion. The administration was, according to Eisenhower, "in a hell of a fix."[40]

As far as Humphrey was concerned, the obvious solution to the administration's difficulties was to reduce defense spending. At a May 22 cabinet meeting he argued that the government had to find another $12 to $15 billion in cuts in order to balance the budget and fulfill its promise to reduce taxes. "We've got to revise whole programs," he said, "and this means surgery." When a stunned Charles Wilson noted that this would mean taking at least another $10 billion from Defense and the Mutual Security Agency, Humphrey responded: "Charley, that's right. You [sic] just got to get out the best damn streamlined model you ever did in your life. And you have to do it in six months, not three years. This means a brand new model—we can't just patch up the old jalopy."

Humphrey was especially strident about this, pointing out that under terms of NSC 162/2 the administration was committed to a "balanced security" that took into account the country's economic well-being. Nor was he impressed with what had thus far been accomplished. He wanted major program cuts, a complete bottom-up keelhauling of the defense establishment. Yet to that point, he said, the administration had not "done a damn' thing but go along with the programs and policies of the past Administration. . . . The cuts that had been accomplished "were only sufficient to take us back to the levels where Truman left off." "Either do better," he warned, or "abandon all hope of being retained in office."[41]

If Humphrey believed the defense budget should be slashed, Charles Wilson insisted that lacking a commitment to redeployment and a clear, forthright statement that nuclear weapons would be employed in small and large wars alike, the Defense Department could not agree to the force reductions needed to achieve a balanced budget. Wilson was strongly seconded by Admiral Radford, who remained committed to the ideas expressed in the August JCS paper. The administration's real problem, he said, was that it was attempting to retain great conventional and nuclear strength simultaneously and that the cost was simply too great. He believed the government should "make every effort to change over to a greater emphasis on the new weapons system since the cost of trying to maintain both systems was plainly too high."[42]

During the first full-scale NSC meeting on the 1955 budget, Eisenhower, who was clearly aware that he was presiding over a divided government, told council members and other participants that he did not want them coming to the table as representatives of a particular department or agency.

He was not interested in arranging a compromise between "varying departmental positions." It was especially important, he said, for members of the JCS to keep this in mind. He told the chiefs that any one of a half dozen officers could direct the day-to-day operations of their particular branch. That is not why he had selected them to head their services. They had a "distinct" and "much more difficult" task, which was "to bring their consolidated wisdom and their corporate experience as statesmen" to bear in solving "the problems of national security." "We want your brains and hearts," he said, "with your background."[43]

The president expected that his message of austerity, so frequently reiterated, and his insistence that the job of the military was to plan an adequate but not necessarily a perfect defense would by this time have taken root. However, the JCS did not prove accommodating. Despite the fact that by this time the fighting in Korea had ended, the services called for an increase of 135,000 in the size of the armed services—to over 3.5 million officers and enlisted personnel. Under this proposal the Army would remain at twenty divisions, the Navy would get a third Forrestal-class aircraft carrier, and the Air Force would grow from its existing 114 to 120 wings. Wilfred McNeil, the Defense Department's comptroller, estimated the cost of this program at $42 billion in new money.[44]

In defense of the JCS position, Radford and Wilson argued that nothing had changed in the world situation to justify reductions. The Soviet Union, now a thermonuclear power, posed at least as serious a threat as before, and America's military forces, widely disbursed at overseas bases, remained overextended. Moreover, redeployment was not to be implemented at any time in the near future. Nor had the administration developed a clear policy regarding the use of nuclear weapons. As a result the JCS saw no rational basis for reducing their estimate of necessary force levels.[45]

An appalled Joseph Dodge, who only moments before had projected an $8.7 billion deficit for the coming year, objected to the fact that in developing its plans the Defense Department had ignored any possible savings that might come as a result of the end of the Korean War. Treasury Secretary Humphrey complained that the only cuts he could find in the Defense Department proposal came from funding for the Mutual Security Agency, which dispensed military aid to the allies.

Responding to the unacceptable gap between the expectations of the military and the ambitions of the budget cutters, Secretary Dulles inquired whether the JCS had as yet begun the review of basic military strategy that the president had requested in July. Radford, who again stressed the failure of the NSC to adopt key provisions of the August JCS paper, replied that the chiefs "did not feel that they had been given sufficiently clear definitions of policy" to be able "to outline a really significant change in the existing composition of our military forces." A little later in the discussion Radford made himself entirely clear when he remarked that unless we were prepared to use nuclear weapons "in a blanket way, no possibility existed of significantly changing the present composition of our armed forces." In supporting Radford, Wilson claimed that it would be impossible for the JCS to "come up with a 'new look' at our military strategy" until two basic questions had been answered. First, "to what degree do we start to change our basic national security policy?" Second, to what degree can we shift emphasis from conventional to atomic weapons? Lacking answers to these two questions, Wilson said, it would be difficult "to get down . . . to 3 million men and still maintain reasonable security for our country."[46]

At last, Humphrey found something he and Wilson could agree upon. Supported down the line by Dodge, he argued that redeployment ought to begin as soon as possible and that it was "absolutely essential" for the Defense Department to plan on the use of nuclear weapons in large and small wars alike since only "their use on a broad scale could really change the program of the defense department," cut military costs, and produce a balanced budget. He again warned that if the 1955 budget did not at least approach balance "the American economy will go to hell and the Republican Party will lose the next election."[47]

Ike was bitterly disappointed by the trend of the discussion. No one had performed well. Charles Wilson had to know, though evidently he did not, that a defense budget of $42 billion in new money, which did not even include funds for the Mutual Security Agency, was entirely unacceptable. Nor was Ike at all satisfied with the performance George Humphrey put on at the meeting. He liked Humphrey enormously, but the man was so utterly fixated on the importance of a balanced budget that he was prepared to gut the military, immediately redeploy American forces from Western Europe, Japan, and Korea to bases back in the United States, and authorize the military to use nuclear weapons in any conflict, large or small, regardless of the impact these actions might have on the national security. During the discussion Ike repeatedly challenged Humphrey's extreme views, reminding him that national security meant more than a balanced budget.[48]

The Joint Chiefs of Staff were, in Eisenhower's mind, the worst of all. They had ignored his repeated calls for austerity and had refused to take into account the importance of a sound economy in making their budget recommendations. Clearly, he felt, it was time to take matters in his own hands. He therefore told Wilson and Radford in plain English that he expected the military to find ways of reducing force levels. He did not want combat units cut, but he saw no reason why support forces could not be sharply reduced, thus producing the savings he required. He wanted the military to take a serious look at how it managed the production of military equipment, suggesting that in order to save money the Pentagon borrow techniques used in the civilian sector by expanding purchasing when the national economy had slowed while cutting back when the economy was overheating. He also reminded Radford that "the utmost we can hope to achieve is, in Washington's words, a respectable posture of defense. We cannot hope for a perfect defense." Therefore, he asked, "can we stretch out more? Do we need everything for our armed forces right now?" In short, he said, he wanted the Joint Chiefs to undertake "a complete reexamination" of the problem.[49]

Following the president's lead, the NSC instructed Wilson and the JCS to return in December with a revised 1955 budget estimate that met the president's requirements. They were also to develop a new strategic plan that would allow for a sharp reduction in the size of the military establishment.[50]

In the aftermath of this meeting Eisenhower decided that he would not put up with any dilatory tactics on the part of the JCS. He instructed Wilson to develop his 1955 budget "on an austerity basis." In this way strategic planning and budget cuts would "go forward simultaneously." If the new strategic plan reduced costs, fine and good. Otherwise old structures would continue in place "but with personnel curtailed so far as appears safe."[51]

At a subsequent White House conference called by the president for the specific purpose of reducing defense expenditures, Eisenhower, Wilson, and John Foster Dulles agreed that some American forces then stationed in Korea could safely be redeployed to the United States, and that while the number of divisions deployed in Europe would remain the same, they would be "skeletonized" in order to allow the administration to bring at least some troops back to the United States from the Continent. At this meeting, no doubt under heavy pressure from Eisenhower, Wilson also changed his mind regarding the nuclear question. Whereas, when discussing this issue before the NSC, the secretary had taken the position that no force reductions could be justified unless the United States committed itself to the unlimited use of nuclear weapons, he now agreed "that the dependence that we are placing on new weapons would justify completely some reduction in" ground and naval forces, and that because of this the Army's request for 1.5 million officers and enlisted personnel would not be approved.[52]

Joseph Dodge, who knew nothing of this White House meeting, grew suspicious when the Joint Chiefs of Staff proved slow in producing either a revised budget or a new strategic plan. He believed that only an entirely new national strategy, accompanied by a full-scale revamping of the entire defense establishment, would produce the sort of results required to balance the budget. Eisenhower told him not to worry. Even if a new strategic plan were put in place, he wrote, it was unlikely to have any immediate effect. For that reason, he explained, he had instructed Wilson "to establish personnel ceilings in each service that will place everything except a few units on an austerity basis." There was, he said, no excuse for keeping the defense establishment at 3.5 million. "We are no longer fighting in Korea, and the Defense establishment should show its appreciation of this fact and help us achieve some substantial savings—and without wailing about the missions they have to accomplish. If they put their hearts into it, they can make substantial savings in personnel with little damage to the long term efficiency of the establishment."[53]

While Eisenhower was taking steps to sharply reduce the size of the armed services, the Army, Navy, and Air Force were at work on their own revised 1955 budget proposals. When these at last found their way to his desk early in December, Wilson was astounded. The total, including carry-over funds and new money, was actually higher than the figure already rejected by the president. With only four days remaining before the upcoming NSC meeting at which he was expected to produce an acceptable budget, Wilson took matters into his own hands. Without consulting the JCS (but with his recent White House meeting very much in mind), he established force levels that called for a 23 percent cut in the size of the Army and reductions of 13 percent and 7.5 percent for the Navy and Marines respectively. The Air Force would receive a slight increase. With these changes Wilson was able to propose a defense budget of $31 billion in new money.

During the same period that the armed services worked on their budget proposals, they also developed the new overall military strategy that Eisenhower had called for earlier. In doing so they were guided by a set of instructions that literally dictated the outcome of their work. Planning for the years 1955 through 1957, Charles Wilson wrote, was to be based on certain fundamentals established in NSC 162/2. First, the chiefs were to emphasize the primary importance of maintaining a vast nuclear retaliatory capability and to make adequate provision for continental air defenses. They were also to keep in mind the vital importance of protecting the American economy as "an essential bulwark in the preservation of our freedom and security." In what amounted to a signal victory for the budget cutters, the JCS was also told that the "size and composition of the armed forces" were to be based on "feasible annual expenditures," the guidelines for which were to be obtained from recent reports issued by Humphrey and Dodge. As a practical matter this meant that by the 1957 fiscal year new money for the military would be limited to at most $33.8 billion. Finally, Wilson made it clear that by the end of the 1957 fiscal year he expected force levels to have been reduced from the current level of nearly 3.5 million to somewhere between 2.5 and 3 million. In a slight concession to Radford and the JCS, as part of his call for a new strategic plan, Wilson authorized the JCS to assume that in the event of any war the United States would use nuclear weapons "whenever it is of military advantage to do so." This concession did not give Radford the blanket authority to use nuclear weapons that he wanted. The president would still decide on a case-by-case basis under what circumstances nuclear weapons might be used, but it at least implied that the administration had come a step closer to recognizing the conventionality of nuclear weapons.[54]

Radford assigned a special ad hoc committee, headed by Air Force General Frank F. Everest, the job of developing a new strategic plan based on Wilson's instructions. Not surprisingly, the plan that the Everest group produced, which came to be known as the "New Look," placed heavy emphasis on air power and its ability to inflict "massive damage upon the USSR" in the event of war. It also called for an elaborate system of continental defenses, the use of tactical nuclear weapons in support of American or allied forces "whenever the employment of atomic weapons would be militarily advantageous," and the creation of a highly mobile, combat ready strategic reserve to be stationed largely in the United States.[55]

Implementing this strategy would require the withdrawal of most American ground forces from Korea and Japan in the near future. For a variety of reasons the Everest committee recognized, however, that it might be necessary to retain ground forces in Europe beyond 1957. Still, the document continued, America's allies in Europe and Asia would ultimately be required to provide the "major share of ground forces for their own defense." In this regard they should be made to recognize that America's "massive retaliatory striking power" was a major contribution to their security and that the "tactical atomic support which can be provided our allies will become increasingly important in offsetting present deficiencies in conventional requirements."[56]

By proposing a sharp reduction in the size of America's overseas commitments while emphasizing nuclear striking power, the Everest committee was able to propose that over the coming three years, the military establishment could be reduced to a total 2.815 million officers and enlisted personnel, a cut of more than 600,000. These new force levels would require the Army to take a one-third cut in its manpower while the Navy and Marines were reduced by 15 and 20 percent respectively. Even the Air Force would be cut from 143 to 137 wings.[57]

Reaction to the Everest Report was by no means universally favorable. General Ridgway warned his colleagues and Secretary Wilson that the proposed cuts called for in the report would "so weaken the Army that it could no longer carry out its missions."[58] Admiral Carney, equally concerned about the cuts and the heavy emphasis the report placed on "massive retaliation," argued that the country required "a flexible strategy capable of countering whatever action the enemy may choose to take."[59] Obviously, Ridgway and Carney were both deeply concerned. Yet in the end, despite their fear that America's limited war capabilities were being sacrificed in the interest of reduced costs, they endorsed the Everest Report as the best strategy available, given the restraints under which the administration required the JCS to operate. At the same time, the chiefs forwarded the new strategic plan to Secretary Wilson with a warning. Their recommendation, they said, was based "on the assumption that present international tensions and threats remain approximately the same." Any change in the world situation would require an entirely new set of estimates.

On December 16, 1953, Admiral Radford presented the new strategic plan and proposed force levels to the NSC. After Radford completed his presentation, Wilfred McNeil announced that by the end of the 1955 fiscal year the military establishment would have been reduced to about 3 million, a good start on the overall plan. He estimated that new money for 1955 would be $31.2 billion and that total defense expenditures for 1955, including carry-over funds, would reach $37.6 billion, far below the current spending level, which was running at about $44 billion.[60]

Following McNeil's presentation, the president asked for comments from the service representatives. Air Force and Navy leaders indicated that the budget would be "a tight squeeze," but raised no serious objection. Secretary of the Army John Stevens, however, had more to say. He read a statement from Ridgway in which the general warned that the administration was weakening the Army to such an extent "that it could no longer carry out its missions." Stevens added his own "very grave concern" not only over the cuts but also over the fact that he had not been allowed to participate in the talks that resulted in the decision to shrink the Army. He urged the president to consider smaller reductions stretched out over a longer period of time.

The president thanked Stevens for his statement but indicated that the decision regarding the Army would stand.[61]

Eisenhower had managed to implement a revised national military strategy that called for a 28 percent decrease in force levels and large-scale budget reductions. As a result his administration was headed toward "solvency" and its first balanced budget. Whether this had been achieved at the expense of "security," however, was a matter that sharply divided the JCS. Earlier, when it became apparent that the president was not going to implement most of the important ideas incorporated in the August JCS paper, Radford proved unwilling to support force reductions and budget cuts. However, when Eisenhower made it clear, as he did at the October 13 meeting of the NSC, that he was not giving the chiefs a choice, Radford fell in line. Air Force Chief of Staff Nathan Twining, who recognized that the New Look made the Air Force the premier service, also gave Ike his complete support. General Ridgway and Admiral Carney, of course, felt differently.

Eisenhower expected, even invited, internal policy debates and was especially cognizant of the importance of giving all sides an opportunity to state their views. However, once a policy had been decided upon he expected all the members of the team to pull together. On that score he had reason to be concerned. Carney kept his opposition to the New Look in-house, but General Ridgway was not so willing to acquiesce. Thus, during his appearance before the House Appropriations Committee, he showed early signs of disaffection, telling the legislators that while it was true, as administration spokesmen claimed, that the JCS had unanimously endorsed the 1955 budget and the lower force levels called for under the Everest Report, they had done so only because of limitations placed upon the planning process by the administration.[62] In early 1954 Ridgway went no further than this, but just how long Eisenhower would be able to keep him from breaking ranks and appealing directly to Congress remained to be seen.

NOTES

1. Lovett to Eisenhower, 11 Nov. 1952, Whitman File, Administration Series, Box 25, Eisenhower Library (hereafter cited as EL). See also Emmet John Hughes, *Ordeal of Power* (New York: Atheneum, 1963), 71–73.

2. Sherman Adams, *First Hand Report* (New York: Harpers, 1961), 404.

3. Warner R. Schilling, Paul Y. Hammond, and Glenn H. Snyder, *Strategy, Politics, and Defense Budgets* (New York: Columbia University Press, 1963), 393 (hereafter cited as Snyder, "The New Look"); Robert J. Watson, *A History of the Joint Chiefs of Staff: The Joint Chiefs of Staff and National Policy, 1953–1954* (Wilmington: Michael Glazier, Inc., 1979), 5:15.

4. Eisenhower to Radford, 18 May 1953, Whitman File, Diary Series, Box 3, EL.

5. Snyder, "The New Look," 412; Robert Donovan, *Eisenhower* (New York: Harper, 1956), 19.

6. Steven Juricka, Jr. ed., *From Pearl Harbor to Vietnam: The Memoirs of Admiral Arthur Radford* (Stanford: The Hoover Institution Press, 1980), 308–309; 312–13 (hereafter cited as Radford, *Memoirs*). Wilson to Eisenhower, 19 March 1953, Whitman File, Administration Series, Box 40, EL. By waiting until May to name his nominees to the JCS, Eisenhower was able to act with at least some discretion. Hoyt Vandenberg was scheduled to leave in June. The terms of two other friends, "Joe" Collins and Omar Bradley, would end in August before their replacements were sworn in. Only the chief of Naval Operations, Admiral William Fechteler, would have to be replaced before his term was up.

7. Eisenhower to Radford, 18 May 1953, Whitman File, Diary Series, Box 3, EL.

8. Radford, *Memoirs*, 314–15; Watson, *History of the Joint Chiefs of Staff,* 5:15.

9. Donovan, *Eisenhower*, 25. Before Wilson offered the new members of the JCS their appointments he cleared these nominations with Senator Taft, who told the press: "Wilson had me to his apartment and showed me the list. I found it entirely satisfactory."

10. Scholars will note that under NSC 68/2 the original date was the end of 1954. However, as the costs of rearmament escalated, President Truman insisted on a stretch-out. NSC 135/3 called for full rearmament by the end of 1956.

11. NSC 149/2, Washington, 29 April 1953, U.S. Department of State, *Foreign Relations of the United States, 1952–1954,* (Washington, DC: GPO, 1984), 2:307–15 (hereafter cited as *FRUS*).

12. Ibid., 378–86.

13. Memorandum for the secretary of defense, 1 July 1953, Whitman File, Administration Series, Box 39, EL.

14. Eisenhower to Wilson, 1 July 1953, ibid.; Watson, *History of the Joint Chiefs of Staff,* 5:16–17.

15. Matthew B. Ridgway, *Soldier:The Memoirs of Matthew B. Ridgway* (New York, Harpers, 1956), 267; Snyder, "The New Look," 413.

16. Because of illness Hoyt Vandenberg retired in June and was replaced by Twining. Radford and the other two members of the JCS were sworn in in August.

17. Kenneth W. Condit, *A History of the Joint Chiefs of Staff* (Washington, DC: JCS Historical Office, 1991), 6:178.

18. Radford, *Memoirs*, 319.

19. Watson, *History of the Joint Chiefs of Staff,* 5:18–19.

20. Ibid.

21. Ibid., 18–21; Snyder, "The New Look," 414; Ridgway, *Soldier*, 268–69.

22. Radford, *Memoirs*, 322.

23. NSC discussion, 27 Aug. 1953, *FRUS, 1952–1954*, 2:443–55.

24. Ibid.

25. Ibid.

26. Ibid.

27. Ibid.

28. Robert Cutler, memorandum of a meeting with the president, 3 Sept. 1953, ibid., 455–57.

29. John Foster Dulles, memorandum of a meeting with the president, 6 Sept. 1953, ibid., 457–59.

30. Ibid.

31. Ibid.

32. Ibid.

33. Eisenhower, memorandum to Dulles, 8 Sept. 1953, ibid., 460–63.

34. NSC discussion, 9 Sept. 1953, Whitman File, NSC Series, Box 4, EL.

35. NSC discussion, 29 Oct. 1953, *FRUS, 1952–1954*, 2:573.

36. NSC discussion, 7 Oct. 1953, ibid., 527–28; Saki Dockrill, *Eisenhower's New Look: National Security Policy, 1953–61* (New York: St. Martin's Press, 1996), 33–47.

37. NSC discussion, *FRUS, 1952–1954*, 2:593–94; NSC discussion, 7 Oct. 1953, ibid., 532–34.

38. Ibid.; Snyder, "The New Look," 436.

39. NSC 162/2, *FRUS, 1952–1954*, 2:582.

40. NSC discussion, 15 July 1953, Whitman File, NSC Series, Box 4, EL; Memorandum for the president, 28 Sept. 1953, ibid., Administration Series, Box 12, EL.

41. NSC discussion, 15 July 1953, Whitman File, NSC Series, Box 4, EL. Humphrey was referring to the fact that Wilson had achieved his $5 billion in cuts largely through accounting maneuvers that had no effect, at least immediately, on the military expansion. See Snyder, "The New Look," 398.

42. NSC discussion, 1 Oct. 1953, ibid.

43. NSC discussion, 13 Oct. 1953, *FRUS, 1952–1954*, 2:535.

44. Ibid., 543.

45. Ibid., 541–42; Watson, *History of the JCS*, 5:26; Snyder, "The New Look," 425–26.

46. NSC discussion, 13 Oct. 1953, *FRUS, 1952–1954*, 2:545.

47. Ibid., 547; Snyder, "The New Look," 427–29.

48. NSC discussion, 13 Oct. 1953, *FRUS, 1952–1954*, 2:545–48; 29 Oct. 1953, ibid., 571–74.

49. NSC discussion, 13 Oct. 1953, *FRUS, 1952–1954*, 2:543–45.

50. Ibid., 549.

51. Eisenhower, memorandum for General Cutler, 21 Oct. 1953, Whitman File, Diary Series, Box 3, EL.

52. Eisenhower, memorandum for the record, 11 Nov. 1953, ibid.

53. Dodge to Eisenhower, 27 Nov. 1953, Whitman File, Administration Series, Box 12; Eisenhower to Dodge, 1 Dec. 1953, ibid.; Eisenhower to Wilson, 30 Nov. 1953, ibid., Box 39; Eisenhower to Wilson, 2 Dec. 1953, Whitman File, Diary Series, Box 7, EL.

54. Wilson to JCS, 16 Oct. 1953, in J.C.S. 2101/108, Enclosure A, CCS 381 (1–31–50), Sec. 46, Modern Military Branch, National Archives (hereafter cited as NA); Watson, *History of the JCS,* 5:26–28.

55. J.C.S. 2101/113, 10 Dec. 1953, "Military Strategy and Posture," CCS 381 (1–31–50), Sec. 32, NA. The high costs of the massive retaliatory capability and continental defenses meant that the strategic reserve was never established.

56. Memorandum for the secretary of defense, "Military Strategy and Posture," 9 Dec. 1953, CCS 381 U.S. (1–31–50), Sec. 32, NA. The final draft of the Everest Report, "Military Strategy and Posture," J.C.S. 2101/113, is dated December 10, 1953, and can be found in CCS 381 (1–31–50), Sec. 32, NA. See also Watson, *History of the JCS*, 5:28–29; Snyder, "The New Look," 432–33, 440–44.

57. Ibid. The Air Force cut six wings of troop carriers. These planes were of no consequence to the Air Force since they existed only to move ground troops.

58. Ridgway, *Soldier*, 288.

59. Memorandum by the chief of Naval Operations, 7 Dec. 1953, JCS 2101/112, 381 U.S. (1–31–50), Sec. 31, NA.

60. NSC discussion, 16 Dec. 1953, Whitman File, NSC Series, Box 5, EL.

61. Ibid., 17 Dec. 1953.

62. *NYT*, March 16, 1954.

Photo 1—President Dwight D. Eisenhower. Photograph used with permission.

Photo 2—Admiral Chester Nimitz and General Eisenhower are smiling here but their disagreements were many. Photograph used with permission.

Photo 3—Admiral Arthur Radford, the principle author of the New Look, served as Chairman of the Joint Chiefs of Staff from 1933 to 1957. Photograph used with permission.

Photo 4—Charles Wilson, the former head of General Motors, served as secretary of defense for more than four years. Photograph used with permission.

Photo 5—General Maxwell Taylor, shown here with Eisenhower, strongly disagreed with the New Look and tried in vain to convince the president to adopt a strategy of "flexible response" instead. Photograph used with permission.

Photo 6—Neil McElroy, shown here at his swearing in ceremony, served as secretary of defense during the 1958 debate over Pentagon reorganization. Photograph used with permission.

6

"If the Administration Decides to Beef Up the Armed Forces along Lines Now Talked Of, the Whole Eisenhower Program Will Take a New Direction, Economic as well as Military."

Although in 1953 Eisenhower managed to establish a new, less costly military strategy as well as budget targets for the years 1955 through 1957, peace did not descend upon the administration. The Budget Bureau, seconded by Treasury Secretary Humphrey, pressed for further defense cuts while the JCS, concerned by recent foreign policy setbacks, an increasingly tense international situation, and Moscow's growing nuclear power, urged a reconsideration of the New Look and more than hinted that a "preventive war" was in order. The president remained the man in the middle, fighting off extreme proposals while continuing to pursue a policy that in his view protected both the economic well-being of the nation as well as its fundamental security requirements.

The debate over budgets and global strategy continued inside the administration throughout the year 1954. General Ridgway, who had reluctantly acquiesced in the decisions taken in 1953, repeatedly criticized the New Look, arguing that the nuclear retaliatory capability it emphasized would be virtually useless after a state of "atomic plenty" had been achieved. Once the Soviet Union developed the capacity to retaliate against the United States, a situation of mutual deterrence would occur in which it would be suicidal to use strategic nuclear weapons. Under such conditions, Ridgway argued, the Soviets were certain to become increasingly confident and aggressive, especially if the United States lacked the conventional forces to respond appropriately to their actions. Ridgway even contended that it would be quite impossible for the United States to successfully conduct a large-scale nuclear war. The extensive employment of such weapons, he claimed, would result in a catastrophe beyond imagining, a disaster for victor and vanquished alike.[1]

Ridgway also disputed the view advanced by Eisenhower, Admiral Radford, and others, that the United States could safely reduce the size of its ground forces because tactical nuclear weapons would vastly enhance the firepower of the remaining units. The assumption that firepower could replace manpower was unproven and, he believed, unfounded. Due to the highly complex technology required in the nuclear age, he argued, the armed services would actually require increased manpower. Ridgway also dared to speculate that in an era when both the United States and the Soviet Union had devastating nuclear power at their disposal, the Soviets might decide to initiate a war using only their conventional strength while keeping their nuclear weapons in reserve. What would the United States do if confronted with a large-scale conventional military challenge? Would we be the first to use the devastating power at our disposal, knowing it would mean our own destruction?[2]

Chief of Naval Operations Admiral Robert B. Carney, while more circumspect than Ridgway, was no less opposed to the administration's new military policies. In a memorandum prepared for the other members of the JCS, he warned: "If we base our strategy upon a predetermined concept of enemy intentions, and in consequence circumscribe our military capabilities by building forces capable of countering only one predetermined enemy course of action, we invite disaster." Carney went on to attack the fundamental assumption of NSC 162/2, noting that the emphasis that document placed "upon massive air retaliatory and counter-offensive capabilities apparently is based upon the premise that such capabilities will deter general war, inhibit local aggression, and dissuade the Soviets from actions which might precipitate all-out war." He agreed that the massive retaliatory power of the United States would most likely deter the Soviets from beginning a general war, but argued that "it will undoubtedly also cause them to pursue their objectives by creating situations in which massive damage techniques would not serve, and would even be detrimental to, the best interest of the United States." These and other considerations led Carney to conclude that the United States should "place greater emphasis upon a highly mobile, combat-ready, U.S. Strategic Reserve." He thought that "[s]uch a mobile reserve, backed up and supported by an adequate mobilization base and supplemented by a massive air retaliatory capability of reasonable proportions, is necessary if we are to continue over the long term to be able to cope with limited aggression and at the same time be prepared for general war should it eventuate."[3]

Before the middle of May 1954, the views advanced by Ridgway and Carney had gained currency as a result of a series of foreign policy setbacks. By that time French forces had suffered a humiliating defeat at Dienbienphu in Indochina; America's allies had refused to join Washington in an attempt to save Vietnam; the Geneva Conference, which had convened in April, gave promise of producing a unified Vietnam under Communist control; the French Government seemed poised to kill the European Defense Community Treaty, the centerpiece of the administration's plan for the defense of Europe; and a major crisis was brewing in the Far East where the Chinese Communists seemed to be preparing for an assault on certain offshore islands held by the Chinese Nationalists.

With the international situation apparently going very badly wrong, press reports indicated that the administration was having second thoughts about its security policy. *Newsweek* noted in an unusually long article that the New Look had "not saved Indo-China" and that this failure "has raised the question of whether it will save other threatened areas." The administration, the magazine observed, seemed to have few attractive choices. It could beef up conventional forces to meet local aggression, thus abandoning the New Look and hopes of reduced government spending; it could decide to employ tactical nuclear weapons in small wars to make up for its lack of conventional strength, an option that was fraught with many dangers; or it could "resign itself to further Communist expansion in Southeast Asia and elsewhere."[4]

Following the French defeat at Dienbienphu one unidentified official who was privy to NSC discussions told *Newsweek* of his "hunch" that military spending would go up, not down, in 1955 as the United States attempted to hold the line against Communist expansion in Southeast Asia. Pentagon sources agreed. "If the administration decides to beef up the armed forces along lines now talked of," *Newsweek* claimed, "the whole Eisenhower program will take a new direction, economic as well as military." All in all, the magazine believed, General Ridgway, whose views were well known, was correct. The loss of Indochina served as a "reaffirmation of the axiom that nothing can take the place of the foot soldier and the weapons of ground warfare that support him."[5]

Newsweek's report correctly reflected concerns that were in fact bubbling up inside the administration. May of 1954 marked the beginning of a period during which the New Look became a matter of hot debate between those who believed the administration should continue in pursuit of a balanced budget, and a growing number of critics who believed the international situation was so threatening that a reconsideration of decisions taken in 1953 was in order.

On May 10, 1954, only days after the French collapse at Dienbienphu, the president received a sobering report on the fiscal situation from his new budget director, Rowland Hughes. After estimating revenues for 1956 as well as the savings that might be made in nonmilitary spending, Hughes informed the president that (assuming there were no dramatic changes in the domestic or international situation that would result in increased spending) the 1956 budget would be out of balance by $6.8 billion. The gap for 1957 would be approximately $5.9 billion. Hughes added that if certain tax reductions, which the Treasury Department considered desirable, were enacted, the gap would rise to $9.7 billion for 1956 and $12 billion for 1957. Hughes repeated his findings at a May 20 meeting of the NSC and warned that it would not be easy to balance the budget even by 1957, that it would "require reductions in expenditures for the basic national security programs at least as large as those that had been made for the FY [fiscal year] 1955 budget."[6]

In a passionate defense of Hughes's report, George Humphrey warned that in the coming weeks the administration would be under pressure to return to "just a little inflation." It would have to resist these pressures, he insisted, since the alternative would ultimately prove "disastrous for the United States." Government revenues were coming down, Humphrey claimed, while Congress seemed determined to put increased pressure on the budget by reducing taxes. The administration, therefore, had no choice but to make further cuts in defense spending. The facts were clear, the treasury secretary argued. The United States could no longer afford to "be prepared to fight two or three or more different kind of wars" but would have to "decide on one kind of war which it will be prepared to prosecute if war comes." Nor was there any doubt which kind of war Humphrey had in mind.[7]

Responding to Humphrey's zealous appeal, John Foster Dulles observed that the national defense required greater flexibility than the treasury secretary implied with his "one war" proposal. If the administration should decide to prepare only for a nuclear confrontation, it would immediately lose all of its allies as well as the overseas military and air bases that were central to its strategy. Moreover, he said, it would have to transform every small conflagration into a big war, and "we could not afford to do that." When Humphrey continued to insist that cuts were essential to preserve the "American way of life" and "a strong and free economy," Dulles retorted that "we must also appraise the nature and degree of the external dangers we face." In the last few months, he noted, the "international situation" had changed "greatly for the worse." Because this was a time of "mounting rather than of lessening danger," Dulles said, "it would increase our peril if either our allies or our enemies concluded that we were sacrificing security to economy."[8]

Like Dulles, Eisenhower too was unprepared to endorse Humphrey's extreme views. There was, he said, an "irreducible minimum" that had to be spent on security measures. "We can never under any circumstances say that we cannot afford to defend our country." The "American way of life" was important, he agreed, but so too was "the physical survival of our nation."[9]

During the next several weeks, the NSC's Planning Board as well as the JCS attempted to convince the president that far from meriting further cuts, defense spending had dropped below the "irreducible minimum" he had referred to at the May 20 meeting. In 1953, when the NSC approved the Everest Report and a sharp reduction in the size of the armed forces, it did so with the understanding that any deterioration in the world political or military situation would require a rethinking of national security policy. A June 14, 1954, report by the Planning Board clearly indicated that the world situation had indeed changed for the worse. The question then became, should the administration continue to adhere to policy decisions taken earlier?[10]

According to the Planning Board the Soviet Union remained strong and in absolute control of its East European satellites. Moreover, Communist China had "gained prestige more rapidly than anticipated" and was growing in power. Soviet military strength was growing too, and now exceeded the levels that existed when NSC 162/2 had been approved. The board was especially concerned about Moscow's growing thermonuclear capabilities. As Soviet nuclear might grew, board members feared that America's willingness to fight a general war would decrease. Echoing views held by General Ridgway, the board also noted that at some point in the not-too-distant future a situation of mutual deterrence would occur when it would prove suicidal for the United States to loose its nuclear lightning. At that point the Soviets would enjoy greater freedom of action than at present and could be counted upon to behave more aggressively. As Eisenhower's special assistant for National Security Affairs, Robert Cutler, made clear, some on the board believed that this would allow the Soviets to avoid atomic war and "nibble the free world to death piece by piece." The United States, these board members believed, should have the capability to fight limited wars without recourse to the use of nuclear weapons.[11]

The board went on to enumerate a number of ways in which the New Look was falling short simply because it was not being implemented. When the new strategy was first approved, it had been assumed that some American ground forces stationed in the Far East and Europe would be redeployed to the United States. American ground forces would then be organized into a highly mobile force capable of moving swiftly to support threatened allies whose own ground forces would provide the majority of military units engaged in repelling the aggression. It had also been assumed that allied forces in Europe would be augmented by twelve new German divisions that would operate as part of the European Defense Community (EDC). Eight Japanese divisions were also to have been organized for the defense of the home islands. Finally, NSC 162/2 called for the creation of a large mobilization base that would include a stockpile of strategic materials and a much improved military reserve.[12]

Though a year had passed none of this had thus far taken place. The planned withdrawal of some American forces from the Far East had been postponed after the French defeat in Indochina. Because the French Parliament had failed to ratify the EDC, it had proven impossible to withdraw the five divisions still stationed in Europe. As a result, American ground forces overseas remained overextended; the "indigenous forces" that were to be the first line of defense against Communist aggression were not in place; the Army and Marines were losing, not gaining, mobility; and little had been done to develop needed reserves. The only aspects of the New Look that appeared to have any momentum were in the area of nuclear retaliatory power and improved continental defenses.

Nor did the world situation appear promising from a political point of view. The growth of Moscow's nuclear power, combined with the soft line being followed by the new Soviet Government of Georgi Malenkov, the board believed, was having a deleterious effect on the allies, who now appeared less willing to accept American leadership and more fearful of actions that could lead to war. Witness the recent failure of the United States to organize allied support for the French in Indochina, the unwillingness of the French to ratify the EDC, and the growing difficulties the United States was experiencing in maintaining its SAC overseas airbases. On top of that, the board added, the allies had not seen fit to cooperate with the United States on East-West trade, and the future of U.S. relations with Japan was still very much up in the air.[13]

The JCS reinforced the concerns of the Planning Board with briefings and papers that claimed that the military threat from the Soviet Union was growing exponentially, that the United States was lagging behind in development of long-range missiles, and that the foreign policies that had been designed to check Communist expansion had been a miserable failure. It was time, the chiefs believed, to reverse the trend toward reduced forces and budgets established under the New Look.

It was the growing Soviet thermonuclear threat that the JCS first brought to the attention of the president and the NSC. During the Truman and early Eisenhower administrations the United States had paid relatively little attention to the development of ballistic missile technology. This was because in the early postwar period weapons experts held that to be effective missiles armed with the nuclear warheads that were then available required a circular error probable (CEP) of at least one-half mile.[14] The guidance systems of that era could not approach this standard. As a result missile research lagged. The situation began to change in June 1953, when the mathematician John von Neuman and the physicist Edward Teller informed the Air Force Scientific Advisory Board that it would soon be possible to produce a thermonuclear warhead with an explosive power of between one and two megatons that would be light enough to be carried on an intercontinental ballistic missile (ICBM). With a warhead of such huge destructive capacity, accuracy counted for much less; even with a CEP of from three to five miles a missile so armed would be able to destroy an entire city. Next, Bruno Augustein, a mathematician working with the RAND Corporation, did calculations that demonstrated that given this fact it would be cost effective to deploy thermonuclear-armed ICBM's far sooner than had earlier been assumed.[15]

In February 1954, von Neuman submitted a report to General Nathan Twining, air force chief of staff, indicating that if weight and accuracy standards were relaxed (changes that would not undermine the effectiveness of the weapons), the United States could by 1960 have a force of 100 operational ICBM's armed with thermonuclear warheads. It also seemed certain that by that time, if not before, the Soviets, who had exploded their first thermonuclear weapon in August 1953, would also have such a weapon. A few weeks after this the Air Force Council decided that the Atlas ICBM project should be given a high priority and that "extraordinary action [should] be taken to accelerate the revised program."[16]

On June 3, in an effort to gain increased funding for the Atlas program, a JCS team briefed the NSC first on "the impact of atomic and thermonuclear weapons on our national security policy and on our over-all military strategy," and then on "the time factor in relation to the developing Soviet capability to inflict severe damage on the United States." The minutes of this meeting do not state precisely what the briefing team proposed beyond a complete reevaluation of national policy. There is at least a hint, however, that the subject of preventive war came up, for the notes on the meeting indicate that the team made "a series of recommended courses of action which were quite drastic in character." In a less radical vein the team also proposed that the United States develop an ICBM as quickly as possible. In supporting this proposal Admiral Radford noted that the enormous areas of damage inflicted by thermonuclear weapons "greatly simplified the old problem of attaining accuracy for guided missiles." He also observed that by 1958 the Soviets would quite probably have an ICBM armed with a thermonuclear warhead, and that possession of this weapon would allow them "to force a showdown" with the United States.[17]

At the same time that the JCS was pressing for increased funding for missile development, it launched a double-barreled attack on U.S. foreign and military policy. In a paper forwarded to the NSC ten days after the briefing on the Soviet missile threat, the chiefs argued that America's postwar foreign policy had been a dismal failure. Since 1945, the chiefs claimed, Moscow had "amassed under its control some 800 millions of people, millions of square miles of territory, and vast material resources." It had accomplished this even though the United States enjoyed, first, a nuclear monopoly and, after that, nuclear superiority. The chiefs were convinced that "the struggle of the Free World against the spread of Soviet-Communist domination of peoples and areas has now entered a precarious if not critical stage, characterized by continuing Communist expansion and military growth on the one hand and the emergence of divisive strains in the Free World coalition on the other." Considering all of this as well as the fact that America's nuclear superiority was a rapidly wasting asset, the chiefs believed that Washington should seek to persuade its allies that time limitations "dictate the necessity of confronting the Soviets with unmistakable evidence of an unyielding determination to halt further Communist expansion," Moscow had to be convinced "that aggression will be met with counteraction which, inherently, will hold grave risks to the maintenance of their regime."[18]

In a second paper, which was also forwarded to the NSC in June, the JCS made the case for the expansion of America's conventional military forces. The deterioration of the international situation as evidenced by recent failures in Indochina, they contended, suggested the necessity of planning for substantial increases in the defense budget and in the size of America's military establishment. The "[p]rolonged continuance" of a situation in which American forces remained poorly deployed in Europe and Asia would, they suggested, "require re-examination of the personnel and major force ceilings" earlier decided upon. They further contended that new programs should be developed "to increase the striking power of all U.S. Forces which can be brought to bear on the enemy." More assets should also be put into continental defense. Finally, the JCS observed, the United States needed to face up to the problem of "limited local aggression" which would become more likely once a situation of mutual nuclear deterrence occurred. In an age of "atomic plenty," the chiefs asserted, "the Soviets might well elect to pursue their ultimate objective of world domination through a succession of local aggressions, either overt or covert, all of which could not be successfully opposed by the Allies through localized counteraction." This made the creation of a highly mobile strategic reserve force, even given the political necessity of retaining forces in Europe and the Far East, immediately desirable.[19]

Like the JCS, Secretary of Defense Wilson appears to have believed the time had come to call a halt to the administration's planned force reductions and, therefore, its economy measures. On April 27, 1954, for example, the *New York Times* carried a story in which Wilson was quoted as saying that the "next few months" were "obviously critical ones in world affairs," and that "what happens in Europe and Asia during this period may force a soul-searching review of our specific policies, plans, objectives and expenditures."[20] In subsequent discussions that culminated in July, the JCS and Wilson agreed that given the dangerous international situation, plans for further reductions in the size of the military establishment should be scrapped. In planning for the 1956 fiscal year, Wilson agreed to slight increases in the size of the Army, Navy, and Marines, and proposed that the Air Force should be provided with extra funding so that it might reach full strength a year ahead of schedule.[21] At a meeting held on July 30, Wilson presented this proposal to the NSC. Budget Director Hughes, startled by this news, which ran directly contrary to agreements made in 1953, asked Wilson if this meant the services would retain 150,000 more men than had originally been planned. Wilson agreed that this was so.[22]

When the JCS produced final proposals for the 1956 fiscal year, the price tag attached to their plans by Comptroller Wilfred McNeil was $37.4 billion in new money, roughly $8 billion more than Congress had appropriated for 1955, and $5.2 billion more than the president had authorized under terms of the three-year plan laid out by the Everest committee. Had Eisenhower accepted that budget proposal, given Budget Bureau revenue projections, he would have run a $12.2 billion deficit in 1956. Even without the costs of the Korean War he would be faced with deficits that outstripped those generated by the Truman administration.

In November 1954, before final decisions had been taken on the budget, the JCS forwarded a doomsday paper to the NSC. Time was running out for the United States, the document claimed. The moment had come to abandon the ineffective policies of the past in favor of more "*dynamic* countermeasures" when dealing with Soviet aggression. Failure to take action, the chiefs argued, would leave the United States "isolated from the rest of the free world and . . . placed in such jeopardy as to reduce its freedom of action to two alternatives—that of accommodation to Soviet designs or contesting such designs under conditions not favorable to our success."[23]

In discussing this JCS paper Admiral Radford told the NSC that once a nuclear balance between the United States and the Soviet Union had been achieved, the chiefs "could no longer guarantee a successful outcome for the U.S." in a war between the superpowers. Nor did Radford believe that war could be avoided indefinitely. Assuming that the Soviets remained committed to the goal of world domination, he said, it seemed clear that at some time in the future "the Soviet Union will elect to force the issue." Having as much as said that the Soviets were certain to start a war when their relative strength was greater than at present, Radford, aware of the president's strongly held views on this subject, nevertheless refused to take the last logical step of recommending "preventive war." However, he did note that the chiefs "had concluded that the United States has only a limited period of time with which to reach an accommodation with the Communists." In summing up, he remarked that the JCS believed that "if we continue to pursue a policy of simply reacting to Communist initiatives, instead of a policy of forestalling Communist action, we cannot hope for anything but a showdown with Soviet Communists by 1959 or 1960" at which time they would be far stronger militarily and especially in terms of thermonuclear might than at present.[24]

These calls by the JCS for a more aggressive foreign policy and a larger, more costly military establishment were received cooly by the president and his civilian advisors. Secretary of State Dulles was, not to put too fine a point upon it, insulted by the argument that his foreign policy had been a failure. On the contrary, he insisted that the administration's policies had been quite successful and warned that the more aggressive policy recommended by Radford and the chiefs would result in America losing its allies and being forced to stand alone against the growing power of the Soviet Union. Only in one area was he willing to admit that the United States faced a deterioration in its overall position. This had to do with the "forthcoming achievement of atomic plenty and a nuclear balance of power between the

U.S. and the USSR." For the life of him, Dulles said, short of provoking a general war he did not know how that could be prevented.[25]

Not surprisingly, Treasury Secretary Humphrey was especially angered by what appeared to him to be a transparent attempt by the armed services to use scare tactics to force increases in the defense budget. Eisenhower, too, no doubt distressed by the possibility of escalating deficits, most vehemently opposed abandoning his foreign and military policies. He was especially unimpressed with the argument for a buildup in conventional forces, warning that if we did so "we might just as well stop any further talk about preserving a sound U.S. economy and proceed to transform ourselves forthwith into a garrison state." Priorities had to be established. High on Ike's list was "the capability to deter an enemy from attack and to blunt that attack if it comes." That could be achieved by "a combination of effective retaliatory power and a continental defense system of steadily increasing effectiveness." He also believed that "we should base our security upon military formations which make maximum use of science and technology in order to minimize numbers in men."[26] In local wars, he said, the victims of aggression would be able to count on the support of the Air Force, the Navy, and possibly small contingents of American troops, a few battalions at most. It had been basic to Eisenhower's thinking that the United States could not and should not engage in more Korea-style limited wars. He had not altered his opinion on this point. Countries threatened with aggression would themselves have to bear the burden of fighting on the ground. If people would not fight for their own freedom, he said, there was not much the United States could do about that.[27] Nor did Eisenhower entertain for a single moment the idea advanced by Ridgway and the Planning Board that a condition of mutual deterrence might result in a general war in which neither side used nuclear weapons. On the contrary, he argued, the more numerous these weapons became, the more likely it was that they would be employed. Moreover, as far as he was concerned, this was not a question within the purview of the Soviets to decide. "Since we cannot keep the U.S. an armed camp," he told the NSC, "we must make plans to use the atom bomb if we become involved in a war." The United States would show patience in a crisis and would not attack first, but if there was a war with the Russians it was going to be fought with nuclear weapons no matter what the other side did.[28]

Eisenhower's conviction that the United States should depend on "indigenous forces" to do most of the fighting in local wars, and that a war with the Soviets would inevitably involve a full-scale nuclear exchange, explains why conventional forces were of so little importance in his scheme of things. He thought the current military plan, which called for the United States to have seventeen divisions in Europe within six months after the beginning of a general war, was utter nonsense. Try as he might, he could not imagine how he would have managed the cross-channel invasion of Europe in 1944 if the enemy had been armed with nuclear weapons. Such a landing would have been inconceivable. He envisioned the first twenty-four to forty-eight hours of a nuclear war as a holocaust of unimaginable proportions, and doubted that "any nations as we now know them would continue to exist at the conclusion" of such a war. Under the conditions he envisioned, it would be literally impossible to move troops to Europe. The Army's role, he believed, would be to establish and preserve order at home, to aid in the reconstruction and reorganization of a society that had been laid waste. That would be its primary responsibility. A large combat-trained and-equipped ground force was not essential for such a purpose.[29]

Nor was Eisenhower impressed with the chiefs' view that the nation stood at some sort of precarious crossroad. In fact, during Radford's recitation he showed visible anger, remarking "with considerable forcefulness," that while the chiefs had been quick to criticize, they had offered no substantive alternative to established policies. He then remarked that "if our present security policy was as completely futile as Admiral Radford was saying, there would obviously be no need for the Soviet Union to go to war with us; they would achieve their objectives readily enough without resort to war." [30]

While these discussions were taking place at the NSC level, the Joint Strategic Survey Committee of the JCS, evidently having assumed that a deteriorating international situation was about to result in the abandonment of New Look planning, began reworking the numbers for the 1957 fiscal year. The committee's proposals called for an increase in the size of the Army to 28 divisions and 1,352,000 officers and enlisted personnel. It also envisioned an increase in the size of the Marine Corps and a larger Navy to include two more Forrestal-class aircraft carriers, for a total of sixteen. Early in December 1954, the JCS met with Wilson to discuss these proposals, which at the time were still at the talking stage. Wilson should have told the chiefs to leave well enough alone. Instead, probably out of concern for the developing crisis in the Taiwan straits, he and Radford went to the White House for a meeting with the president where they laid out these as yet sketchy ideas.

No memorandum is extant describing what happened at that conference. From the results, however, it seems clear that the president lost his temper. He rejected the tentative 1957 budget proposals *and* insisted on sticking to the planned reductions agreed upon for 1956 with one exception. To save additional funds, he ordered the cuts that were originally to have been made gradually over three years to be completed in two.[31] The following day he announced his decision at a meeting of the NSC, turned to Admiral Radford, and with a smile said that "he did not know if Radford went along with this idea, but that he'd better." Radford, a smile planted on his face, said that "he went along with the proposal." That was not quite good enough for Eisenhower, who warned the admiral "that he had better be pretty eloquent" when explaining and defending the military program in upcoming public statements.[32]

At this same meeting a chastened Charles Wilson announced that the 1956 defense budget would probably run to about $34.275 billion in new money with total expenditures of $35.750 billion. He also indicated that there was a good chance an extra 5 percent might be cut, leaving a total of $34 billion. Subsequently, Budget Director Hughes informed the president that he and Wilson had agreed upon a defense budget of $32.5 billion in new money for 1956, $5 billion less than the military had earlier requested. With carryover funds, total defense expenditures would reach $34 billion. "The Secretary," Hughes remarked in a special aside to the president, "has taken a principal part in effecting these solutions."[33]

Eisenhower had been able to hold the line on spending for 1955, but again, only by imposing his will. He was not able to do so, however, and at the same time sustain the administration's united front. Earlier it had been Hoyt Vandenberg who used Congress as a sounding board for Air Force complaints. On this occasion it was Matthew Ridgway who broke ranks. During his first year as army chief of staff, Ridgway had been torn by conflicting emotions. He owed an enormous debt to Eisenhower, who had brought him to the pinnacle of his profession. At the same time, he felt an even deeper loyalty to the Army, which, he came to believe, was being gutted for partisan political purposes.[34] He was also angry and frustrated by what he considered to be the unethical tactics used by Eisenhower and Wilson to win JCS approval for their policies. These feelings boiled over when, in his January 1954 State of the Union Message, Eisenhower told Congress that the "defense program recommended in the 1955 Budget . . . is based on a new military program [the New Look] unanimously recommended by the Joint Chiefs of Staff."[35] This passage requires an extremely careful reading. The unwary will understand it to mean that all of the members of the JCS had approved the New Look and the proposed budget. However, the JCS had not approved the budget. Moreover, Ridgway and Carney endorsed the Everest Report not because they believed in it, but because it was the best option available given the military priorities established in NSC 162/2 and the rigid fiscal restraints imposed by the administration.

Ridgway was furious. Not surprisingly, he was also the first high-level military leader to publicly break ranks with the administration. In testimony before the Appropriations and Armed Services committees of the House and Senate he expressed doubts about the New Look and the budget, claiming that with Moscow "increasing the combat effectiveness, the training level, and equipment of its ground forces," the cutbacks being recommended by the administration jeopardized national security. At the same time, in a remark that revealed his own conflicted state of mind, he said that he "whole-heartedly accepted" the budget and the policy that lay behind it as the work of "duly constituted civilian authorities." In testimony before the House Armed Services Committee he was more forthright, stressing that the nation's security was being jeopardized by the sharp reductions in Army manpower. He also warned that should the crisis between the Nationalist Chinese and Mao Zedong's Communist government over the islands of Quemoy and Matsu in the Formosa straits blossom into war, the United States would be in no position to protect the islands militarily.[36]

Following Ridgway's statement, a number of Democrats moved eagerly to the attack, claiming that defense cuts were being made simply for budgetary reasons. The powerful Senator Richard Russell of Georgia warned that with the crisis over Quemoy and Matsu at the boiling point "[t]his is no time to engage in any wishful thinking about Communist intentions." Missouri's Stuart Symington was even more critical, remarking in part: "Nothing Wilson has said so far has changed my opinion that these heavy cuts in our Armed Forces are not justified from the standpoint of national security."[37]

Eisenhower, who considered Ridgway's statement an act of disloyalty, responded sharply in public. At a press conference he described the general's views as "parochial" and went on to point out that Ridgway did not "have the overall responsibility that is borne by the Commander in Chief, and by him alone, when it comes down to making the recommendations to Congress." Privately, he denigrated Ridgway's comments regarding the offshore islands as absurd. The Nationalist Chinese had a large, well equipped army with which to defend Taiwan and the straits, he said. If they could not hold against Mao's forces, what good would an extra American division be?[38] When members of the Republican leadership in Congress expressed concern that Ridgway's comments were damaging the administration, they received a lecture. Ridgway, Ike said, was like any other service chief. "They all want additional manpower and they always will." He, on the other hand, had to consider "the very delicate balance between the national debt, taxes, and expenditures" and what was essential for national security. He thought it ironic that he had spent a large portion of his life "fighting for an increase in the strength of the Army from 118,000 to 121,000," only to be confronted now by the argument that "a million-man army backed by a large trained reserve was inadequate."[39]

Ridgway's defection had no significant effect on the budget debate then going on in Congress. The Republican majority rejected Democratic-sponsored amendments that would have added $400 million to the budget to retain current force levels for the Army, Navy, and Marines.[40] It did, however, have an immediate effect on the president, who quickly decided that the general would not be appointed to a second two-year term.

On February 18, 1955, General Maxwell Taylor, commander of U.S. Forces in the Far East, was in his office in Tokyo when he received a message from Secretary of the Army John Stevens calling him back to the United States. Taylor arrived a few days later and was immediately brought to the Pentagon for an interview with Charles Wilson. The secretary began with a "long, rambling discussion of conditions in the Orient," which of course had nothing to do with why Taylor had been summoned home. Taylor later wrote: "He then began to cross-examine me on my readiness to carry out civilian orders even when contrary to my own views." "After thirty-seven years of service without evidence of insubordination," he continued, "I had no difficulty of conscience in reassuring him, but I must say that I was surprised to be put through such a loyalty test."[41] A few days later Taylor was summoned to the White House where the president "went over essentially the same ground as Mr. Wilson with regard to loyalty to civilian leadership." At the end of their discussion the president told Taylor that at an appropriate moment he intended to nominate him to replace Ridgway as army chief of staff.[42]

Admiral Carney too was replaced. Unlike Ridgway, Carney had been a "team player," keeping his opposition to the New Look inside the national security establishment. However, he ran afoul of Secretary of the Navy Charles Thomas, who believed that Carney was making executive decisions, especially with regard to appointments and assignments, that were not within his purview. Carney did not deny it. On the contrary, he believed the fault lay with the 1953 reforms that assigned to Thomas "blanket responsibilities that are so all-encompassing as to require him to extend his supervision into the operating forces" where, Carney believed, he had neither the professional nor technical expertise to make sound decisions.[43] This was definitely not an argument that Eisenhower was prepared to accept, believing, as he did, that "the Chiefs . . . have no powers which are independent of the power of the Secretaries —they are totally subordinate to them." It is not surprising then that when Thomas informed the president that he did not intend to recommend Carney for a second term, the president agreed.

Thomas moved swiftly to find a replacement for Carney. In May, nearly three months before Carney was scheduled to leave his post, he brought Admiral Arleigh Burke for an interview at the White House. In a reprise of what he had told Taylor, Ike used this opportunity to make his views on the role of the JCS absolutely clear. He told Burke he had only two requirements. First, he said, he valued teamwork and loyalty above all else. A man might, indeed should, fight for his views "within the family." However, once a decision had been reached he had to accept it "as he would a decision in an ordinary battle." He would have to say to himself "well, the old man is crazy but these are his orders, nevertheless." Once, he said, the military had lived by this simple idea. In recent times "we began to break out, write articles ourselves, argue about whether a decision [was] good or not and to hell with what the President or anybody else thought." "There could be no going to Congress to override the President," Ike told Burke. "I am very much annoyed at the habit that seems to be springing up of a man seeking, or inadvertently finding, opportunities to talk on the outside. That habit might belong to a bunch of politicians, not to the military."[44]

Eisenhower's second point, delivered on so many different occasions that it might well have become known as "the lecture," was that a member of the JCS should separate himself from the day-to-day operations of his service. His principal duty was in the joint work he undertook with the other chiefs, who were to function as a corporate body, giving the president the best military advice possible, regardless of how it affected individual services. A chief's "first loyalty," he said, "is to the Joint Chiefs of Staff." Ike made it clear that if Burke could not live by these principles he should not agree to join the JCS.[45]

Admiral Carney retired from the service quietly. At a farewell meeting with the president, he delivered a long letter in which he discussed the many deficiencies he found in current policy, wished the president "Godspeed," and went into retirement.[46] Ridgway, on the other hand, whose service had been far more seriously affected by budget cuts than the Navy, decided that he could not leave without at last speaking his mind publicly.

On June 27, 1955, three days prior to his departure, he sent a final report to Charles Wilson in which he reviewed his numerous objections to the New Look. He forwarded his message as an unclassified document, assuming it would be widely disseminated. In an attempt to avoid embarrassment, Wilson classified the document Top Secret. Several weeks after Ridgway left the Pentagon, however, someone leaked Ridgway's "farewell" to the *New York Times*. Embarrassed, the secretary then belatedly released the original, which, he claimed, was after all "a matter of very little consequence."[47]

Despite Wilson's clumsy attempt to block publication of Ridgway's farewell message, its effect on the public consciousness was minimal. In May the United States, the Soviet Union, Britain, and France signed the Austrian Peace Treaty, ending ten years of military occupation for that small country. Soon thereafter plans for the Geneva Conference, the first meeting of the leaders of the Big Four in a decade, gathered momentum. The conference itself, which opened on July 18 and lasted for a full week, produced no significant breakthroughs. However, it did leave the public thinking of peace, disarmament, and "the spirit of Geneva." It was the wrong moment to challenge Eisenhower's military policy.

NOTES

1. NSC discussion, 25 March, 3 Dec. 1954, *Foreign Relations of the United States, 1952–1954* (Washington, DC: GPO, 1984), 2:639–40, 804–806 (hereafter cited as *FRUS*); Ridgway to Wilson, 27 June 1955, in Ridgway, *Soldier*, 323–32.

2. Ridgway to Wilson, 27 June 1955, in Ridgway, *Soldier*, 323–32.

3. Memorandum by the chief of Naval Operations, 7 Dec. 1953, JCS, 2101/112, 381 U.S. (1–31–50), Sec. 31, Modern Military Branch, National Archives (hereafter cited as NA).

4. *Newsweek*, 24 May 1954, 31.

5. Ibid., 26 July 1954, 20–21. In this issue *Newsweek* gave General Ridgway's views an even more direct endorsement, remarking that he was fighting the most important battle of his life and that what was at stake might "be the survival of what is left of the Free World." Due to the crisis in the Far East, both Ridgway and Carney called for upward revisions in their respective budgets. See Memorandum by the chief of staff, U.S. Army, 11 March 1954, JCS 1800/215, CCS 370 (8–19–45), Sec. 44, NA; "Memorandum by the chief of Naval Operations," 3 June 1954, JCS 2101/135, CCS 381 (1–31–50), Sec. 39, NA.

6. Hughes to Eisenhower, received at the White House on 10 May 1954, Whitman File, Administration Series, Box 20, Eisenhower Library (hereafter cited as EL); NSC discussion, 22 Nov. 1954, *FRUS, 1952–1954*, 2:785–87; see also ibid., 17 Dec. 1954, 828–31.

7. NSC discussion, 20 May 1954, Whitman File, NSC Series, Box 5, EL; Hughes to Eisenhower, 10 May 1954, Whitman File, Administration Series, Box 20, EL.

8. Ibid.

9. Ibid.

10. NSC discussion, 24 June 1954, *FRUS*, 2:649–79, 686–90.

11. Ibid., 689.

12. Ibid., 649–79.

13. Ibid., 654, 672.

14. CEP can be interpreted in this way. If an attacker were to fire two missiles, each with a CEP of one-half mile, he could be confident that one of these would fall within a radius of one-half mile of the target. Modern missiles have a CEP measured in a matter of feet.

15. Fred Kaplan, *The Wizards of Armageddon*(1983; reprint, Stanford: Stanford University Press, 1991), 114–16; Robert A. Divine, *The Sputnik Challenge* (New York: Oxford University Press, 1993), 22–23.

16. Ibid.

17. NSC discussion, 4 June 1954, Whitman File, NSC Series, Box 5, EL.

18. NSC discussion, 23 June 1954, *FRUS,* 2:680–86; Memo by secretary of defense to executive secretary of the NSC, 22 Nov. 1954, ibid., 785–97; NSC discussion, 24 Nov. 1954, ibid., 787–801.

19. Ibid. On June 8, 1954, the chief of naval operations submitted a paper calling for a reversal of the policies that had reduced the Navy's presence in Far Eastern waters. See JCS 2101/135, CCS 381 U.S. (1–31–50), Sec. 39, NA. the Army followed with its own appeal a few days later. See JCS 1800/215, in CCS 370 [8–19–45], Sec. 44, NA.

20. *New York Times* (hereafter cited as *NYT*), 27 April 1954.

21. Radford to Wilson, 1 July 1954, CCS 370 [8–19–45], Sec. 46, NA. On June 29, Wilson and the JCS agreed on force levels that included a twenty-division Army of 1.173 million; a 130-wing Air Force of 975,000; a Navy of 682,000 including fourteen attack carriers; and a Marine Corps of 215,000. Total forces under this agreement would have reached 3.045 million.

22. Hughes to Wilson, 23 July 1954, CCS 370 (8–19–45), Sec. 46, NA. This long memorandum explains what Hughes expected of Wilson at this time.

23. Hughes to Eisenhower, Nov. 1954, Sec. 46, NA; NSC discussion, 22 Nov. 1954, *FRUS, 1952–1954*, 2:785–87; see also 17 Dec. 1954, ibid., 828–31.

24. Ibid.; NSC discussion, 24 Nov. 1954, 788–801.

25. Ibid.

26. Ibid.

27. Ibid.; NSC discussion, 4 June and 5 Aug. 1954, 686–98, 700–715.

28. Ibid.; NSC discussion, 3 Dec. 1954, Whitman File, NSC Series, Box 5, Eisenhower Library (hereafter cited as EL).

29. James Haggerty diary entry, 4 Jan. 1955, in *FRUS, 1955–1957* (Washington, DC: GPO, 1988), 19:5–6.

30. NSC discussion, 24 June and 24 Nov. 1954, *FRUS, 1952–1954*, 2:686–98, 787–803.

31. JCS 1800/228 encloses note from secretary of defense to JCS, 9 Dec. 1954, CCS 370 [8–19–45], NA; Watson, *History of the Joint Chiefs of Staff*, 5:72–76.

32. NSC discussion, 10 Dec. 1954, Whitman File, NSC Series, Box 6, EL; *NYT*, 8 Dec. 1954. Two days before this meeting Wilson had implied that given the seriousness of the international situation the administration's economy drive had come to an end.

33. Ibid.; Hughes to Eisenhower, 20 Dec. 1954, Whitman File, Administration Series, Box 20, EL.

35. Ridgway, *Soldier*, 272.

36. *Public Papers of the Presidents, Dwight D. Eisenhower, 1954* (Washington, DC: GPO, 1962), 12.

37. U.S. Congress, House Committee on Appropriations, *Hearings, Department of Defense Appropriations for 1955*, 83rd Cong., 2d sess., 43–45; ibid., Senate Committee on Appropriations, *Hearings, Department of Defense Appropriations for 1955*, 83rd Cong., 2nd sess., 106–08; ibid., *Department of the Army Appropriations for 1955*, 83rd Cong., 2nd sess. 53–61; *NYT*, 1 Feb. 1955.

38. *NYT*, 1 Feb. 1955.

39. Eisenhower's telephone conversation with Radford, 1 Feb. 1955, Whitman File, Administration Series, Box 29, EL.

40. *Public Papers of the Presidents, Dwight D. Eisenhower, 1955* (Washington, DC: GPO, 1959), 226–27.

41. Senator Symington did manage to add $46 million to the budget to keep the Marine Corps at its then current strength, but Wilson sequestered the funds.

41. Maxwell Taylor, *An Uncertain Trumpet* (New York: Harper, 1959), 28.

42. Ibid.

43. Diary entry, 11 Aug. 1955, Ann Whitman Diary, Box 6, EL; Carney to Eisenhower, probably 10 Aug. 1955, Whitman File, Administration Series, Box 10, EL.

44. Diary entry, 17 May 1955, Ann Whitman Diary, Box 5, EL.

45. Ibid.

46. Carney to Eisenhower, n.d., delivered on 11 Aug. 1955, Whitman File, Administration Series, Box 10, EL. Before leaving, Carney had a last meeting with the president in the Oval Office. He presented Ike with this private letter in which he detailed the many problems he had faced as chief of naval operations and those the Navy faced as a result of attempting to carry out expanded commitments with reduced resources.

47. Ridgway, *Soldier*, 323–32; David Halberstam, *The Best and the Brightest* (New York: Random House, 1969), 472.

7

"The Day that Discipline Disappears from Our Forces . . . We Would Be Foolish to Put a Nickel into Them."

Eisenhower's decision to replace General Ridgway and Admiral Carney by no means ended his difficulties with the military. On the contrary, the seemingly endless struggle over strategic doctrine, roles and missions, and the size of the defense budget continued, leading Eisenhower to conclude that his 1953 reforms had failed and that another attempt at reform was in order.

The first sign of trouble ahead came as a result of developments behind the Iron Curtain. In May 1955, during rehearsals for Moscow's annual May Day parade, the Soviets put on display a new intercontinental jet bomber that appeared to be comparable to the American B-52. Not long after this, at a meeting of the NSC, Allen Dulles, the director of the Central Intelligence Agency, estimated that eleven of these planes, dubbed *Bison* by the Air Force, had been seen. Now the Soviets not only had the hydrogen bomb, they seemed to have aircraft capable of delivering those bombs over American targets from air bases inside the Soviet Union.

Dulles's news created consternation among some of those sitting at the table since at the time the Air Force had fewer than twenty operational B-52's in its inventory. The Soviets, it appeared, were developing and deploying long-range bombers much faster than had been anticipated. Admiral Radford, apparently rattled by Dulles's revelations, lashed out at the intelligence community for springing this news on the administration with absolutely no forewarning. He was even more distressed because it appeared that "the Soviets had done just as good a job in the development of the *Bison* as the United States had managed to do with . . . the B-52." It was going to be extremely embarrassing for him, he said, to explain this development to Congress. When Charles Wilson interrupted to argue that the Defense Department knew nothing about the Russian plane's performance characteristics, Radford refused to back down. He seemed convinced that in every respect the *Bison* compared favorably to the B-52. Noting that the new Russian plane was powered by four jet engines larger and more powerful than the eight that powered the B-52, he even claimed that the Soviets had "outdistanced" the United States in jet engine design.[1]

Radford's outburst notwithstanding, the president does not appear to have been surprised or even especially concerned by the appearance of the *Bison.* Sooner or later the Russians were bound to develop such an aircraft. His problem was political. The 1956 defense budget was still before Congress and the Democrats would certainly try to take advantage of the situation. To preempt his critics and undercut any possible call for an increase in the number of bombers to be produced, Ike instructed Wilson to seek an extra $356 million to accelerate production of the 471 B-52's then on order and authorized a speedup in the production schedule of the F-100 interceptor aircraft. In order to limit possible political repercussions, he also kept news of the Soviet plane under wraps until after the House of Representatives had acted on the budget.

On May 13, one day after the lower house finished its work, the Pentagon broke the news that the Soviets had developed a new intercontinental bomber. The *New York Times* carried the story on page one, including in its coverage an artist's rendering of the aircraft. Not surprisingly Missouri's Stuart Symington was quick to take advantage of the announcement, pronouncing himself "shocked and astounded" at the news. The former air force secretary warned that "we may have lost control of the air," and said: "It is now also clear that in quality as well as quantity of planes the Communists are at least in the process of surpassing the United States; and I am confident they are well ahead with the production of the possible ultimate weapon, namely the intercontinental ballistic missile." Taking dead aim at the secretary of defense, Symington claimed: "Throughout his tenure of office Mr. Wilson has underestimated the strength of the Communists and their ability to produce modern arms. Nor has he taken the steps necessary to obtain adequate arms for this country." As a result, he continued, "the lights of freedom will soon be going out, all over the world." Symington concluded his condemnation of Wilson with a call for an investigation into the B-52 bomber procurement program.[2]

Eisenhower was not surprised to find his defense policy under partisan attack. He was, however, embarrassed by the reaction of some high-ranking Air Force officers who immediately jumped for a place on the Democrats' bandwagon. On the same day that he personally rejected allegations of a "Bomber Gap," Brigadier General William Burgess, deputy chief of staff of the Continental Air Defense Command, charged that the Russians "had planes as good as ours and more of them." No doubt under intense pressure from Eisenhower, Air Force Chief of Staff Nathan Twining then issued a statement indicating that Burgess's statement was inaccurate. At the same time, however, Twining refused to give Eisenhower the backing he expected. The general, who wanted a B-52 force nearly twice as large as the one approved by the president, told the press, "We are ahead today," but made it clear that America's lead might not hold up for long.[3]

Following Twining's lukewarm endorsement of administration policy, the White House began actively seeking statements of support. From NATO headquarters in Brussels, Eisenhower's close friend, General Albert Gruenther, issued a statement indicating that "Russia is quite a long way behind," while Secretary of the Air Force Harold Talbot described the B-52 program as "just about right." Even so, it was a disgruntled Air Force officer, General Thomas Power, deputy air force chief of staff for research and development, who had the last word on the issue. In a prepared speech, he declared flatly that Moscow "has the world's largest air force" along with human and material resources that "we could not possibly match." Pentagon censors eliminated that claim from the speech as delivered, but much to the president's annoyance the uncensored speech was leaked to the press.[4]

Democratic criticisms notwithstanding, aided by a Congress that was even more cost conscious than he, the president weathered this initial phase of the "Bomber Gap" controversy. His original budget proposal called for $32.9 billion in new money. Congress passed a 1956 military budget of only $31.9 billion, including the $356 million he had requested for a speedup in B-52 production. Even so, the president's difficulties were just beginning. The presidential election campaign was just over the horizon, and the Democrats seemed certain to revisit the issue of national security as the time for campaigning approached.

Eisenhower took cognizance of this late in 1955 as his administration hammered out its budget proposal for the 1957 fiscal year. After intense negotiations between the Bureau of the Budget, the Defense Department, and the JCS, all sides agreed that the administration would ask for $34.9 billion in new funding, which, along with $785 million in carryover funds, would produce total defense expenditures of $35.7 billion for 1957. This figure was substantially less than the services had originally requested, but it was also $3 billion more than Congress had actually approved for 1956 and $2 billion more than the president had originally planned to recommend.

Eisenhower made this concession to the military, expecting that in return the armed services would support his budget proposal and remain on the sidelines during the political skirmishing that preceded the 1956 election. He was, in fact, assured of this by Charles Wilson, who told him flatly that the program "would be fully supported by the services." Responding sternly, Ike told Wilson "that he expected this to be done." He wanted no repetition of the public criticism Ridgway and Hoyt Vandenberg had leveled against his previous budgets.[5]

Only days after Eisenhower sent his 1957 budget proposal to Congress, his hopes for keeping the military in line began to fall apart when the *Saturday Evening Post* published the first of six weekly excerpts from General Ridgway's memoir, *Soldier*. In the second installment, entitled "Keep the Military out of Politics," Ridgway alleged that time and again during his tenure as army chief of staff, Charles Wilson had made decisions that weakened the Army for political and fiscal, not military, reasons. Ridgway blasted Wilson for repeatedly proposing "actions, which . . . would have seriously impaired the Army's capability to accomplish its missions and would have weakened esprit, which are the basic strengths of any military organization." In another part of the article, Ridgway wrote: "I think the tendency, which was manifest many times during my tenure as Chief of Staff, of civilian secretaries making military decisions on a basis of political considerations constitutes a danger to this country."[6]

Not long after this, the White House suffered another blow when assistant secretary of the air force for research and development, Trevor Gardner, suddenly resigned, charging that the administration was providing inadequate research funds for missile development. The resignation of a fairly obscure Washington bureaucrat might not have made headlines had it not been for its timing. The ballistic missile was already being discussed in the American press as "the ultimate weapon." The thought that the Soviets might achieve it first was a daunting prospect. Indeed, not long before Gardner launched his salvo, *Time* published a "nightmare" scenario in which the Russians launched the world's first ICBM. Should that happen, the magazine contended, Moscow would hold "the whip hand at last." It was for this reason, the article claimed, that the administration had undertaken a crash program of missile development. America's missile makers, the magazine continued, "are racing that day when an enemy made meteor glows like a spark in the sky."[7]

Was the administration doing enough? Gardner certainly did not think so. Nor did Senator Henry Jackson, who, only days before Gardner resigned, gave a widely reported speech in which he charged that the Soviets were on the verge of test firing a ballistic missile with a range of 1,500 miles. "The political effect of such a breakthrough," the Washington Democrat said, "would be so devastating that Western Europe's public opinion would force its leaders, no matter what their own inclinations, to withdraw at least into neutrality if not out-and-out collaboration with Communism." Jackson thought the psychological impact of a Soviet breakthrough on the missile front would destroy "America's trump military card," its claim to technological superiority over the Soviets. Once we lost that, he concluded, the Kremlin would "very likely take over Europe without firing a shot."[8]

Jackson was joined in the attack by the seemingly ever-present Stuart Symington, who, in an appearance on "Meet the Press," claimed that the Soviets "have fired, tested, long range ballistic missiles hundreds of miles farther than anything this country ever tested." The Russians were, he claimed, "ahead of us in the development and production of long range missiles. Of that there is no question in my mind whatsoever." Why were they ahead? Because the Soviets were working night and day to develop long-range missiles while Eisenhower's penny-pinching administration refused to authorize overtime pay for American technicians working on missile development. In like fashion, he charged that "our Strategic Air Command is over 90% manned by obsolescent if not obsolete airplanes." The number of modern intercontinental bombers being built, he said, "is just a small trickle of what it should be."[9]

At his regular press conference Ike attempted to calm the tempest, telling reporters that his administration was "doing everything that human science and brains and resources can do to keep our position in the proper posture." To Republican legislative leaders who met regularly at the White House, he noted that Stuart Symington's views notwithstanding, missile development was not on a "business as usual" basis. There were 25,000 people including 10,000 scientists working in the missile field, and more than 50,000 hours of overtime were being worked, which, he added, was "the maximum for a program of long duration." In another move designed to reduce the hysteria, Eisenhower authorized the appointment of a missile czar who would be responsible for coordinating the entire missile development effort.[10]

Eisenhower could not quiet the nerves of a nation growing increasingly fearful of Soviet military might. Even his friend, the financier Bernard Baruch, told Ike that he had to do everything possible to develop medium- and long-range missiles as soon as possible. He was convinced that whichever nation developed them first would enjoy a huge strategic advantage and that if the Soviets won this race NATO would collapse. The business community, he wrote, had focused too much attention on the bottom line and not enough on national security. He urged Ike to leave no stone unturned in the quest for missile superiority.[11]

Eisenhower refused to admit this publicly, but at the time it did appear that the Soviets were ahead of the United States in the area of missile development.[12] In fact, late in 1955, before the Democrats took up the issue, the State Department had come to conclusions startlingly similar to those advanced by Senator Jackson. If the Soviets were the first to develop an intermediate range ballistic missile (IRBM), a State Department planning group warned, this would undermine "the free world's confidence in U.S. technological superiority and enhance its fears as to the consequences of war." One result of this would certainly be the weakening of the NATO alliance. If Moscow achieved an intercontinental ballistic missile first, that would be even worse for it would "raise doubts in the free world as to the U.S. willingness to resist—and hence the U.S. ability to deter—Communist peripheral expansion, in view of the increased U.S. vulnerability to instant devastation." The "threat to the cohesion of the Western coalition" under such conditions, the department experts averred, "would be greater than under any other circumstances envisaged in this paper."[13]

At the time Eisenhower received this report he had serious doubts about the utility of the ballistic missile as a weapon, and he certainly did not believe that if the Soviets developed one first they would have the whip hand in the cold war. On the contrary, he believed that in the event of war with the Soviets, "in a matter of hours" the United States would be able to "inflict very great, even decisive, damage upon the productive power of the Soviet Union and its satellites." The guided missile was, he thought, "merely another, or auxiliary, method of delivering over the Soviet Union the kind of destructive force that is represented in the hydrogen bomb."[14]

Nevertheless, Eisenhower did agree with those, including Secretary of State Dulles, who believed in the "profound and overriding political and psychological importance of the U.S. achieving such a weapon before the Soviets."[15] He therefore authorized what amounted to a crash program designed to develop both an IRBM and an ICBM as quickly as possible. The program was given the highest priority with a budget for 1957 of $1.2 billion. Overall funding for military research and development in that year amounted to $5 billion.

Did Eisenhower believe he was spending enough on missile development? Absolutely. As he explained to Bernard Baruch, "we are already employing so many of the nation's scientists and research facilities that even the expenditure of a vastly greater amount could scarcely produce any additional results."[16] Because his science advisors and Secretary Wilson believed that the quickest way to a breakthrough in the missile field was to support existing programs then being carried out independently by the three services, Eisenhower even abandoned his own strong predilections against duplication of effort. He allowed the three services to continue to work on separate IRBM projects and the Air Force to work on two ICBM projects, Atlas and Titan, simultaneously. Reflecting his deep concern, he also insisted on special monthly, instead of quarterly, reports regarding progress in this field.[17]

Influenced by the fact that 1956 was an election year and by increasing popular concern over charges that the administration was sacrificing the nation's security in the interest of a balanced budget, Senator Richard Russell, the Democratic chairman of the Senate Armed Services Committee, authorized Stuart Symington to launch an inquiry into the strength and effectiveness of American air power. Russell appointed three Democrats to the subcommittee: Symington, who would act as chairman, was joined by Democrats Henry Jackson and Sam Ervin, Jr., of North Carolina and by Republicans Leverett Saltonstall of Massachusetts and James H. Duff of Pennsylvania.

Soon after Russell announced the formation of the Symington subcommittee, Eisenhower began to feel pressures building from inside Republican ranks for increased defense spending. At a meeting with nervous Republican leaders held just four days after Russell announced the formation of the Symington subcommittee, Senator Saltonstall informed him that a move was on in Congress to add as much as $1.5 billion to the budget for the purchase of additional B-52 bombers. From the way Saltonstall spoke, it was clear that many Republicans were not entirely averse to increased spending. It was an election year and Republican legislators did not want to be caught on the wrong side of what was developing into a hot issue.[18]

Eisenhower reminded the legislators that B-52 production had been stepped up in 1955 and argued that going beyond what had already been done would be a waste of money. Nor was he moved by Democratic allegations that the United States had a "second-rate Air Force." He told the legislators that talk of a huge and growing Soviet bomber force was just that—talk. U.S. intelligence, he said, had no certain knowledge of how many aircraft the Soviets had or whether the Soviet *Bison* was as good as the B-52.[19]

Eisenhower came under similar pressure from the JCS as well as from Secretary Wilson. Early in March, at Admiral Radford's suggestion, the members of the JCS left Washington for a week-long retreat at Ramey Air Force Base in Puerto Rico. Radford thought the time had come to develop a second installment on the New Look by establishing policy and planning guidelines for the years through 1960. On returning from Puerto Rico the chiefs forwarded a memorandum to Wilson, a copy of which Radford presented separately to the president. In it they reiterated their long-standing view that postwar American foreign policy had been a dismal failure. In part the document stated: "The deterioration of the free world position leads the Joint Chiefs of Staff to the conclusion that either the programs for general strategy have not been resolutely implemented or that the general strategy is inadequate to cope with the situation now confronting the United States as the leader of the free world." Unless a more aggressive policy was soon developed, the chiefs warned, the country would find itself in "great jeopardy." They also insisted that defense spending would have to be substantially increased and called for an annual budget of from $38 to $40 billion for the years 1958 to 1960, exclusive of funds provided for military aid to America's allies. These numbers stood in sharp contrast to a Bureau of the Budget planning document that assumed an estimated defense budget of $34.5 billion for these same years.[20]

Eisenhower, angered by both the tone and substance of the JCS paper, immediately called Admiral Radford and Secretary Wilson to the White House for a conference. He told them that he did not agree with the "dark picture" the JCS had presented. If their portrayal of the world political situation was in fact correct, he said, "we should go to field conditions, declare an emergency, increase the military budget and even go to a garrison state." "In that case," he added meaningfully, "the services would have to go to a much more Spartan mode of living." He told Radford that the paper simply would not do. In fact he refused to accept it, demanding that the chiefs produce a more positive evaluation of the world situation, one that emphasized the progress that he said had been made in the military field during the preceding three years.[21]

Nor was he in the least sympathetic to the chiefs' call for increased defense spending. In a private letter to Wilson he noted that the "one disappointing feature" of his experience with the Defense Department was that "every recommendation made by the military authorities seems to be for an increase in strength or in money or both." Such recommendations, he noted, were never accompanied by money-saving proposals. Moreover, even though over the last few years "[f]ire power" had been "miraculously increased," overall strength remained high. He wanted Wilson and Radford to do something about this.[22]

In the past when the president had objected to Defense Department spending proposals, Wilson had dutifully returned to his offices and found ways of meeting the president's demands. This time, however, the situation was beyond him. Wilson told Eisenhower that costs were spiraling out of control, that huge sums, nearly $5 billion annually, were going into research and development, and that inflation was eating another 5 percent of the budget each year. The Air Force and Navy were losing another $1 billion a year in downed or damaged aircraft. He also pointed out that America's aging fleet of B-36 bombers had probably become vulnerable to modern Soviet air defenses and that the administration would have to replace them by adding to the number of B-52's on order. If this was not done, he said, he could not honestly go before the people of the United States (or the Symington committee, which was soon to convene) and assert that we were staying ahead of the Russians.[23]

The frustrated Wilson also noted that the Defense Department was currently spending at a rate several billion dollars in excess of authorized funding, a fact made possible only because of carryover funds and a variety of one-time savings. In brief, Wilson told the president, his bag of tricks was empty. As he saw it, "simply to carry out current national security policies is certain to cost billions more over the next few years" than the administration was spending at the current time. Something had to give, he said. He simply could not fulfill the department's commitments "on the basis of the budgets on which the Defense Department now operates." He told the president that unless the nation's global military commitments were sharply reduced, the budget would have to be increased. The administration's 1957 budget proposal of $34.9 billion, which White House aide Sherman Adams correctly described as "an exercise in ingenuity," could not be replicated. In 1958 and thereafter, he said, the department would need as a bare minimum $38.5 billion. To make the point that he was dead serious, Wilson followed up by submitting to the president a supplemental budget request for the current 1956 fiscal year. Much of the extra $550 million he was requesting would go for increased purchases of intercontinental bombers.[24]

Wilson's appeal for higher defense spending in 1958 shocked the outgoing director of the Bureau of the Budget, Rowland Hughes, who believed that the secretary's call for more money meant that the administration "had reached a vital crossroads." As he saw it, the question was "whether or not we proposed to adhere to our total budget program as it had originally been formulated." The unspoken alternative, of course, was for increased taxes or deficits.[25]

Treasury Secretary George Humphrey, whose concerns paralleled those of Hughes, jumped into the fray, warning that for the past four years the administration had controlled defense spending with "one-shot" savings, "which would not be repeated in the forthcoming fiscal years." Though the government had achieved back-to-back balanced budgets, he thought it deserved little credit for this. The year 1956 had been the "biggest year in terms of income and Gross National Product in our history." Yet the fact of the matter was that "we are barely going to break even this year." Given what Wilson had indicated, it was clear the administration would not be able to produce another balanced budget in the future. The simple fact, he said, was that "our programs were bigger than our pocketbook." It was essential, he concluded, that we undertake "a basic review of our troop deployments and . . . our national security policies.[26]

Not long after Wilson, Hughes, and Humphrey laid out the parameters of the problem the administration faced, Percy Brundage, who had replaced Hughes at the Budget Bureau, added his voice to the growing chorus of concern. In a paper that sought to look four years into the future, Brundage too warned that as the new and costly research programs undertaken in the past few years moved to the stage of development, and deployment, they would place enormous new burdens on the government. The threat was such, Brundage warned, that the federal budget for 1958 and later could not be balanced without new taxes. Under the circumstances, he added, it seemed vital that the administration undertake "a fundamental reexamination of the military program for 1958 and subsequent years."[27]

Ike was caught on the horns of a dilemma that had dogged him throughout his first administration. The original study produced by the JCS in August 1953 called for a radically redesigned defense policy that was intended to reduce costs. Had it been implemented American forces would have been withdrawn from overseas bases in Europe and Asia back to the United States. The ground forces would have been drastically reduced in size, and nuclear weapons would have been completely integrated into the military establishment at all levels and would be used as conventional arms. For a variety of international political reasons Eisenhower had been unable to implement this radical shift in defense policy. Instead he had resorted to piecemeal cuts in support forces, stretch outs, and one-time savings to reduce costs. Now his advisors were telling him they had come to the end of the road, that he would either have to implement policies that remained unpalatable, raise taxes, or face increasing deficits in an election year.[28]

Eisenhower was forced to contend with these pressures while also preparing for the upcoming Symington Air Power hearings. In early April 1956, just days before the Missouri Senator gaveled the hearings to order, he held a series of meetings designed to solidify support for the administration's military program. First, he had a long session with Senators Saltonstall and Duff, the Republican members of the subcommittee. For more than an hour and a half the three men went over the major issues that were likely to be the focus of the investigation. Eisenhower pointed out that missile research and development had the highest priority possible, that great sums were being expended on these programs, and that more would be recommended if that was deemed necessary. On the question of the nuclear deterrent, he warned the senators not to get caught up in a numbers game. If the United States had sufficient power to deter an attack, he said, there was no need or justification for adding to the number of weapons in the arsenal simply for the purpose of attempting to match the Soviets. He also reminded the senators that in measuring deterrent power, naval aviation as well as allied forces should be taken into account. Aware of how difficult it was going to be for the Republicans in Congress to stand pat in the face of the Democratic assault, he also informed the senators that he intended to submit to Congress Wilson's $550 million supplemental budget request, which would be used primarily for the purchase of more B-52 bombers. If anything could stiffen their backs, he thought, that would.[29]

Ike then met personally with the JCS in hopes of convincing them to support the administration's military program. He told the chiefs that he did not expect them to "abandon their . . . convictions . . . about security needs." He understood that they all felt the need for increased resources. However, he added, he did expect the services to operate "on a Spartan basis" and with an awareness that a sound economy was basic to national security. He was aware, he said, that there were powerful pressures coming from the press and Congress for increased defense spending. He expected the chiefs to resist these pressures, which, he argued, could make the defense budget escalate out of control. If they refused to cooperate, he warned, he would intervene personally to make certain that spending remained within reasonable bounds.[30] When testifying before the committee, Ike urged: "Everyone in the Defense establishment should nail his flag to the staff of the United States of America, and think in terms of the whole."[31]

Eisenhower had some specific warnings for General Twining and the Air Force. Noting that in recent testimony before the Senate Armed Services Committee, certain Air Force officers had left the impression that the Navy contributed nothing to this country's strategic-bombing capabilities, he told Twining that when testifying he and other Air Force officers were to take the Navy's contributions into account in their overall evaluation of U.S. capabilities. If an officer "can't bring himself to do this," Ike remarked sternly, "he doesn't belong in the position he holds." He also warned Twining against being tempted to break with the administration simply because Stuart Symington and other Democrats were speaking in terms of an extra appropriation for the Air Force in 1957. He reminded Twining that the Missouri senator also claimed that by eliminating waste he could cut the overall defense budget by more than 20 percent.

Having first lectured his military advisors on his and their responsibilities, Eisenhower then offered what appeared to be a carrot in the form of a moderate increase in future defense spending. He told the JCS that if they would accept $36.5 billion as a "level off figure" for the years 1958 through 1960, that could be done "without damage to the economy." This figure was only $1.5 billion below the low figure that the chiefs had proposed in their recent report to him. Moreover, it was an increase of $2 billion over the Budget Bureau's recommendation and $4.6 billion more than Congress had actually appropriated for 1956. (It was also, although the chiefs may not have known this, $2 billion below the bare minimum Charles Wilson had informed Eisenhower he needed to keep the department afloat.[32]) He also informed the JCS that he had decided to approve the 1956 budget supplement, including the money for more B-52's, that Wilson had earlier submitted.[33]

Wilson added his voice to the message the president was sending, telling Twining that he had gone to bat for the Air Force to get the president's support for the supplemental budget. Now, he said, he expected the Air Force to show its gratitude by supporting the president's program. The new money already approved by the president would give the department what was needed. He would be very disappointed, he added, "if all top people do not battle it out on this basis."[34]

Although Eisenhower did what he could to solidify support for the administration's military program prior to the opening of the Air Power hearings, it was not enough. The opportunity to criticize administration policy before a friendly Democratic majority at hearings that were being given wide national attention in an election year was too good for high-ranking Air Force officers to pass up.

The Symington subcommittee, which was obviously designed to serve partisan political purposes, held its first hearing on April 16 and adjourned three months later just before the presidential campaigning season moved into high gear. The subcommittee held forty-one public as well as executive sessions, and heard witnesses that included Secretary Wilson and other civilian representatives of the Defense Department, scientists, and weapons experts. The stars of this show were, necessarily, high-ranking Air Force officers. Despite concessions made to them by the administration, to a man they offered wide-ranging criticisms of administration defense policy as not only inadequate but threatening to the national security.

Up to this point in time General Nathan Twining, the air force chief of staff, had played the good soldier on the JCS, joining Arthur Radford as a stalwart defender of the New Look. Nevertheless, when asked to describe "areas of weakness" in the Air Force program, Twining produced a long list that included among other things an inadequate supply of officers and enlisted personnel with technical skills, insufficient research funds, and, above all, a serious need for more B-52's.[35]

Basing his testimony on Air Force intelligence estimates that subsequently proved to be completely erroneous, Twining testified that the Soviets were producing more intercontinental bombers than the United States. He went on to state that because of this he had asked the administration to authorize the procurement of an additional 300 B-52's beyond the 500 already approved by the administration for the Strategic Air Command. This request, however, had thus far been ignored and was currently resting in administrative limbo.[36] Twining refrained from offering a total cost figure for the budget increases he sought, but told Congress that to get a start on these changes the Air Force would need $23.6 billion for the next fiscal year. This compared with $15.6 billion, which the administration had included in its 1957 budget.[37]

General Earle E. Partridge, head of the Air Defense Command and the Continental Defense Command, was if anything more pessimistic than Twining in his assessment of Soviet and American capabilities. In testimony before the Symington subcommittee he pointed to an inadequate radar network, obsolescent interceptor aircraft, and inadequate missile defense systems as problems faced by his command. "We need additional radar and we need to improve the capability of the radar equipment which we already have," Partridge said. In addition, he noted, "We need to bring into the inventory as rapidly as possible better aircraft and new guided missiles with improved range. . . . Even in our present-day interceptor aircraft the unreliability of our fire-control equipment downgrades our capability to achieve operational effectiveness." Partridge estimated it would cost $61 billion over fifteen years to bring the air defenses of the United States up to an appropriate standard.[38]

General Curtis LeMay, the head of SAC who was known to be seeking a force of 1,800 B-52's, told the committee that "under any reasonable set of assumptions, we believe we now have the capability of winning any war the Soviets might start," although not "without this country receiving very serious damage." However, he continued, on the basis of current levels of production in this country and the Soviet Union, "we will be inferior in striking power to the Soviet long-range air force by 1958–60." After stating that the Soviets were well ahead of the United States in the development of long-range missiles, he offered the "guess" that within three years Moscow would be able to deal a devastating blow to the United States in a surprise attack.[39]

The Symington subcommittee hearings made headlines and set part of the agenda for the coming presidential elections. However, it was the appropriations committees that had the power to make or break the administration's control of the budget process. For four successive years the administration had been able to make its case before Congress. Indeed, never before had Congress voted as much for defense as Eisenhower had requested, even after the Republicans lost control of Congress in 1955. However, the 1957 budget was different. Symington and his Air Force allies had successfully made the case that a "bomber gap" existed.

The Symington hearings were still under way when Curtis LeMay testified on the budget before the Senate Appropriations Committee. He told that committee that he supported the administration's 1957 budget proposal for SAC only "because that is the way my boss wants it done." He went on to urge the senators to add $3.8 billion annually to the SAC budget, arguing that "it is more necessary now because intelligence sources had provided additional information regarding Soviet capabilities." LeMay insisted that given the Soviet Union's large building program, the old goal of a 137-wing Air Force should be scrapped in favor of something much larger.[40]

In responding to LeMay's testimony, the president urged caution while noting that the general had taken an extremely narrow view, excluding as unimportant all aspects of this nation's overall deterrent power save the Strategic Air Command. When Defense Department witnesses had finished making the case for the administration, he said, he was confident all would see that he had not been "indifferent to the security of the United States."[41] Eisenhower, of course, had the facts on his side. America's deterrent power was overwhelming. Moreover, the Soviets had not undertaken to build the huge bomber force LeMay and Twining claimed. Unhappily for the president, however, reason did not prevail in the panicky political environment of 1956. Congress voted a defense budget, exclusive of military construction costs, of $34.7 billion in new money. Though not especially out of line, this figure included an extra $900 million earmarked for the purchase of more B-52's.

The president had nothing to say publicly about Congress's decision to add almost $1 billion to the Air Force budget, but he was furious. In direct opposition to his own wishes, and without the sanction of either the JCS or the Defense Department, LeMay and a few other officers had successfully appealed to Congress for increased funding. That was simply unacceptable.

According to White House assistant, Sherman Adams, soon after the successful Air Force raid on the budget, Eisenhower called Wilson and a few of the secretary's key civilian aides to the White House for preliminary discussions on the 1958 budget. He wanted to be absolutely certain that none of the services would ever again go to Congress with a spending program that differed from his own. When Wilson observed that the services seemed to have goals of their own and were not easily controlled, Ike replied angrily: "Put every single person on the spot to justify every single nickel." He did not want to hear the service chiefs talk of their *requirements* ever again. "I have listened to the term all my life. Next year the demagogues will all be gone and everybody will be looking to save money. You people never seem to learn whom you are supposed to be protecting. Not the generals," he exploded, "but the American people." Then, fixing Wilson with a steely-eyed stare, he said: "You have got to be willing to be the most unpopular man in the government."[42] Wilson took the hint and sequestered the extra funds Congress had voted for the Air Force.

Eisenhower's 1956 run-in with the Air Force was the first in a series of challenges that led him to conclude that the 1953 reforms had failed and that more changes were essential. Other issues included a very public ongoing dispute between the Air Force and the Army over the control of guided missile systems, and the Army's desire to develop a large organic aircraft component as well as its unwillingness to accept the limited role assigned to it under the New Look.

In an earlier era the roles and missions of the services had been relatively easy to define. The Navy operated at sea and the Army on land. As technology changed the nature of warfare, however, it became more difficult to decide, as James Forrestal once put it, "who will do what with what." The introduction of missiles in the 1950s represented the latest manifestation of this problem. Did responsibility for the development and deployment of surface-to-air missiles rest with the Army, which had traditionally operated anti-aircraft defenses, or should the Air Force, which deployed interceptor aircraft, have that responsibility? Was a surface-to-surface missile a long-range artillery weapon to be developed and deployed by the Army, or a pilotless bomber that was in the Air Force's province? In a long interview published in *U.S. News and World Report*, Army Chief of Staff General Maxwell Taylor described the missile as "the artillery of the future." When asked whether he believed the Army ought to respect certain range limitations regarding the missiles it deployed, he noted that it was the Army's role to destroy enemy ground forces wherever they might be found. He recognized no range limitation regarding the Army's mission. The Air Force, of course, felt quite differently about this and bitterly opposed what it considered to be the Army's intrusion into its fundamental mission.[43]

The Air Force and Army were also at odds over whether the Army should be allowed to develop an organic aviation component. Appearing on the CBS television program "Face the Nation," General Taylor indicated that the Army hoped to develop a force of about four or five thousand aircraft for the purpose of artillery observation, to move small numbers of troops quickly from one point to another, and to transport supplies. In another television interview General James Gavin, the Army's head of Missile Research and Development, denied that the Army wanted an air force of its own, but, he continued, "wherever we can use the air vehicle" to aid the infantryman through new forms of air mobility, "we certainly want to do it, and we are going to do it." Gavin, whose ambitions far exceeded Taylor's, thought that "[t]wenty thousand planes for the Army might indeed not be too many."[44] The Air Force, of course, viewed this as not only heretical but dangerous to its interests and did all in its power to deny the Army this capability.

By the spring of 1956, largely as a result of these and other doctrinal issues, the Air Force and the Army found themselves embroiled in a major public relations war. The conflict began to take shape in the latter part of 1955 when, with the tenth anniversary of SAC near at hand, General Robert L. Scott, who headed public relations operations for the Air Force, developed plans for a two-year public relations campaign that he dubbed "A Decade of Security Through Global Air Power." The campaign, which was designed "to mold opinion and channel the vibrant tensions of public thinking" in support of "peace through airpower," emphasized the "spectacular mobility" of the Air Force, which, when "coupled with a complete arsenal of destructive weapons, outmodes the most modern surface forces."[45]

On learning of Scott's plans, the Army, one of the "modern surface forces" Scott seemed to be denigrating, decided to go public with its own case. Beginning in late 1955 and escalating thereafter, high-ranking Army officers and civilians in the Department of the Army began a campaign that was clearly intended to strengthen the Army's claim to play an important role in the new world of the missile, while at the same time questioning the usefulness of the Air Force.[46] Thus, in a speech given in November 1955, Secretary of the Army Wilbur Brucker described the Army's NIKE anti-aircraft missile as "the first combat ready surface-to-air guided missile for our air defense." He also claimed: "This deadly missile which can reach, outmaneuver and destroy any aircraft either available at the present time or under development is now our principal anti-aircraft weapon." In a public statement that followed, General Gavin claimed: "Our NIKE system can destroy any airplane present or planned, regardless of great height or speed." One did not have to be particularly perceptive to understand that both Brucker and Gavin were claiming that piloted aircraft, theirs and ours, had been made obsolete by modern missile defense systems.[47]

In commenting on the power of the new missiles generally, Gavin took an even more direct swing at the Air Force when he remarked, "it seems apparent that these weapons eventually may replace piloted aircraft and so greatly alter the structure of our armed forces." A month later, in an article published in *Army*, the monthly publication of the Association of the United States Army, he attacked "the confused thinking" that had "obscured defense matters since World War II." The United States, Gavin wrote, clearly could not rely on a single service or weapon system to win wars. Because the United States had to be prepared to fight small and large, nuclear and conventional wars, it needed an Army with "sizeable forces in being, ready to move by land, sea, or air and fight any time, any place."[48]

Early in January 1956, in a direct assault upon the strategy of massive retaliation generally and the Air Force in particular, Taylor argued that those Pentagon planners who believed the next war would begin with a full-scale nuclear exchange were not thinking clearly. "Personally," he said, "I rate this concept of war as only one of the forms, and not necessarily the most likely, which war may take." As the destructiveness of nuclear weapons grew, he thought it "increasingly improbable that an aggressor would intentionally embark on the gamble of atomic world war." He was even more direct in a subsequent interview, remarking: "It seems to me that, as the day of atomic parity approaches, no sane leader of any country will ever embark intentionally on this kind of big war."[49]

In declaring the idea of full scale nuclear war to be "increasingly improbable," Taylor challenged the Air Force's basic raison d'être. He then made the case for the Army as that service with the "unique ability to proportion punishment to fit the crime of aggression." With "versatile and flexible military forces," the Army was "preparing to fight either the short war or the long war, the small war or the big one." The Army (unlike the Air Force he seemed to be saying) was "equipped and trained to apply military power with discretion, to discriminate between friend and foe, and to temper its application of force from the admonitory whistle of the military policeman to the terrible destruction of atomic weapons." Two weeks later Taylor struck even closer to home when he said: "We must have forces which are flexible, which can apply military power with intelligent selectivity" and which have "the ability to make their retaliatory punishment fit the crime of aggression with measured, not simply massive blows."[50]

The Air Force gave as good as it got. The April issue of *Air Force Magazine* was entirely devoted to singing the praises of SAC. Arthur Godfrey, a radio and television personality who was both a civilian pilot and a great booster of the Air Force, gave enthusiastic mention to the magazine several times on the air. Godfrey generated 160,000 requests for copies, which the Air Force was pleased to provide. According to *Time*, the next issue of *Air Force* "almost wrote off the Army as a combat service."[51]

By early April 1956, Admiral Radford, who blamed the growing discord among the services entirely on the Army, was clearly worried. He urged the president to intervene, claiming that the Army's aggressive public relations campaign had produced serious discord and that unless the various disputes between the Army and the Air Force were resolved, "a situation may develop in which the Services are involved in increasing public disagreement among themselves." In simple terms, a revolt was brewing and Radford wanted Eisenhower to put a stop to it.[52]

It was not Eisenhower's style to step into a situation such as this. The job was Wilson's and he resented having it thrust upon him. Even so, in a meeting with Maxwell Taylor he made it abundantly clear that he would not support the Army's extreme claims regarding organic aviation and missile development. He was especially discouraging with regard to air transport, which he insisted should remain an Air Force responsibility. He also held a long meeting with the entire JCS at which he reminded them once again that it was their responsibility to think and act as a group in the national interest. Their service loyalties had to be set aside in favor of their "corporate opinion."[53]

Eisenhower's efforts went unrewarded. The Army and Air Force continued to snipe at one another. At the same time it became increasingly common for the JCS to deadlock on important issues, presenting "split papers" to Secretary Wilson, who was left to make judgments as best he could, usually with the aid of Admiral Radford and definitely not to the benefit of the Army.

During the first half of 1956, as the quarrel between the Army and Air Force gained momentum, General Taylor made a serious effort to convince his colleagues on the JCS as well as the president that the New Look, with its emphasis on massive retaliatory power, was seriously flawed. During the chiefs' March retreat at Ramey Air Force Base in Puerto Rico, he presented "A National Military Program," a paper in which he spelled out his critique of the New Look and advocated instead a new "flexible response" doctrine that, in addition to the ability to retaliate massively in the event of general war, called for expanded conventional forces and limited war capabilities. Taylor failed to win any support for his views.[54]

Taylor's inability to gain even a hearing for "flexible response" was the last straw for a number of younger staff officers on the Army's Policy Coordinating Group who saw him and the theory he represented as the only hope for saving the Army from the ravages of Admiral Radford, the Air Force, and the budget cutters. The Policy Coordinating Group had developed staff studies designed to emphasize the Army's importance to the nation, and to expose the danger of overemphasizing air power at the expense of the other services. Now, several of the younger officers assigned to the group decided to use their studies to expose the weaknesses of the New Look publicly; they hoped to make "flexible response" an election year issue.

Colonel Donovan Yeuell, one of the most outspoken of the colonels involved in this minirevolt, contacted his brother-in-law, Wallace Carroll, the news editor of the *New York Times*, hoping to interest the paper in publishing their views. At first the *Times* editorial staff showed little interest. However, when they learned that Taylor and the Army hierarchy supported the views the colonels were expressing, they changed their minds.[55]

Yeuell and his colleagues provided Anthony Leviero of the *Times* with a number of classified staff studies that stated the Army's case for flexible response as well as its claim that the New Look, with its overemphasis on air power, was leading the nation toward disaster. Leviero then went to the public relations division of the Air Force, outlined the Army's claims, and asked if they had a rebuttal. The Air Force public relations men provided Leviero with studies of their own. Armed with secret studies developed by both services, Leviero published two articles, the first of which, ironically enough, appeared on Armed Forces Day, May 19, 1956. The Army's argument, now plainly stated for the public to consider, was that though the United States had expended vast resources on national defense, "our outlay has not been correctly related to the nature of the threat." Despite the fact that the United States and the Soviet Union were fast approaching the point when neither nation could safely launch a nuclear attack on the other, the

Army contended, "we continue to pour excessive manpower and money into an Air Force which has been substantially neutralized." At the same time, funds were lavished on the Navy even though America's potential adversary had "practically no naval experience or tradition." In the meanwhile, the Army had been starved to the point that it would probably be unable to meet threats of a limited nature with appropriate levels of force. "We have violated the first principle of strategy—indeed, of common sense—by failing to shape our military strength to meet the likely dangers," the study concluded. "[U]nless there is an immediate revision of our military structure it is probable that the international position of the United States may disintegrate to a point where we shall be forced into either total war or subjugation."[56]

On May 20 Leviero published a second article, this one based on the leaked Air Force materials. Whereas the Army's studies had focused on the weakness of relying too heavily on a massive ability to retaliate, and emphasized the importance of having a variety of war-fighting capabilities, the Air Force studies more or less indiscriminately lashed out at the other two services. One claimed that the big Forrestal-class aircraft carriers, on which the government had lavished billions of dollars, would play no significant role in a strategic bombing campaign and in the event of war would be highly vulnerable to enemy counteraction. A second took on the Army's claim that manned bombers had become obsolete by charging that the Army's NIKE anti-aircraft missile, already deployed at over 100 sites around the United States, was ineffective and would be unable to defend the country against an air attack.[57]

Eisenhower was infuriated by this latest outburst of feuding among the services. At a press conference held some days after the Leviero articles appeared, he told reporters that while debate and disagreement among the services were to be expected, he would not tolerate revolt. "The day that discipline disappears from our forces, we will have no forces, and we would be foolish to put a nickel into them." Then, in a remark clearly directed at the Army, he added: "The sole use of armed forces, so far as war between the two great countries possessing atom and hydrogen bombs today is this: their deterrent value." One of the worst aspects of the entire affair, Eisenhower thought, was the amount of security information that had been leaked to the press and *ipso facto* to the Soviets as a result of this infighting. Referring to the published Air Force studies, he remarked: "We shouldn't tell the enemy our weaknesses—if they are weaknesses—and shouldn't damage the confidence of our people and our allies in these weapons," especially, he thought, if they were as effective as he believed.[58]

Soon, the press was filled with stories indicating that big changes were in store for the military. *Newsweek* noted that Congress was "fed up" with the constant squabbling among the services, while *Time* remarked approvingly that the turmoil was pushing the country toward "a unified military establishment."[59] In a long piece, *Time* observed that it was Eisenhower's job to make certain that all elements in the military establishment meshed, that only in this way could the machine work "to keep war away by its total retaliatory power." "That aim," the magazine noted, "no longer permits the luxury of the three services and their many sub-services wrangling for power and heading in different directions." As a result, *Time* reported that the president had made "one of the most important decisions of his administration: to move for a truly unified armed service that will work in practice as well as on paper, as a single machine." According to the magazine, he had ordered the White House staff to "start work immediately on mapping out a unification plan" that would be presented to Congress in 1957, after the election.[60]

Time's report was not entirely inaccurate. At this time Ike told Radford that he envisioned an entirely new system in which the powers of the secretary of defense and the chairman of the JCS would be vastly enhanced. The service chiefs, on the other hand, would be reduced in status to become mere assistants to the chairman, who would have the power to choose and reassign them. Distressed by the fact that security information was regularly leaked to the media, Ike also considered requiring that a new oath be taken by military and civilian employees of the Pentagon requiring them, even after they had left government service, to "disclose nothing which the Department of Defense determines to be security information."[61] In a subsequent meeting with Radford and Taylor he once again observed that if the chiefs could not develop "corporate judgment on the great issues" of the day, "the system as we now have it will have failed and major changes must come."[62]

In the immediate aftermath of the brief and unhappy "Revolt of the Colonels," Charles Wilson attempted to demonstrate that the services were not as badly divided as press reports indicated by holding a staged press conference that included top Pentagon civilians and members of the JCS. According to Wilson, the importance of inter-service rivalry had "without question" been exaggerated by the press. None of the reporters who attended were fooled. *Time* described the chiefs as showing "mock solidarity." Nathan Twining, was clearly unwilling to go beyond "restrained tribute to the Army," and when reporters asked General Taylor about the revolt, he denied that one had taken place, refused to "flatly disavow everything that has been published," and was vague about whether he would pursue possible court-martial proceedings against the officers who had leaked top secret documents to the press.[63]

Nor did the back stabbing stop. Immediately following the "Revolt of the Colonels," Admiral Radford, who had previously been invited to address the graduating class of '56 at Annapolis, *did* warn the graduates against making "a fetish of tradition." He also urged them to remember that the services "must think as a team, work as a team, and when necessary fight as a team." Only a few days later Assistant Secretary of the Navy James H. Smith, Jr., delivered a speech in Akron in which he asserted a much more significant role for the Navy in the field of strategic bombing than the Air Force would ever sanction. Secretary of the Army Wilbur Brucker, meanwhile, gave one speech filled with encomiums for the "magnificent Navy" and the "great Air force with its intrepid pilots," and another in which he infuriated Air Force officials by asserting the Army's right to develop and deploy long-range ballistic missiles. Meanwhile, in Palo Alto, California, Brigadier General Carl Hutton, head of the Army's air arm, denied that the Air Force had a "divine right to a monopoly on flying machines just because they fly" and discounted the view that "everything that walks belongs to the Army, that swims belongs to the Navy, and that flies belongs to the Air Force."[64]

Late in November 1956, Charles Wilson made another futile attempt to resolve the ongoing disputes between the Army and the Air Force over missilry. He ruled that the Army would have responsibility for "point defense," and for that purpose it would control the NIKE and ground-based TALOS air defense missile systems, each with a range limited to no more than 100 miles. Beyond that, however, the Army suffered a series of setbacks. Although Wilson's directive did not prohibit the Army from continuing to work on the Jupiter IRBM, it limited the Army's other surface-to-surface missile forces to a range of no more than 200 miles and assigned the Air Force responsibility for deploying all long-range surface-to-surface missiles. Under this ruling the Army could develop the Jupiter, but was denied the right to deploy the finished weapon. Wilson's ruling also sharply curtailed the ability of the Army to develop a large organic aviation component. "We're not going to set up an air force within the Army," declared Deputy Secretary of Defense Reuben Robertson.[65]

Wilson had issued his ruling, but few paid much attention. Said one Army planner: "This thing [Wilson's order] isn't going to stop us." Other Army officials claimed that the Wilson memorandum on missiles contained so many loopholes that the Army could actually expand its missile work. In like fashion the Army continued adding aircraft to its inventories. In 1953, at the beginning of the Eisenhower era, the Army claimed 3,200 operational aircraft. In 1956, when Wilson issued his ruling the figure stood at 3,573; and in 1961, as Ike prepared to leave office, the number had jumped to 5,564.

Nor did the dismal outcome of the "Revolt of the Colonels" discourage Maxwell Taylor from making another attempt to convince the president of the merits of "flexible response." He believed he had a case. Earlier, stung by criticisms of its massive retaliation doctrine, the administration had included in NSC 5602, the latest revision of NSC 162/2, new wording indicating that in the event of local aggression the government's intention was to apply force discreetly. Specifically, the revised policy stated that Washington would develop forces that, in concert with its allies, would be effective in establishing "a deterrent to any resort to local aggression" or in suppressing "local aggression in a manner and on a scale best calculated to avoid the hostilities broadening into general war." These forces, the document continued, "must not become so dependent on tactical nuclear capabilities that any decision to intervene against local aggression would probably be tantamount to a decision to use nuclear weapons."

The document also stipulated:

With the coming of nuclear parity, the ability to apply force selectively and flexibly will become increasingly important in maintaining the morale and will of the free world to resist aggression. The United States and its allies must avoid getting themselves in a position where they must choose between (a) not responding to local aggression and (b) applying force in a way which our own people or our allies would consider entails undue risks of nuclear devastation.[66]

Taylor thought that these passages from NSC 5602 supported his claim that flexible response was in fact a stated national security policy. The other members of the JCS, however, insisted that the emphasis should remain on nuclear retaliatory capability and continental defense. As a result, work on the Joint Strategic Objectives Plan for 1960, the basic planning document from which all else in the military field, including budgets and force levels for the next three years would be derived, ground to a halt. At length, when it became clear that the Joint Chiefs were deadlocked on this key paper, Taylor and Radford took the issue directly to the president.[67]

Taylor, the first to speak, began by explaining that there was a sharp difference of opinion between himself and the Marine commandant, General Pate, on the one hand, and Admiral Radford, Admiral Burke, and General Twining, on the other, over the proper interpretation of NSC 5602. Taylor then noted that the first issue dividing the chiefs had to do with the proper definition of general war. Those who disagreed with him believed that planning ought to be based on the assumption that a war with the Soviets would begin with a large-scale nuclear exchange. Taylor believed that in the unlikely event a nuclear war did take place it would probably develop "step by step" from smaller encounters involving conventional forces to larger actions. NSC 5602, he said, called for a flexible military strategy that required strong conventional as well as nuclear forces. However, Taylor argued, if planners began with the assumption that a general war would begin with a nuclear exchange, the "programs for fighting" this war "would absorb all available funds," thus denying the military the flexibility NSC 5602 required.

The second difference among the chiefs, Taylor explained, stemmed from the fact that those who disagreed with him advocated a "firm commitment for the use of atomic weapons" in small and large conflicts alike. He noted, this too contravened the principle of "flexibility" called for in NSC 5602. The adoption of such a policy would result in an overemphasis on nuclear forces and a tendency "to freeze out" the conventional forces that would be required "to handle small war situations."[68]

Despite the fact that Taylor was able to cite chapter and verse from NSC 5602, Eisenhower categorically rejected his views. He thought it "fatuous" to believe that the United States and the Soviet Union might be locked in a full-scale struggle and not resort to the use of their most powerful weapons. As to local conflicts, he believed that the United States should make every effort to encourage the development of indigenous forces able to conduct local wars on the ground. The United States, he said, would back them up with air and naval forces and perhaps some small, specialized military units. However, he continued, he would never tie up American forces in small wars "on the Soviet periphery." Regarding the question of the use of nuclear weapons, Ike told Taylor that tactical nuclear weapons had "come to be practically accepted as integral parts of modern armed forces" and that planning "should go ahead on the basis of the use of tactical atomic weapons against military targets in any small war in which the United States might be involved." Eisenhower admitted that there would be no great role for the Army to play in the sort of war he envisaged. Indeed, in the aftermath of the holocaust that he believed would result from a nuclear exchange between the superpowers, he could not imagine how Army units could even be transported to Europe. However, he said, as a civil defense agency "the Army would be truly vital to the establishment and maintenance of order in the United States."[69]

Toward the conclusion of this conference Taylor remarked that the president's decision was bound to produce some "fundamental and rather drastic changes." Radford agreed. It would, he said, have "far-reaching effects."[70]

Following their meeting with the president, Radford, Taylor, and the other members of the JCS went back to work on the Joint Strategic Operating Plan for 1960. Ike's ruling left little to debate. The new operating plan stated that "atomic weapons will be used from the outset" of a general war and that in lesser conflicts they would be used "when required to achieve military objectives." In April 1957, during a subsequent NSC discussion, the president went further, indicating that because the United States did not have the resources to fund both large conventional as well as nuclear forces it would be necessary to sharply curtail the non-nuclear forces. As a result nuclear weapons would in the future be viewed as conventional in nature.[71]

Although Eisenhower had, at least for the remainder of his administration, resolved the doctrinal dispute between the supporters of the New Look and those who advocated increased conventional capabilities, his differences with all of the armed services over budgeting continued. Early in July 1956, when the three service chiefs submitted a proposal to Admiral Radford calling for annual defense budgets for the years 1958 to 1960 of $48.5 billion, he told them to think again. Their proposal came in at $12 billion (33%) more than the president had indicated he would support. In an effort to produce a plan that would meet the president's fiscal objectives, and, not incidentally, finally implement key provisions of the original August 1953 JCS paper, Radford presented the chiefs with his own plan, which called for a force reduction of 800,000 officers and enlisted personnel over three years.

Under Radford's plan the Army would be reduced from its current level of 1,040,000 to a force of 580,000. The Navy and Marines would be reduced by 200,000 to 663,000, and the Air Force would be cut from its optimum size of 970,000 to 820,000. Radford based his thinking on a number of assumptions gleaned from his many discussions with the president. First, in keeping with Eisenhower's emphasis on the importance of a healthy domestic economy, the defense budget had to be kept below $40 billion, no easy task given the enormous costs of modern weaponry. Second, he assumed that the United States would not involve itself in any significant way in future limited wars. Therefore, the United States need plan only for a general war that was certain to be violent and short, involving the large-scale use of nuclear weapons. This second assumption led to a series of important conclusions. First, the ground forces that were currently stationed at overseas bases would be of no consequence in such a struggle. Therefore, it would be possible to redeploy all but small nuclear-armed contingents from Europe and Asia. Second, the Army would have no role in such a conflict except in terms of a civil defense responsibility within the United States, and therefore could be sharply reduced in size. Third, the Air Force could all but eliminate its tactical air and troop carrier units, while at the same time strengthening SAC. Fourth, the Navy's role would be limited, and its primary responsibility would be antisubmarine warfare.[72]

At a July 9 meeting of the JCS held in Radford's office, Taylor entered a strong dissent to Radford's plan. He argued that the chairman's "concept" would prepare the United States for the least likely type of war while stripping the country of its ability to meet "the most probable type of threat." He warned that it also represented a return to a "Fortress America" concept that would cost the country its allies abroad and that it played directly into the hands of the Soviets, who no doubt longed for the day the United States would withdraw its forces from Europe and Asia. Despite the extraordinary nature of Radford's proposal, Taylor received no support during this meeting from the other chiefs, who, he later wrote, listened "in strained silence."[73]

Taylor left the meeting in a gloomy frame of mind. That was not the end of this matter, however, for once again the Army took its case to the public. On July 13, Anthony Leviero published the first of two blockbuster articles on the Radford plan in the *New York Times*. Taylor later recalled that the Leviero stories caused "a tremendous hullabaloo in the Department of Defense" and "in Washington generally."[74]

The Leviero stories also caused consternation among the NATO allies, especially in Germany. Chancellor Konrad Adenauer was in fact so distressed at the thought that American forces would soon be withdrawn from Europe that he immediately dispatched a high-ranking German officer, General Adolf Heusinger, to Washington for meetings with the appropriate American officials. Heusinger left Washington with assurances that American forces would not be leaving.

This is not to say that the president, who was on vacation at the time the Leviero stories appeared, entirely disapproved of what Radford had proposed. Of course, he could not support the admiral's ideas regarding redeployment of American forces. Nor was he prepared to make a clear unequivocal statement that nuclear weapons would be used in any future war, a concept Radford had long advocated. These proposals continued to have serious negative foreign policy implications. Nevertheless, it is clear from what followed that Radford and the president were on the same wavelength.[75]

Indicative of his feelings, on his return to Washington Eisenhower gave Radford a pat on the back for his efforts, while expressing disappointment with the performance of every other member of the JCS. "Individually," he said, they were "the finest men he" knew, "but in their jobs" they seemed unable "to rise above a service approach." A few weeks later he unburdened himself to his old friend "Swede" Hazlett. He had, he complained, made "little or no progress in developing real corporate thinking" among the chiefs. He had tried repeatedly but unsuccessfully "to make [them] understand the importance of striking a balance between minimum requirements in the costly implements of war and the health of the economy." He was appalled, he said, at what "one or two [whom] I have known all my life" had done. He was especially astonished that it should be the Navy under Admiral Burke that had been most cooperative, while the Army had refused to accept its mission.[76]

Even though he was not prepared to go as far as Radford proposed with his "super New Look," Eisenhower knew that fiscal considerations would require a substantial reduction in the size of the armed forces.[77] Because he also knew that to reveal planned force reductions before it was absolutely necessary would in all likelihood produce another outburst of opposition from the services, he decided to exclude them from any direct involvement in planning the 1958 defense budget until after the presidential election. Instead, from August until November 1956, Wilson, Radford, Wilfred McNeil, and a few other Pentagon insiders worked secretly on the numbers.[78]

Given the escalating cost of modern weaponry, and an inflation rate running at roughly 6 percent, Eisenhower agreed to $38.7 billion ($10 billion below the original proposal made by the services) as a reasonable target figure for the 1958 military budget. This figure was considerably higher than Eisenhower had originally planned. However, he surrendered to Wilson's argument that to go any lower would threaten whole programs. Following up on Radford's original proposal, he also authorized Wilson to begin planning a force reduction of 350,000.[79]

For the next two months Wilson and McNeil struggled to produce a budget. Then, however, came the Anglo-French-Israeli invasion of Gamal Abdel Nasser's Egypt, followed quickly by the Soviet invasion of Hungary. With the world in crisis Wilson temporarily abandoned plans for further cuts in force levels and informed the president that a budget of less than $41 billion would make it "very difficult for him to hold his people in line." At that point the question became, where was the money to fund the missile development programs, other high technology priorities, and current force levels to come from? For a moment, the president was near despair. The picture was so bleak, he even considered seeking a tax increase.[80] Fortunately, the crises of late 1956 passed like a summer storm. By December, the Anglo-French invasion force had withdrawn from Egypt; the Israelis had stopped their advance in the Sinai; and the Soviets had crushed the Hungarian uprising. The election was over, too.

In mid-December Eisenhower met with Wilson, Radford, and the few others who had been involved in planning the 1958 budget. At this meeting he personally went over Wilson's $39 billion defense budget proposal line by line, and ordered further cuts of $500 million. It must have been at about this time that he entered the following in his diary: "During my term of office, unless there is some technical or political development that I do not foresee—or a marked inflationary trend in the economy (which I will battle to the death)—I will not approve any obligational or expenditure authorities for the Defense Department that exceed something on the order of $38.5 billion."[81]

In December, with the election behind him and the 1958 budget in its final form, Eisenhower set out to require the services to support his budget when it was presented to Congress. That process began when he and Wilson met with the service secretaries and the JCS. The chiefs believed that given the Hungarian Revolution and the 1956 Middle East crisis, war had become more likely and budgets ought to be increased. Eisenhower disagreed. Arguing that Moscow's intervention in Hungary had proven to the world the failure of communism, he opined that the Soviet Union was weaker than at any time since 1950. He also claimed that the manner in which the administration had handled the Suez crisis had dramatically raised America's credit in the Arab world. Eisenhower complemented this upbeat interpretation of the world situation by noting that those members of the JCS who had doubts about the budget would have to understand that many different programs had to be brought together to make the country strong, and that he was the only person in a position to see the entire picture. Overspending on defense, he once again warned, would produce inflation, which would be a disaster for the entire country including the military.[82]

A few days after this, at an NSC meeting held for the specific purpose of discussing the 1958 budget, Eisenhower listened as each member of the JCS explained how the amount of funding assigned to his particular service would be used. Each member was also given the opportunity to discuss the gaps in his program that could be closed if funding was increased. Following these presentations, Eisenhower turned to Secretary of the Army Wilbur Brucker and asked: "Are you confident that the Army program previously described is the best Army program for the money?" The startled Brucker expressed certain doubts. When the president replied that the issue was the appropriateness of the "balance between the proposed strength of our Army and the general economic strength and well-being of the country," Brucker folded, agreeing with the president's assertion that to increase the Army's budget would risk "inflation and serious damage to the nation's economy." Navy Secretary Charles Thomas and Air Force Secretary Donald Quarles were each in turn subjected to the same sort of questioning and forced to agree that under the circumstances they had devised the best program possible for the money.[83]

Eisenhower had placed enormous pressure on the service secretaries and the JCS in order to gain their assent to a budget that he knew they viewed as inadequate. The question then became, Would the services acquiesce in his decision? The immediate answer seemed to be no. One week following the NSC meeting, Wilson and Radford informed the White House that a rebellion was brewing. Although, to quote Radford, the members of the JCS had sat "like bumps on a log" when being briefed by the president on the budget, they appeared ready to denounce it as soon as the opportunity presented itself. Air Force leaders, who had not been prepared to challenge the president face to face, nevertheless took the position that their budget allocation was an "imposed ceiling," and were planning an end run around the White House to Congress. Their attitude was "that they were 'not going to let the President get in the way.' "[84]

Two days later, on December 31, the White House staff secretary, General Andrew Goodpaster, went to the Pentagon for a meeting with the service secretaries and the JCS. He carried with him a document describing the president's understanding of what had transpired at the two preceding meetings. It stated that those present had been given the opportunity to express their views on the military program, that while each had pointed out areas where "increases in the program would be desirable," they had nevertheless agreed that the program was "well-balanced and satisfactory." The document further stated that each service secretary and member of the JCS had "assured the president that he can and will give the program his wholehearted support, as involving an acceptable degree of risk and providing a reasonable and wise degree of security." Following a general discussion of the document, Goodpaster asked those who agreed with the president to endorse it in writing. Those who disagreed might of course refuse to sign, but it was clear that would be risky. Everybody signed.[85]

Eisenhower's military advisors might be unhappy with his 1958 budget, but the president, true to his commitment to a balance between security and solvency, felt he was being as forthcoming as possible. The administration was caught in a developing financial squeeze. When Raymond J. Saulnier, chairman of the President's Council of Economic Advisers, gave a briefing to the NSC on budget prospects for the period through 1961, he used only two models, the first projected continued growth for the entire period, the second assumed a slight recession on the order of one experienced in 1953–54. He chose not to develop any other models because, he explained, even given uninterrupted growth the budget picture was grim with "no substantial outlook for improvement in the balance of receipts and expenditures." The reason for this, Percy Brundage, the director of the Budget Bureau, pointed out, was obvious. Even if no new programs came on line, those that had already been approved by Congress and the president were going to increase in cost faster than federal revenues. The only solution Brundage could see was to freeze federal expenditures at levels established in the 1957 budget, a solution that Defense Secretary Wilson noted would have a devastating effect on his department.[86]

At the same time that Eisenhower was getting this bad news from his economic advisors, Wilson informed him that actual spending at the Pentagon was spiraling out of control, and that he might not be able to hold to the target figure of $38 billion the president had earlier established as a sort of unofficial spending ceiling for the 1957 fiscal year. Actual spending during the last half of 1956 had been pegged at $40.2 billion and according to Wilson would reach $42 billion during the 1958 fiscal year unless something drastic was done soon. The problem, Wilson explained, was that overspending by the Air Force had "thrown the program of obligations out of balance." "Inflated costs and acceleration of the missiles program" were the chief causes of the problem. Another part of Wilson's problem was the unexpectedly high cost of research and development, which was gobbling up 15 percent of the total defense budget. While admitting that the real savings were to be found by cutting back on big ticket items such as missiles, aircraft, naval vessels, and research and development, he told the president that the only option open to him was to immediately begin a large-scale reduction in force levels. Unhappily, he said, he had already cut procurement to the point where further reductions would be dangerous.[87]

The secretary wanted to know if Eisenhower was willing to show some flexibility regarding the $38 billion spending limit earlier agreed upon. The president refused to bend, indicating that since he was disinclined to seek an increase in the federal debt limit or a tax increase, Wilson would have to get tough with the services.[88] Wilson then initiated a series of stopgap measures designed to slow the pace of spending. He placed a freeze on military construction and ordered the services to purchase nothing they could not pay for with existing funds. Against his better judgment he also cut procurement by another $500 million, and began planning large-scale force reductions.[89]

In his January 16, 1957, budget message to Congress, Eisenhower announced that the Air Force, which had just achieved its long sought-after goal of 137 wings, would drop to 128 wings by mid-1958 while the Army would be cut from 19 to 17 divisions.[90] Similar cuts would be made in the size of the Navy and Marine Corps. Though it was clear that these reductions were being made for fiscal reasons, he justified them by pointing out that the new weapons being brought into the nation's arsenal were far more technologically advanced and costly than those they replaced, and by observing that "a whole new family of even more advanced weapons," ballistic missiles, was also being acquired. The firepower of these new weapons, he said, was so extraordinary that it no longer made any sense to measure strength merely in terms of numbers of ground troops, planes, or ships.

While preparing his 1958 budget, Ike had gone to extraordinary lengths to be certain that the armed services would not raise an outcry when it reached Congress. He was spared having to find out whether his efforts would succeed or not because when the budget arrived on Capitol Hill, legislators on both sides of the aisle were in an economizing mood and literally stumbling over one another in search of things to cut. The administration should, therefore, have had clear sailing for its defense budget proposal. What followed, however, was a comedy of errors in which the administration badly mismanaged the situation. First, Treasury Secretary Humphrey encouraged Congress to wield the fiscal axe by announcing that there were many places in the budget where cuts could be made. He also predicted "a depression that will curl your hair" unless reductions were made. When questioned about Humphrey's statement, the president inadvertently made matters worse by defending Humphrey and suggesting that it was after all Congress's duty to go over his budget with a fine tooth comb.

While he may have had the Constitution on his side, the president had made a mistake. He soon found himself defending his already bare-bones defense proposals against Democrats and Republicans alike who were calling for budget cuts that he believed went too far. When House Democrats invited the president to suggest where cuts might be made, he replied by listing $1.8 billion in spending, which, he said, could safely be postponed. He rejected any outright cuts in his budget proposal, however, as unjustified.[91]

In July while a congressional conference committee was in the last stages of hammering out a budget, Wilson brought the president a memorandum on the military program that called for a force reduction of 300,000 over two years, with half the cuts to be absorbed by the Army. Eisenhower approved the overall figure but refused to commit himself to the precise cuts recommended for each of the services. He also rejected Wilson's suggestion that he discuss the plan with the JCS on the ground that the chiefs "would know that he was being purely arbitrary" especially about the 150,000 cut in the size of the Army.[92]

While Eisenhower and Wilson were agreeing on force reductions that no doubt would have taken place under any circumstances, Congress enacted a $33.8 billion military budget for 1958. This fell $15 billion short of what the services had originally requested and was $4.7 billion less than the president was asking, a fact that created a whole new set of problems for the Defense Department. Half of this shortfall, Secretary Wilson admitted, could be taken care of through "bookkeeping adjustments," but the other half would "cut into the program." On instructions from the president, Wilson urged Congress to restore $1.2 billion of the proposed cuts, but was turned down.[93] The legislators having taken a stand, Eisenhower decided that they could also take the heat. He told Wilson that after Congress adjourned the public should be informed "that sufficient funds have been appropriated to support a force of only 2.5 million rather than the present 2.8 million."[94]

Force level reductions solved part but not all of Eisenhower's fiscal problems. It was as though he was revisiting the problems he had first addressed during his 1952 campaign for the presidency. The costs of research and development had escalated beyond imagination. Weapons systems were proliferating and changing with such speed that they sometimes became obsolescent before they could be deployed. At the same time the variety of weapons being produced made it financially impossible for any nation to acquire them all. As Nelson Rockefeller noted in a memo to the president, it seemed clear that to avoid financial ruin a nation had to make sound choices because an "organization which produces constant friction and duplication of effort will sap our economy without adding to our military effectiveness."[95]

At an NSC meeting held in early July Eisenhower prodded Wilson into undertaking a complete review of the various missile programs then under development, several of which duplicated one another. Considering the financial difficulties the administration faced, he said, choices had to be made. Wilson's response was less than satisfactory. He promised a cut in the

NIKE-HERCULES air defense system, dropped the already obsolete F-103 interceptor, a Navy bomber, and the NAVAHO, an air-breathing missile system that the Air Force no longer wanted.[96] Eisenhower himself fought off an attempt to expand funding for the proposed nuclear-powered airplane and reduced funding for the B-70, which was to have been the follow-on bomber to the B-52. Overtime for workers involved in missile development and the production of B-52 bombers was cut, and funding for research and development was reduced by 10 percent. As a result of these and subsequent reductions, the administration was able to keep actual expenditures for 1957 to $38.436 billion and for 1958 to $39.070 billion.[97]

With the aid of a parsimonious Congress, the president had managed to keep the lid on spending. Even so, by early 1957 he was thinking in terms of another effort at reforming the military establishment. Nothing was working as he had hoped. The 1953 reorganization had, he said, been a "useless thing." The Army and the Air Force continued to quarrel over roles and missions and had been contestants in disputes that involved the publication of highly classified security information. There had also been a minirevolt reminiscent of the more famous "Revolt of the Admirals." Moreover, each member of the JCS remained the champion of his particular service. None seemed willing to think in terms of the broader national interest or pay the least attention to that aspect of NSC 5602 that required them to consider the economic health of the country in developing their thinking regarding the nation's security. Finally, and no doubt most importantly, the budget process was a shambles, in part at least because the services were duplicating one another's efforts in the extraordinarily costly area of weapons development. The solution to many if not all of these problems, Eisenhower still believed, was wrapped up in a single word, *unification*.

NOTES

1. NSC discussion, 5 and 26 May 1955, *Foreign Relations of the United States, 1955–1957* (Washington, DC: GPO, 1988), 19: 78, 82–83 (hereafter cited as *FRUS*).

2. New York Times (hereafter cited as *NYT*), 18 May 1955. Richard Russell, the powerful chairman of the Senate Armed Services Committee, showed little enthusiasm at this time for allowing Symington to run an investigation. Later, however, he authorized Symington to act. For a complete analysis of Symington's career as a leading opponent of the Eisenhower administration's defense policies, see Linda G. M. McFarland, "From Cold Warrior to *Realpolitik* Statesman: Stuart Symington and American Foreign Policy" (Ph.D. diss., University of Missouri, 1996), 146–350.

3. *Time*, 30 May 1955, 11–12.

4. Ibid.

5. Goodpaster, memorandum of a conference with the president, 22 Dec. 1955, Ann Whitman Diary, Box 7, Eisenhower Library (hereafter cited as Goodpaster Memcon, and EL).

6. Matthew Ridgway, "Keep the Army out of Politics," *Saturday Evening Post,* 28 Jan. 1956, 34, 72.

7. *Time*, 30 Jan. 1956, 52. For Eisenhower's reaction to the Gardner resignation, see Supplementary notes on the Legislative Leadership Meeting, 14 Feb. 1956, *FRUS, 1955–1957*, 19:198.

8. *NYT*, 2 Feb. 1956.

9. Transcript of "Meet the Press," 5 Feb. 1956, Office of the Staff Secretary, White House Sub-series, Box 6, EL.

10. *NYT*, 2 Feb. 1956; *Time*, 9 April 1956, 34. Edger V. Murphree, a former member of the Atomic Energy Commission's General Advisory Council, was chosen to head up the missile program.

11. *Public Papers of the Presidents of the United States: Dwight D. Eisenhower, 1956* (Washington, DC, GPO, 1958), 236; Baruch to Eisenhower, 6 Feb. 1956, Whitman File, Administration Series, Box 5, EL; Eisenhower to Baruch, 13 Feb. 1956, ibid.; Eisenhower diary entry, 30 March 1956, *FRUS, 1955–1957,* 19:275; NSC discussion, 1 Dec. 1955, 169, ibid.

12. NSC discussion, 4 Aug. 1995, *FRUS, 1955–1967*, 19:10; NSC discussion, 15 March 1956, ibid., 259; Notes on Legislative Leadership Meeting, 14 Feb. 1956, ibid., 196–98.

13. Ibid.; "Memorandum Prepared in the Department of State," n.d., delivered to the secretary of state on 30 Nov. 1955, ibid., 160; NSC discussion, 1 Dec. 1955, ibid., 168.

14. Eisenhower diary entry, 30 March 1956, ibid., 275.

15. NSC discussion, 1 Dec. 1955, ibid., 169.

16. Eisenhower diary entry, 30 March 1956, ibid., 275.

17. Report on missile development, n.d., delivered to NSC on 30 Nov. 1955, ibid., 161–66; see also ibid., 170n; Draft of a letter to the Republican leadership, 23 Feb. 1956, Whitman File, Diary Series, Box 13, EL.

18. Legislative Leadership Meeting, 28 Feb. 1956, ibid.

19. Ibid. Eisenhower was right to be suspicious. Though Air Force intelligence estimates indicated the existence of a huge Soviet bomber fleet, Moscow never invested heavily in intercontinental bombers. For the story of how the Air Force arrived at this completely erroneous conclusion, see Fred Kaplan, *The Wizards of Armageddon* (1983; reprint, Stanford: Stanford University Press, 1991), 156–60.

20. Memorandum for the secretary of defense, 12 March 1956, *FRUS, 1955–1957*, 19:234–38. The chiefs also estimated that there would have to be a

sharp increase in foreign military aid. In all they were recommending a defense budget of between $42 billion and $45 billion.

21. Goodpaster Memcon, 13 March 1956, White House, Office of the Staff Secretary, Box 4, EL. Eisenhower expressed considerable displeasure with both Radford and Wilson for not holding the chiefs under a tight rein. See NSC discussion, 22 March 1956, *FRUS, 1955–1957*, 19:268–74; Diary entry for March 29–30, Ann Whitman Diary, Box 8, EL.

22. Eisenhower to Wilson, Whitman File, Administration Series, Box 41, EL; see also Diary entries for March 29–30, Ann Whitman Diary, Box 8, ibid.

23. NSC discussion, 22 March 1957, *FRUS, 1955–1957*, 19:269–71. Wilson wanted to add twenty-nine B-52's to the inventory for a total of five hundred.

24. At the Puerto Rico conference Wilson told the JCS that the department could not function on less than $40 billion. Minutes of a White House meeting, 29 March 1956, Ann Whitman Diary, Box 8, EL; Memorandum for the president, 29 March 1956, White House, Office of the Staff Secretary, Defense Department Sub-series, Box 7, ibid. In a budget conference held on May 23, Assistant Secretary of Defense Wilfred McNeil, comptroller for the Defense Department, was even more specific than Wilson, telling the budget director that since 1954 spending had regularly exceeded the established budget level and that this had been made possible by a series of one-time savings. See Goodpaster Memcon, 23 May 1956, White House, Office of the Staff Secretary, Defense Department Sub-series, Box 2, ibid.; see also NSC discussion, 17 May 1956, *FRUS, 1955–1957*, 19:306–11.

25. NSC discussion, 22 March 1956, Ann Whitman File, NSC Series, Box 7, EL.

26. Ibid.

27. Brundage to Eisenhower, 23 May 1956, Whitman File, Administration Series, Box 8, EL.

28. Goodpaster Memcon, 13 March 1956, Whitman File, Diary Series, Box 13, EL. Eisenhower's anger with Wilson quickly subsided. At a meeting with his economic advisors he admitted that it was unlikely that defense spending could be brought below current levels and decided to approve the entire supplemental budget submitted by Wilson. See Memorandum for the record, 3 April 1956, White House, Office of the Staff Secretary, Department of Defense Sub-series, Box 2, EL.

29. Memorandum for the record, 4 April 1956, Ann Whitman Diary, Box 8, EL.

30. Goodpaster Memcon, 2 April 1956, Whitman File, Diary Series, Box 15, EL.

31. Ibid.

32. White House meeting, minutes, 29 March 1956, Ann Whitman Diary, Box 8, EL; Goodpaster Memcon, 2 April 1956, White House Office of the Staff Secretary, Box 4, EL. Wilson and Radford had both earlier expressed the view

that in all probability, given new and developing programs as well as the need to replace obsolete equipment, the services would have difficulty getting along on $38 billion in 1957 and thereafter. Eisenhower's total package, including the approved budget supplement, came to just over $37 billion.

33. Percival Brundage to Eisenhower, 3 April 1956, Whitman File, Administration Series, Box 8, EL.

34. Goodpaster Memcon, 5 April 1956, Whitman File, Diary Series, Box 15, EL.

35. U.S. Congress, Senate Committee on Armed Services, *Hearings before the Subcommittee on Airpower*, 84th Cong., 2d sess., 21 June 1956, 1482–87; 1510–34.

36. Goodpaster Memcon, 14 March 1956, Whitman File, Diary Series, Box 13, EL; Kaplan, *The Wizards of Armageddon*, 156–160.

37. U.S. Congress, Senate Committee on Armed Services, *Hearings before the Subcommittee on Airpower*, 84th Cong., 2d sess., 21 June 1956, 1482–87, 1510–34.

38. Ibid., 30 April and 1 May 1956, 244–73.

39. Ibid., 105, 116, 219–20.

40. *NYT,* 12 June 1956. Civilians at the Pentagon estimated that the extra 1,300 B-52 bombers that LeMay wanted would require an appropriation of $55 billion.

41. *Time*, 14 May 1956, 27.

42. Sherman Adams, *Firsthand Report* (New York: Harper, 1961), 404; for a less colorful but more complete discussion of that meeting, see Goodpaster Memcon, 31 July 1956,Whitman File, Diary Series, Box 17, EL.

43. *U.S. News and World Report*, 3 Feb. 1956, 64–73; see also "The IRBM: The Artillery Support Weapon," "Promise of Ballistic Missiles," and "Requirement: Guided Missiles for the Army," *Army*, March 1956, 11, 14–15, 19–24.

44. *Time*, 4 June 1956, 21. For more on this see W. B. Bunker, "Why the Army Needs Wings," *Army*, March 1956, 19–24; "The Wrong Way," *Army,* Oct. 1956, 15.

45. *Washington Post*, 19 May 1956. When the press obtained a copy of the public relations campaign agenda and questioned Air Force leaders about it, they held their ground. Said one official Air Force spokesman: "The Air Force would be derelict in its duty to the American people if it allowed citizens to be brainwashed by claims of the other services that they, not the Air Force, are the true path to peace and security."

46. *Time*, 4 June 1956, 20–23.

47. Wilbur Brucker, speech dated 21 Nov. 1955, and James Gavin, speech dated 22 Oct. 1955, found in Papers of Nathan Twining, Box 117, Manuscript Division, Library of Congress (hereafter cited as LC).

48. A. J. Bacevich, *The Pentomic Era: The U.S. Army between Korea and Vietnam* (Washington, DC: National Defense University Press, 1986), 43.

49. Maxwell D. Taylor, "How the U.S. Army Plans to Assure Peace or Win War," *U.S. News and World Report*, 6 Jan. 1956, 86–87; Statement to the Senate Armed Services Committee, 20 Feb. 1956, in Bacevich, *The Pentomic Era*, 44.

50. Maxwell D. Taylor, "Nuclear Weapons Can't Replace Ground Forces," *U.S. News and World Report*, 9 Nov. 1956, 58–59. For more on this theme, see James D. Atkinson, "The Single Weapon Fallacy," *Army*, June 1956, 23–27. The Air Force carefully monitored the media for statements such as this. For a large collection of these, complete with the Air Force's responses, see the Twining Papers, Box 117, LC.

51. *Time*, 4 June 1956, 22.

52. Goodpaster Memcon, 30 March 1956, Whitman File, Diary Series, Box 15, EL.

53. Ibid.

54. NSC discussion, 21 Dec. 1956, Whitman File, NSC Series, Box 8, EL; Taylor, *An Uncertain Trumpet*, 36–37.

55. David Halberstam, *The Best and the Brightest* (New York: Random House, 1969), 473–77.

56. *NYT*, 19 May 1956.

57. Ibid., 20–21 May. For the Air Force staff studies on these and other issues dividing the services see the Twining Papers, Box 117, LC.

58. *Time*, 4 June 1956, 22–23.

59. *Newsweek*, 16 July 1956, 22; *Time*, 11 June 1956, 32.

60. *Time*, 4 June 1956, 19.

61. Goodpaster Memcon, 14 May 1956, Whitman File, Diary Series, Box 31, EL; Goodpaster Memcon, 18 May 1954, *FRUS, 1952–1954*, 2:303–305.

62. Goodpaster Memcon, 24 May 1956, Whitman File, Diary Series, Box 31, EL.

63. Halberstam, *The Best and the Brightest*, 473–77; *Time*, 4 June 1956, 19; *Baltimore Sun*, 22 May 1956; *New York Herald Tribune*, 22 May 1956.

64. *Time*, 11 June 1956, 32.

65. Memorandum for members of the Armed Forces Policy Council, 26 Nov. 1956, in Alice Cole et al., eds., *The Department of Defense, Documents on Establishment and Organization, 1944–1978*, (Washington, DC: Department of Defense Historical Office, 1978), 306–11; *Time*, 10 Dec. 1956, 25. Subsequently President Eisenhower overruled Wilson with regard to a 200-mile range limit on Army missiles, expanding the range to 500 miles.

66. For a copy of NSC 5602, see *FRUS, 1955–1957*, 19:242–67; Kenneth Condit, *A History of the Joint Chiefs of Staff* (Washington, DC: JCS Historical Office, 1991), 6:12–19.

67. Condit, *A History of the Joint Chiefs of Staff*, 6:32–37.

68. NSC 5602, ibid., 247. The document stipulated that the United States must have ready forces that, with such help "as may realistically be expected from allied forces, are adequate (a) to present a deterrent to any resort to local aggression,

and (b) to defeat or hold, in conjunction with indigenous forces, any such local aggression, pending the application of such additional U.S. and allied power as may be required to suppress quickly the local aggression in a manner and on a scale best calculated to avoid the hostilities broadening into general war. Such ready forces must be sufficiently versatile to use both conventional and nuclear weapons. . . . Such forces must not become so dependent on tactical nuclear capabilities that any decision to intervene against local aggression would probably be tantamount to a decision to use nuclear weapons." The document also stipulated: "With the coming of nuclear parity, the ability to apply force selectively and flexibly will become increasingly important in maintaining the morale and will of the free world to resist aggression. The United States and its allies must avoid getting themselves in a position where they must choose between (a) not responding to local aggression and (b) applying force in a way which our own people or our allies would consider entails undue risks of nuclear devastation."

69. Goodpaster Memcon, 24 May 1956, Whitman File, Diary Series, Box 31, EL.

70. Ibid.

71. Robert J. Watson, *The History of the Office of the Secretary of Defense: Into the Missile Age* (Washington, DC: Historical Office of the Office of the Secretary of Defense, 1997), 7:104.

72. *NYT*, 13 and 15 July 1956. This description of the Radford Plan is taken from a newspaper report done by Anthony Leviero, Washington correspondent for the *Times*, and is based on extensive but authoritative leaks. Condit, *A History of the Joint Chiefs of Staff*, 6:36–37.

73. Taylor, *An Uncertain Trumpet*, 40–41. In two stories that appeared in the *New York Times* on July 13 and 15, Leviero claimed that all of the chiefs objected to Radford's ideas. Goodpaster Memcon, 17 Aug. 1956, Whitman File, Diary Series, Box 17, EL. In commenting on these events, Radford lent support to Leviero's claim that all the members of the JCS opposed his ideas by remarking: "There was such an expression of opposition that action was suspended on the memorandum."

74. Ibid.

75. Goodpaster Memcon, 31 July 1956, Ann Whitman File, Diary Series, Box 17, EL; Robert A. Ferrell, ed., *The Eisenhower Diaries* (New York: Norton, 1981), 337.

76. Eisenhower to Everett Hazlett, 20 Aug. 1956, in Dwight D. Eisenhower, *Mandate for Change* (Garden City: Doubleday, 1963), 606–607. Total military personnel on active duty dropped from 2,806,441 in 1956 to 2,600,581 in 1958. The Army sustained a loss of 100,000 officers and enlisted personnel, the Air Force, Navy, and Marines in combination absorbed the rest.

77. Watson, *The History of the Office of the Secretary of Defense*, 7:78.

78. In fact the services were allowed to believe they still had a significant role to play in planning the 1958 budget. See Wilson to the Service Secretaries, 21

Nov. 1958, White House Office of the Staff Secretary, Defense Department Sub-series, Box 2, EL.

79. Goodpaster Memcon, 17 Aug. and 2 Oct. 1956, Whitman File, Diary Series, Box 17, Box 19, EL. As late as October 2, with the Suez crisis about to break into open warfare, Undersecretary of Defense Robertson informed the president that to reach an acceptable budget level it would be necessary to plan for a cut of 250,000 in the size of the armed forces with most of the reductions to come from the Army. The old issue of redeployment arose once again, but as before Eisenhower indicated it would be impossible to withdraw the five divisions from Europe.

80. Goodpaster Memcon, 8 Nov. 1956, Whitman File, Diary Series, Box 19, EL.

81. Goodpaster Memcon, 15 Dec. 1956, White House, Office of the Staff Secretary, Department of Defense Sub-series, Box 2; *Ferrell, Eisenhower Diaries*, 337.

82. Goodpaster Memcon, 20 Dec. 1956, White House Office of the Staff Secretary, Defense Department Sub-series, Box 2, EL.

83. NSC discussion, 21 Dec. 1956, Whitman File, NSC Sub-series, Box 8, EL.

84. Goodpaster, memorandum for the record, 12 Jan. 1957, Whitman File, Office of the Staff Secretary, Defense Department Sub-series, Box 2, EL.

85. White House memorandum for Wilson, Brucker, Thomas, Quarles, Radford, Taylor, Burke, Twining, and Pate, 31 Dec. 1956, Whitman File, Administration Series, Box 41, EL; Goodpaster, memorandum for the record, 1 Jan. 1957, White House, Office of the Staff Secretary, Department of Defense Sub-series, Box 2, EL; Goodpaster, memorandum for the record, 12 Jan. 1957, White House, Office of the Staff Secretary, Department of Defense Sub-series, Box 2, EL.

86. NSC discussion, 28 March 1957, *FRUS, 1955–1957*, 19:446–55; Goodpaster Memcon, 24 May 1957, Whitman File, Diary Series, Box 24, EL.

87. Goodpaster Memcon, 5 March 1957, White House, Office of the Staff Secretary, Defense Department Sub-series, Box 1, EL; Goodpaster Memcon, 21 May 1957, Whitman File, Diary Series, Box 24, EL.

88. Goodpaster Memcon, 28 June 1957, Whitman File, Diary Series, Box 25, EL.

89. Watson, *History of the Office of the Secretary of Defense,* 7: 91–92.

90. General Taylor had already reduced the size of each Army division from 17,500 to 12,000 officers and enlisted personnel.

91. Watson, *History of the Office of the Secretary of Defense*, 6:86–90.

92. Goodpaster Memcon, 10 July 1957, *FRUS,* 1955–1957, 19:547–48.

93. Goodpaster Memcon, 21 May 1957, Whitman File, Diary Series, Box 24, EL.

94. Goodpaster Memcons, 12 July and 2 Aug. 1957, White House, Office of the Staff Secretary, Defense Department Sub-series, Box 1, EL. On July 16, 1957,

Wilson announced the first of two 100,000-man cuts in the size of the armed services that took place before the end of 1957. In the following year another 100,000 men were cut from the forces. Over this two-year period the Army was reduced in size by 140,000 officers and enlisted personnel.

95. Goodpaster, memorandum for the record, 28 Oct. 1957, White House Office of the Staff Secretary, Miscellaneous Series, Box 1, EL.

96. NSC discussion, 3 July 1957, *FRUS, 1955–1957*, 19:535–37; Wilson to Eisenhower, 9 Aug. 1957, Whitman File, Administration Series, Box 41.

97. The total size of the American military dropped to 2.6 million in 1958.

8

"I Tried to Persuade the President That It Would Really Be Better for Me to Take Another Year on This."

On October 4, 1957, a Soviet rocket successfully placed Sputnik, the world's first man-made satellite, in Earth orbit. Two more Russian satellites soon followed.[1] The news of these Soviet achievements sent a shock wave reverberating throughout the world. Prior to Sputnik, it had been widely assumed that America's technological superiority was unassailable. Eisenhower was well aware of the importance of this. In fact, two years before, when it became clear that the Soviets were making rapid advances in the ballistic missile field, he ordered a speedup in America's missile development programs. From a psychological point of view, he believed it would be a disaster if the Soviets even appeared to challenge the U.S. claim to scientific and technological preeminence. Unhappily, the speedup came too late. Now every night, a large portion of humanity could see and even hear the Soviet satellite as it made its way across the heavens.

The history of the Eisenhower administration's reaction to Sputnik and the so-called missile gap has been well told elsewhere. It is also generally understood that the president, who gauged the significance of the Soviet achievement better than his critics, refused to be carried along on the wave of panic that for a time gripped the nation. It is less well known, however, that Eisenhower saw in the Sputnik crisis a golden opportunity to move further down the road toward the unification of the military establishment and simultaneously reduce the exploding costs of preparedness. Yet there can be no doubt about this. Shortly after the Sputnik launch, he instructed Nelson

Rockefeller, the head of his Advisory Commission on Government Organization, to develop new ideas on military reorganization. He also informed his economic advisors that "the present climate," by which he meant the public hysteria over Sputnik, had created the opportunity to take "a giant step toward unification" and that huge cost savings would result.[2]

Eisenhower's pursuit of military reform in the aftermath of the Sputnik launching was complicated by the fact that he would be working with a new secretary of defense. Neil McElroy, the former head of Procter and Gamble, seemed a good choice for the job. Former Secretary of Defense "Engine Charlie" Wilson had a disturbing penchant for putting his foot firmly in his mouth and keeping it there, often to Eisenhower's great embarrassment. McElroy, on the other hand, was a marketing man, skilled at selling a product and at ingratiating himself to others. At the same time, there was a downside to the new secretary's personality that was not obvious at the time of his appointment. He lacked toughness and was often too anxious to avoid confrontation. These could be serious disadvantages in a city where, as Harry Truman once remarked, "[i]f you want a friend, get a dog." McElroy suffered from another weakness as well. He knew absolutely nothing about the Defense Department and would have to learn on the job during a moment of national hysteria while his every move was subject to microscopic examination.

McElroy's primary responsibility during the last months of 1957 was to develop a defense budget for the coming fiscal year. That was not going to be easy. With Sputnik decorating the night sky, the pressure to increase military spending was intensifying. At the same time the new secretary of the treasury, Robert Anderson, and Budget Director Percy Brundage both warned that a deficit would result if the defense budget rose much beyond $38 billion. At that level of funding, given inflation and the escalating costs of new weapon systems, there would have to be further reductions in force levels, base closings, and other cutbacks. McElroy was certain to have his hands full.[3]

Eisenhower encouraged the secretary to think of unification as the means by which he could achieve the economies the fiscal situation seemed to require. Thus, at a White House meeting that took place a bare three days after McElroy was sworn in, the first item of business was military reorganization. The president suggested that McElroy contact Rockefeller and others who had crafted the 1953 reforms. These men firmly believed in unification, he said, and would "have specific ideas that might be of value to him." Not long after this, Eisenhower again informed McElroy that he was considering a major reorganization of the Defense Department, including the possible creation of a chief of staff who would be separate from and superior to the other members of the JCS.[4]

The president's hints notwithstanding, the secretary showed little interest in attempting to reorganize the Pentagon. "I tried to persuade the President that it would really be better for me to take another year on this," McElroy later recalled. He told Ike that in the interim he would be working on some ideas for change with two separate groups inside the military establishment, but that his method was to "go slowly."[5]

If McElroy was in no hurry to undertake a major reform effort, the same cannot be said of Nelson Rockefeller, who, soon after the president first suggested that the time for reform was at hand, turned up at the White House with a nineteen-page paper that included both an analysis of the problem and the outline of a solution.[6] Rockefeller argued that the military's basic problem was the "obsolescent division of function among the services." The obvious solution, he believed, was "a greater degree of unification." Because it was not politically feasible to create a single military service, Rockefeller proposed reorganizing the services according to "broad mission areas which represent clearly distinguishable tasks." As an example, he proposed organizing America's ground, sea, and air forces into two basic commands. The "strategic force" would be made up of those units from each of the services intended for use in an all-out war while a "tactical command" would have responsibility for fighting limited wars. Once such an overall organization had been created, he argued, service differences as well as the deplorable waste and inefficiency of the established order would disappear.[7]

Eisenhower was impressed with Rockefeller's analysis but thought his reform proposals politically unrealistic. He let the New Yorker know that he was on the right track and encouraged him to come up with a set of more moderate solutions.[8]

On November 4, Rockefeller was back at the White House for a breakfast meeting with the president. He brought with him Arthur Flemming, the director of the Office of Emergency Preparedness, and Budget Director Brundage. At that meeting the four men hammered out a series of reform proposals that they agreed should be part of any final set of recommendations. These included the creation of real, unified commands for the armed forces; a new chain of command that bypassed the service secretaries and ran from the secretary of defense through the JCS directly to the unified commanders; and an integrated staff for military planning to replace the Joint Staff. The group also agreed that in order to eliminate unnecessary duplication all research and development projects should be controlled by the

Office of the Secretary of Defense. Neither the JCS nor the individual services would have any power in these vital areas.[9] These changes were designed to enhance the power of the secretary of defense and the chairman of the JCS, reduce the power of the service chiefs, and downgrade the military departments, which would in the future only be responsible for handling administrative and logistical chores.

Not long after this meeting Rockefeller and Brundage, who doubted McElroy's willingness to act, urged Ike to instruct the secretary to give military reorganization "a high priority" and establish "a special committee on organization, similar to the one" Charles Wilson had established in 1953.[10] In a separate memorandum Brundage, who saw reorganization as the key to gaining control of spiraling defense costs, suggested that the president include a call for reorganization of both the Defense and State departments in his upcoming State of the Union Message, and again urged him to jar McElroy into action. The defense secretary, he wrote, did not appear to "appreciate the value that would attach to your submission" of reform proposals at the earliest possible moment.[11]

Impressed by the arguments of Brundage, Rockefeller, and Dr. James Killian, the head of the President's Science Advisory Committee, who also supported a renewed effort at reform, Eisenhower instructed Brundage to forward a copy of the reform proposals worked out at the November 4 meeting to McElroy. He was to inform the secretary that he had "read these papers with great interest," that there was "no doubt in his mind" that the proposed reforms would bring about great improvements, and that he wanted the secretary's views regarding these ideas.[12]

Left in no doubt as to the president's wishes, McElroy created a special committee and made it responsible for coming up with a reorganization proposal. The group included two former chairmen of the JCS, General Omar Bradley and the recently retired Admiral Arthur Radford; the current chairman, General Nathan Twining; Eisenhower's close friend, General Alfred Gruenther; Nelson Rockefeller; and William Foster, a former deputy secretary of defense under Robert Lovett. McElroy recruited Charles Coolidge, an old friend whom he knew through his connection with Harvard University, to head the committee. A well-known Boston attorney, Coolidge had served as an assistant secretary of defense under Robert Lovett and was the author of the Coolidge Report, which Lovett had used as the basis for his 1953 reform proposals. McElroy and his deputy, Donald Quarles, also met regularly with the group.[13]

In his State of the Union Message delivered in January 1958, Eisenhower laid out a series of new defense initiatives ranging from a stepped-up long-range missile program to increased foreign military aid. The matter of greatest consequence, he told Congress, was the reorganization of the Pentagon. Interservice rivalry, which he blamed for many of the nation's current travails, had to be stopped. It was vital, he said, that the country have "real unity in the defense establishment in all the principle features of military activities." Strategic planning as well as research and development efforts needed to be brought under "unified direction," while civilian control over the military had to be made truly effective. Though by this time Ike had some well defined ideas about what needed changing, he made no specific recommendations. He did say, however, that military reorganization would be his primary goal for the coming legislative session.[14]

Eisenhower's unwillingness to make detailed reform proposals in his State of the Union message was the result of two considerations. First, of course, the Coolidge committee had not yet even begun its deliberations. Second, Eisenhower believed that there should be a wide-ranging debate on military reform before he made specific proposals.[15] That is why three days before the president delivered his address, Nelson Rockefeller released to the press "International Security—The Military Aspect." This report, produced under the auspices of the Rockefeller Brothers Fund, advocated a series of reforms that, if enacted, would have vastly reduced the power of the JCS and the separate services, while centralizing authority in the hands of the secretary of defense and the chairman of the JCS.[16]

The use of the Rockefeller Brothers Report as a trial balloon was a sound opening gambit. The public discussion of the report's recommendations provided Ike and his advisors with a method of gauging the level of support they might expect, as well as the nature and strength of the opposition. This seemed especially important because military reform was not a partisan issue; one could not easily assess how members of Congress from either party would fall out over this question.

No sooner had the Rockefeller Brothers Report been released, than certain key players in the developing debate made their positions clear. The members of the JCS strongly opposed any system that focused power in the hands of the chairman of the JCS. So, too, did Richard Russell, chairman of the Senate Armed Services Committee, and "Uncle" Carl Vinson, chairman of the House Armed Services Committee. Vinson equated the changes proposed in the Rockefeller Report with "national suicide" and denounced those "alarmists" who sought a "scapegoat" to blame for Soviet achievements in space. "I refuse to be stampeded into precipitous and dangerous changes merely because a Soviet-built satellite is circling the earth." Vinson also rejected the president's claim that interservice rivalry was responsible for the fact that the Soviets appeared to be ahead in the missile race. The problem lay not with the services, Vinson argued, but with the Pentagon's bloated civilian bureaucracy, with amateurs who came and went through the Pentagon's revolving door and interfered with the sound operations of the military.[17]

Not long after this, the influential Texas Democrat, Congressman Paul Kilday, followed up on Vinson's suggestion by introducing a bill based on the premise that it was the Office of the Secretary of Defense and not the armed services that needed reform. Kilday charged that "the principal difficulty in the Defense Department is the impossibility of securing prompt decisions." This was the case, he argued, not because of anything the services did but "because of the administrative jungle created by layers of secretaries, assistant secretaries, and deputy assistant secretaries." The Kilday bill (H.R. 11001), which was enthusiastically supported by Vinson and Les Arends of Illinois, the ranking Republican on the Armed Services Committee, would have limited to 600 the number of civilians the department could employ, eliminated fourteen under-and assistant secretaries, restricted the members of the Joint Staff to three-year terms, and forbidden the comptroller of the department from exercising "any supervision, control, or judgment over the military justification for programs and requirements of the military departments."[18]

Eisenhower and the members of the Coolidge committee learned a great deal from the responses to the Rockefeller Report. They now understood that the House and Senate were not in a mood to be stampeded by "Sputnik hysteria" and that the JCS posed a formidable obstacle to radical change. As Ike himself explained at a press conference in mid-January, he now understood that if reorganization was to succeed he would have to reach a compromise "with Congress [and] with the people who have the job of operating the services."[19]

It was clear that it would be self-defeating to propose the creation of a powerful chief of staff or any other major change in the structure of the JCS. It only made sense, therefore, to take the alternative tactic of seeking to strengthen the secretary of defense. By emphasizing civilian authority Ike could undercut accusations of "Prussianism" or fears of "a man on horseback," arguments that had been used effectively by opponents of reform during earlier stages of this long drawn-out battle. Published reports also made it apparent that the Air Force and the Army were likely to support moderate reform proposals, that the Navy was more problematic, and that the Marines, fearing that some future secretary of defense might support the

Army's long-standing contention that the Corps was a duplicate army, would fight any change that further centralized power and authority.[20]

Immediately following the president's State of the Union Address, the Coolidge committee began holding bi-weekly meetings at which it heard from witnesses including the service secretaries, current and past members of the JCS, and, according to Coolidge, "every top commander from the military services, wherever he was stationed."[21]

Eisenhower did not want to appear to be guiding the deliberations of the committee. He thought Congress would be more sympathetic to a reform package if it appeared to come directly from the Pentagon. At the same time he kept tabs on the committee and influenced its deliberations through contacts with Omar Bradley, "Bill" Foster, and above all Nelson Rockefeller.[22]

On January 20, Eisenhower called Rockefeller to be certain that he was attending committee meetings and that he remained committed to one reform in particular. Ike wanted the service secretaries, who had in the past frequently challenged the authority of the secretary of defense, removed from any operational role and relegated to purely administrative functions. This would have the effect of strengthening the secretary of defense, weakening the services, and clarifying the military chain of command, which would then run from the president and secretary of defense functionally through the JCS directly to the unified commanders. The president informed Rockefeller that he had discussed this point with both "Bill" Foster and Omar Bradley, and that they agreed with him. Aware that any attempt to further strip the service secretaries of real power was certain to produce withering criticism from the likes of Carl Vinson, Ike cautioned Rockefeller that for the moment it would be best to "say nothing at all or we defeat ourselves."[23]

Toward the end of their conversation, Rockefeller, who did not feel McElroy was moving fast enough, suggested that a presidential visit to one of the committee's regular meetings might energize the group. Disturbed by what Rockefeller had said, Ike met with McElroy for the purpose of straightening him out. The meeting apparently went well since, according to Eisenhower's secretary, Ann Whitman, "the President appeared in a fine mood when it was over." Later, however, she amended that judgment, noting that McElroy "seemed to be coming around, though not completely." The president, she wrote, was still less than pleased with his attitude.[24]

Four days after his meeting with McElroy, Ike, accompanied by his legislative aide, Bryce Harlow, and the White House staff secretary, General Andrew Goodpaster, went to the Pentagon for a meeting with the Coolidge group. For two-and-a-half hours he listened as the discussion droned on. He was unimpressed. It seemed to him that the majority of those at the meeting were content to nibble around the edges of what he considered a very big issue. At length, he took control of the meeting, challenging the committee "to do something real instead of glossing over the problem." He warned the group against trying to "laugh off the criticisms" then being leveled against the military establishment. Big changes were needed. Specifically, he mentioned establishing real control over the lobbying and public relations activities of the services, creating an integrated joint staff, removing the service secretaries from the chain of command, and at least thinking about ways of reforming the JCS.[25]

Eisenhower's appearance at the Pentagon marked the moment when the Coolidge committee moved into high gear. Coolidge himself later recalled: "President Eisenhower started the ball rolling by coming to the Department of Defense and speaking to our group and as many of the future witnesses as could be assembled." After four weeks of hearing from witnesses and batting ideas around, the entire group traveled to Ramey Air Force Base in Puerto Rico. There, Coolidge presented the committee with a set of tentative conclusions that the entire membership debated and discussed over the next several days. "Getting away from all the telephones," he later said, "meant that the thinking of the group crystallized in a way that I think couldn't have been done otherwise."[26]

A memorandum that Coolidge prepared immediately following the Puerto Rico meeting clearly indicates that the committee members had, as Eisenhower insisted they should, dealt with fundamental issues. They considered creating a single service to replace the current three, but rejected that idea, both because it was politically unfeasible and because in the midst of the cold war it would have proven dangerously disruptive. Before finally rejecting the idea, the committee also gave serious consideration to transforming the service secretaries into assistant secretaries of defense. They agreed that the current JCS system was not functioning properly and should be reformed. However, given the fierce congressional opposition to creating a powerful chief of staff, they went no further than to recommend that the chiefs be required to spend the majority of their time on their joint work as members of the JCS, and that their offices be placed next to those of the secretary of defense. The committee also recommended that the service secretaries be removed from the chain of command, that true unified commands be established, that Congress should vote "some or all" Defense Department monies to the secretary rather than to the separate services, that all research and development projects as well as all lobbying and public relations activities be centralized in the Office of the Secretary of Defense, and that all promotions to three-star rank and above should be in the Armed Forces of the United States, not in an individual service. It was an extraordinary list of proposals. The problem then became to decide what was feasible. [27]

Toward the end of March, after four separate meetings during which Eisenhower, Coolidge, and McElroy agreed upon a final list of reform proposals, the president instructed the secretary to prepare a clear, straightforward message to Congress in which the entire reorganization plan was explained in detail. He did not get it, at least from McElroy, who had never been enthusiastic about reform and who, in an attempt to pacify the service secretaries and the JCS, drafted a message that compromised the work done by the committee. When Rockefeller saw the proposed draft he went up in smoke. In a nasty confrontation with McElroy, he attacked it as "a weak watered down version" of what the committee had recommended. He warned that compromising "on wording in order to placate the Secretaries of the Services and the Chiefs of Staff simply confuses and weakens the basic concepts and will not give a clear and convincing picture to the public and the Congress." According to Rockefeller, McElroy did not deny the charge, saying only: "Well, the President will use what he wants and eliminate what he doesn't want." In a memorandum to General Goodpaster that reached the president's desk, Rockefeller guessed that McElroy did not care what the White House did with the speech after it was out of his hands. His major concern, Rockefeller continued, was to defend himself against critics inside the Pentagon.[28]

Eisenhower had Bryce Harlow rewrite the message. Then he himself spent an entire weekend working on the piece. He told Henry Cabot Lodge, Jr., that he was "going to town" on the question of defense reorganization. "Over the weekend I spent a great deal of time on the final draft of the document; I am determined to make it in all respects 'mine.' "[29]

While the special message was being written, the president met with key legislative leaders to discuss his reform proposals. A meeting with Leverett Saltonstall and Georgia's Richard Russell went off uneventfully. After meeting with House leaders he told Ann Whitman that he expected trouble from "Uncle" Carl Vinson, who "thinks the legislature should control the Defense Department."[30]

On April 3, Eisenhower sent a special 7,000-word message to Congress, outlining his plan for reorganizing the defense establishment. In it he stated that "as a result of well-meaning attempts to protect traditional concepts and prerogatives, we have impaired civilian authority and denied ourselves a fully effective defense. We must cling no longer to statutory barriers that weaken executive action and civilian authority. We must free ourselves of emotional attachments to service systems of an era that is no more." He then offered a reorganization proposal based on six points that bore a close resemblance to ideas first discussed at the November 4 White House meeting with Rockefeller, Brundage, and Flemming.[31]

The president sought the establishment of truly unified commands "separate from the military departments." The unified commanders would have absolute authority over all ground, sea, and air forces under their control. He also wanted the chain of command to run directly from the secretary of defense to the unified commands. This would eliminate the possibility of any involvement in the operations of a unified command by either an individual service chief or a service secretary. Toward this end he asked Congress to "repeal any statutory authority which vests responsibilities for military operations in any official other than the Secretary of Defense." If Congress agreed, Ike believed he would be well on his way to eliminating from existing law the legislative descriptions of service roles and missions that had been in place since 1947 and that he considered anachronistic.

To aid the JCS, who would serve as advisors to the secretary of defense for strategic planning and for the operations of the unified commands, Ike asked Congress to replace the Joint Staff committee system, which suffered from the same problems as the JCS, with a larger integrated Joint Staff. Because he believed the secretary of defense "must have full authority to prevent unwise service competition in the areas of Research and Development," he also proposed creating a director of Defense Research and Engineering with the power to "eliminate unpromising or unnecessarily duplicative (*sic*) programs" and to initiate needed projects. Ike also suggested that all appropriations for research and development go directly to the secretary of defense so that the services could not develop duplicate programs.

The key aspect of Eisenhower's reform plan was enhanced power for the secretary of defense. Here, money was the key. Though loath to remark on this publicly, Ike believed that interservice rivalry would quickly end and that the services would be blocked from going "over the Secretary of Defense's head to grind their own axes in Congress" if the secretary had absolute control of the funds Congress voted for the military.[32] In fact, had it been politically realistic Ike might have proposed that Congress vote all defense funds in a lump sum to the secretary of defense. Since that was not a possibility, however, he contented himself with asking Congress to grant the secretary "adequate authority and flexibility" in the use of funds. To further enhance the secretary's power, he also asked the legislators to abolish that part of the existing law that stated that the services should be "separately administered by their respective Secretaries under the direction of, authority and control of the Secretary of Defense." Ike called this clause in the law "confusing" and "a hindrance to efficient administration." In making this recommendation he pointed out that the idea "that three military departments can be at once administered separately, yet directed by one administrator who is supposed to establish 'integrated policies and procedures,' has encouraged endless fruitless argument. Such provisions," he thought, "unavoidably abrade the unity of the Defense Department."[33]

Prior to sending his message on defense reorganization to Congress, Eisenhower issued a series of executive orders designed to complement his legislative initiative. He removed the responsibility for strategic planning from the separate services, vested it in the JCS, and warned the chiefs against performing "any of their duties independently of the Secretary's direction." He also removed the service secretaries from the chain of command so that orders from the secretary of defense went directly to heads of the various military commands, and abolished the Joint Staff committee system, establishing in its place an integrated "operations unit" that he attached to the JCS.[34]

Eisenhower, who had long deplored the extreme parochialism manifested by many senior officers, also announced that in the future he would not promote any officer to the rank of Lt. General or above save on the recommendation of the secretary of defense. These officers, he added, "must have demonstrated, among other qualities, the capacity for dealing objectively—without extreme service partisanship—with matters of the broadest significance to our national security." The message was clear, those officers who hoped to rise to four-star rank were expected to spend a substantial portion of their careers working jointly with officers from the other services.[35]

Finally, Eisenhower ordered McElroy to strengthen his control over all public relations functions by taking control of these activities. Providing information to Congress was an important function, and, he said, he had every intention of keeping the country well informed. "But surely," he added, "personnel charged with such duties should not seek to advance the interests of a particular service at the expense of another, nor should they advance a service cause at the expense of overall national and defense requirements." Then he remarked: "We do not want defense dollars spent on publicity and influence campaigns in which each service claims superiority over the others and strives for increased appropriations or other Congressional favors."[36]

The 1958 defense reorganization plan did not go as far as Eisenhower would have wished. Nevertheless, he told the National Security Council that if he could succeed in abolishing the "artificial roles and missions of the services" and instead focus military planning around the unified commands; get rid of the concept that the services were to be "separately administered" and place them under the direct control of the secretary of defense; and win for the secretary real "financial flexibility," he would have "achieved three great legislative changes which very much needed to be made."[37]

Eisenhower's proposals touched off an intense public debate. The influential columnist, Hanson Baldwin, reiterated an argument he and Carl Vinson had made in February, blaming a bloated civilian bureaucracy for America's recent difficulties. Interservice rivalry was not "the crux" of the country's problem. On the contrary, he wrote, competition among the services had produced many positive results and no doubt saved thousands of lives. The really bad decisions, by which he meant postwar demobilization, inadequate defense budgets, and the emphasis that Eisenhower placed on massive retaliation, had not been taken by the military but were all the result of civilian decision making. Writing in the *Wall Street Journal*, Henry Gemmill echoed Baldwin's argument when he claimed that career military men were far better positioned to discern their true needs than the amateurs who came to and left the Pentagon with such frequency. The country's current military problems, he argued, were the result of "bad management" by "a hierarchy of amateurs." Even the influential gossip columnist, Walter Winchell, became involved in the debate, explaining "the present paralysis of our armed forces" as the work of "a bungling bureau of bureaucracy."[38]

This is not to say that the president lacked for defenders. On the contrary, newspapers from coast to coast carried articles and editorials supporting his ideas. "We have heard opposition cries that grave constitutional issues are involved," said the *Kansas City Star,* "but if the opposition prevails," the secretary of defense "will continue to be the only head of an executive department who is prevented by law from administering all its activities." Writing in the *New York Herald Tribune*, the influential columnist, Roscoe Drummond, remarked that if it were possible to develop a military organization from scratch, given recent technological developments, it would be absurd to organize the armed services "on the basis of how they travel—whether on land, sea, or air." Drummond admitted that a fresh start was not in the cards, but warned "we can't stand still and preserve all the past if we are to use modern weapons effectively." Describing the president's plan as the "way of reason, efficiency, and security," the *Los Angeles Times* said: "We have heard enough nonsense about the uses of competition among the services." The paper then remarked archly, "[W]e have also seen some of its results."[39]

Despite the fact that there was in general a good deal of support for reform, some of the president's proposals ran into stiff opposition on Capitol Hill. One of the most controversial was his suggestion that Congress grant the secretary greater control over defense spending. Some in Congress also believed that the reorganization plan was designed to give the defense secretary the power to abolish the services and achieve unification by executive fiat. Senator Mike Mansfield, the majority whip and an ex-Marine who was sensitive to this threat, said: "It appears to me that under the reorganization proposal" the secretary of defense would amass sufficient power "that he could create a supreme command and that he could bring into being a chief of staff based on the German pattern."[40] Senator Styles Bridges of New Hampshire, a conservative Republican, agreed, warning that if the White House plan was enacted as drawn, the Congress would have surrendered one of its basic constitutional powers to the president and at the same time provided the secretary with such power that he could, if he wished, "practically abolish the services."[41] Mansfield more or less summed things up for the opponents of reform when he remarked: "The battle lines are being drawn between the executive arrogation of power and the Constitutional prerogatives of Congress."[42]

The leader of the opposition in the House of Representatives was the Georgia Democrat, seventy-four-year-old "Uncle" Carl Vinson. As the chairman of the House Armed Services Committee, Vinson was perfectly positioned to fight the president, and he had every intention of doing so. He told the press that he was not adverse to any small changes in the military establishment the president might have in mind, but he insisted that its "basic structure" was sound. Vinson promised that his committee was going to be tough on any reorganization proposal that came before it. For some administration witnesses, he said, "it may be a painful experience . . . similar to the Spanish bullfighter's 'moment of truth' when he stands, sword in hand, before the horns of the charging bull."[43] If Vinson was confident he could win this fight, so too was Louisiana's F. Edward Hebert, another member of the Armed Services Committee who predicted even before the hearings began that the reorganization plan would die in committee.[44]

Neither Vinson nor Hebert was prepared for the Eisenhower they met in this encounter. Ike's style of leadership led some to believe that he was neither tough enough nor committed enough to fight for his policies. This was definitely not the case with regard to the reorganization plan. When a reporter asked him how he intended to achieve reform given the powerful opposition he faced, Ike angrily replied that he did not care "how strong they are or how numerous they are." He was prepared to go on television, he said, "as often as the television companies will let me on." He would continue to speak until the people realized "that it is their pocket books first of all; more than that it is their safety. . . . I don't care who is against this thing. It just so happens I have got a little bit more experience in military organization and the direction of unified forces than anyone else on the active list." The reporters were impressed. The *New York Daily News* thought: "The President is entering perhaps the biggest battle of his political life." *Newsweek* called the reorganization fight "the first momentous struggle between the executive and legislative branches since he [Eisenhower] moved into the White House."[45]

Newsweek was correct. This was to be an intensely fought legislative battle. The White House knew it and prepared for it in that way. The first item on its agenda was to prepare a bill. That job went to Robert Dechert, the general counsel for the Defense Department, and Maurice Stans, who had replaced Percy Brundage as budget director.[46] Save for one important point, the bill was an exact reflection of what the president had proposed in his April 3 message. It had become clear in the days following the unveiling of the president's plan that a bipartisan majority in Congress was opposed to granting the secretary of defense significantly increased control over the defense budget and that to insist on that point would endanger the entire reform package. Therefore, the draft bill that Ike submitted to Congress did not include any provisions regarding the appropriations process. So that there would be no confusion on this point, Eisenhower wrote to the leaders of the House and Senate making his changed position clear.[47]

Because the president expected the fight over Pentagon reorganization to be long and difficult, he authorized the creation of a special legislative task force under the direction of Bryce Harlow. Its purpose was to influence legislative thinking and generate public support for the president's program. Harlow ran a high-powered, all-out campaign, personally contacting nationally important political figures, including former Presidents Hoover and Truman, in hopes of convincing them to endorse the president's plan. He also contacted former Secretary of War Robert Stevens, the head of J. P. Stevens and Co., one of Georgia's largest employers, urging him to work on Vinson. At Harlow's request members of the cabinet contacted friends and business associates seeking support.[48]

Harlow also created a special subcommittee under Oliver Gale, a former public relations man for Procter and Gamble, who was then serving as a special assistant to Secretary of Defense McElroy. Gale's group produced a legislative history of the original National Security Act. It also searched out past congressional testimony on the subjects of unification and military organization given by those currently in the administration so that when testifying before Congress these persons would not be caught up in contradictions. The Gale subcommittee also constructed a "black book" or "speaker's manual" that it used to provide useful information to "sympathetic columnists," to those who would be speaking on behalf of the president's program, and to those called upon to testify before congressional committees. The Gale group also monitored the House and Senate hearings and provided up-to-date summaries of testimony to those who were about to testify. The object here was to ensure consistency or if possible correct errors that had been made by earlier witnesses.[49]

The president kicked off his personal efforts on behalf of Pentagon reorganization on April 17, the day after the bill went to Congress, with a fighting speech before the American Society of Newspaper Editors. "Billions for defense but not one cent for needless waste," he told the newsmen. Americans deserved "safety with solvency," and he was determined to see that they got both. Responding to a charge that had been used repeatedly by opponents of reform, he categorically denied that his plan would create some sort of "monstrous general staff" or that there was anything "Prussian" about it. That was the sheerest nonsense, a "straw man" created by the enemies of reform to distract the public from the real issues. "We shall have neither military nor civilian Czars," he said. "The Secretary will stay directly under the President and Congress."[50]

On his evening broadcast the political commentator, Eric Severeid, was impressed with Ike's fervency. "Rarely," he said, "has the president delivered a sharper, franker speech. The vigor of his proposals was matched by the bleakness of the picture he painted of present Pentagon conditions." Severeid thought the president had "momentum" going his way and would probably be able "to get most of what he wants." Reflective of this, Lyndon Johnson, who had earlier scoffed at the idea of more reform legislation, now said: "I not only favor a complete reorganization and unification of the Defense Department, but I favor early consideration by the Congress of the recommendations which the president has made."[51]

While certain powerful Senate Democrats including Johnson and Richard Russell believed the wise course was to seek accommodation with the president, in the House of Representatives Carl Vinson did not appear to be similarly inclined. That became clear on April 22 when the House Armed Services Committee opened its hearings on the president's plan with Neil McElroy as its first witness.

According to the *New York Times,* the secretary of defense was greeted by "a hostile hail of questions" from Vinson.[52] Inadequately briefed by his staff and always too anxious to avoid confrontation, McElroy proved a poor witness for the administration and a boon to the opposition. Under questioning he took positions that were at variance with those Eisenhower himself used to explain why reform was necessary. For example, Ike insisted that interservice rivalry was a problem that could not be dealt with unless the system was changed fundamentally. When committee members questioned McElroy on the significance of interservice tensions, he responded in contradictory ways. At one point, he told the committee that rivalry did not exist. At another, he indicated that harmful interservice rivalry was caused by the congressional lobbying and public relations activities of the services, but that inside the Pentagon all was in harmony. On still another occasion, he said that he believed competition among the services was good for morale. He even told the committee that he already had "considerable power to correct inter-service rivalry under present law," leaving opponents of the bill free to ask why he did not use the power he already possessed instead of asking them to change the law.[53]

Again, although the president had repeatedly stated that by centralizing authority in the hands of the secretary of defense huge sums of money could be saved, McElroy told the committee that the bill would produce "no material dollar savings, save in the area of research and development." Nor did he strengthen the economic case for reform when he admitted that under the bill the Defense Department, which already employed more than 29,000 persons, was certain to expand further.[54]

When the secretary was not undermining the basic arguments favoring reform, he simply appeared confused. For example, he denied that the reorganization plan would significantly expand the powers of his office, claiming instead that it would merely clarify existing authority. At the same time he admitted under sharp questioning that given the unified command structure proposed in the bill, a secretary of defense might, if he chose, effectively abolish the separate services by assimilating all service personnel in those commands. In other words, the secretary of defense would, if the bill were passed, have the power to unify the armed forces by executive order.

Nor did McElroy seem at all adverse to letting Congress change key aspects of the bill. When committee members objected to the fact that under the bill the JCS and the service secretaries would not have the right to appeal directly to Congress when they opposed the secretary's policies, he told the committee that he would not object if Congress struck that provision from the bill. In an ill-advised attempt to pacify his questioners, he even agreed that the bill's wording was "unnecessarily broad" and expressed a willingness to allow congressional staffers to rewrite the bill. When Congressman Hebert asked incredulously: "You are not wedded to the language of the President's bill?" McElroy replied: "That is correct." "My approach is flexible."[55]

Writing in the *New York Times*, Russell Baker observed that Vinson had put the secretary to flight, that he was in full retreat and appeared willing to accept a sweeping rewrite of the bill. "The net effect of the Secretary's four-day appearance," Russell wrote, "was . . . a severe mauling for the letter of the President's bill."[56]

Eisenhower was in Augusta on a brief golfing vacation when he learned what McElroy had done. He told Ann Whitman that the secretary had made "a serious mistake" and that the problem now was "to get McElroy out of the box he is in without too much loss of face."[57] After thirty minutes on the telephone with the defense secretary, Ike dictated a statement to the press indicating there would be "no compromise on—or retreat from—the essentials of this legislation." Press Secretary Jim Haggarty then informed the White House press corps that McElroy "has confirmed to the President that no change in the meaning of any feature of the modernization program has been implied by any testimony of his." Haggarty also read a statement from McElroy in which he denied the accuracy of recent press reports and reiterated that with regard to the reorganization plan there would be no "retreat" and "no compromise in the objectives sought by that recommendation."[58]

To make certain that no one could possibly misunderstand his purposes, Ike followed this up with a surprise appearance at a Chamber of Commerce dinner where he told these leading businessmen that he would not accept any changes in his reorganization plan that would hamper his objectives by limiting the powers of the defense secretary. This country would spend itself into bankruptcy, he said, unless there was a "unified strategy" established "by a unified command under the Secretary of Defense." Only in that way could the country have "security with solvency." A week later he made the same point before the Washington Conference of the Advertising Council and in a radio speech to a meeting of the Republican National Committee.[59] Early in May, Eisenhower also sent letters to 450 of America's leading businessmen, urging them to do everything possible to support his plan for Pentagon reorganization. Thousands of letters poured in, no doubt influencing many in Congress, even, one suspects, Carl Vinson.[60]

McElroy's miscues were only the first in a series of embarrassments that Eisenhower suffered during the House Committee hearings. During his testimony General Twining, the chairman of the JCS, helped Vinson and other opponents of reform when, under intense questioning, he contradicted the president's claim that modern technologies made the old distinctions between the services obsolete. Chief of Naval Operations Admiral Arleigh Burke then expressed serious doubts about key aspects of the reorganization plan. Burke actually called on Congress to rewrite the bill. Marine Commandant Randolph McC. Pate, more hostile to the bill than any other military witness, supported only that part of the proposal that called for the centralization of research and development. Pate made no bones about it, telling the committee that the powers the bill vested in the secretary of defense might tempt some future secretary to "rationalize the Marine Corps out of a job," to give it "the bum's rush."[61]

As a result of the drubbing the administration had taken during the hearings, some believed the president had lost the battle. According to one Defense Department legislative analyst, witnesses who testified in support of the reorganization plan failed to make the administration's case or explain why change was necessary. Another summed the situation up this way: "The Defense Department Reorganization Bill has two chances—slim and none." In his judgment a "vast majority" of the committee opposed "the creation of a single joint staff or general staff." Moreover, the administration's efforts notwithstanding, they believed the bill would allow the secretary to create one. They also opposed reducing the powers of the service secretaries and the separate services, and feared that a powerful secretary of defense could unify the armed forces by transferring, abolishing, or consolidating roles and missions not assigned to the services by law.[62]

A vote count seemed to confirm the worst. Bryce Harlow could find only five of the thirty-seven members of the Armed Services Committee who supported the president. He assumed that Vinson, who ran his committee with an iron hand, would rewrite the bill and that it would contain many "severe restrictions" on the president.[63] Harlow was mistaken. The majority of Democrats, who controlled both houses of Congress, did not want to appear to be playing partisan politics with a grave national security issue. They wanted a bipartisan bill. Moreover, despite the nasty going-over that McElroy experienced, a majority in Congress agreed with the president that reforms were necessary.

On May 12, over the objections of a number of Republican members who apparently believed that the bill was destined for the rubbish heap, Carl Vinson adjourned the hearings. In doing so the chairman, his tongue no doubt planted firmly in his cheek, said that the committee had "sufficient information to make an intelligent decision" and that if he extended the hearings "the press and the country would say the Committee is engaged in dilatory tactics."

In fact, Vinson had decided to offer the president a compromise. On that same day he sent an amended version of the administration bill to the White House for the president's consideration. Harlow and McElroy both supported it as a reasonable compromise that, Harlow claimed, gave the president most of what he wanted.[64] Neither Eisenhower nor Robert Dechert, chief counsel for the Defense Department, was quite so sure. Dechert weighed in with a twenty-page single-spaced analysis of the amended bill that called for fourteen changes, two of which he considered to be of the "utmost importance."[65] Ike focused on the need to change three points in the House version of the bill, all of which tended to undermine the power of the secretary of defense.[66]

On May 16, Harlow came to the White House for a conference with the president. He brought with him a copy of the reorganization plan as amended by the Armed Services Committee, the draft of a public letter endorsing the bill as amended, and a warning from Vinson that unless he received such a letter signed by the president, the compromise bill would not be reported out of committee.[67] The letter congratulated Vinson and his committee for their "constructive efforts" at correcting "the main difficulties" that troubled the defense establishment, and for the "progress" they had made in creating "a sound defense structure." It also stated that the amended bill "by and large" dealt "positively with every major problem I presented to the Congress."

A "leery" Eisenhower signed the letter but only after removing some of the more congratulatory remarks from the text. He also added a paragraph in which he noted that he still had certain problems with the bill, two of which were "quite important," and that he would be sending a member of his staff to negotiate further with Vinson.[68] The Georgian quickly released the letter. However, in subsequent discussions with Harlow he refused to make any further concessions. Vinson had "reached the point," Harlow wrote, "where he believes he should not change the bill any further."[69] On May 21, the House Armed Services Committee voted 36–0 to send the amended reorganization plan to the House floor.

Eisenhower, who had been outmaneuvered, felt betrayed. He was angry with the Republican members of the committee, who, by supporting the revised measure, made it appear that it had his support. He was angry with Vinson, who he believed had deceived him. Finally, he was angry with himself for having sent that congratulatory letter to Vinson in the first place.

The House Committee's action left Ike with a set of unattractive options. He could endorse the Committee's bill, which he considered badly flawed, or he could fight for amendments on the floor of the House. Though he was bound to appear grossly inconsistent since he had just publicly congratulated the House Armed Services Committee on its work, he decided to make a fight of it.[70]

On May 28 Eisenhower issued a strongly worded press release attacking the committee's version of the reorganization plan, which, he said, continued "to emphasize disunity and separatism within the Defense Department." He insisted that language in the bill that required the secretary of defense to exercise his authority "through the respective Secretaries" of the armed services should be stricken. It was a "legalized bottleneck" that limited the secretary's authority, placed "a premium on intransigence by lower level Pentagon officials," and if implemented would "block normal staff processes" and cause "administrative chaos." To retain this language, he said, would give "frictions, delays, duplications in the Defense Department . . . the color of legality."

Ike also opposed a clause in the bill that allowed Congress to block by concurrent resolution any action taken by the secretary of defense to make changes in the combat functions of the services. He was particularly incensed because the House version of the bill authorized any individual service secretary or member of the JCS to initiate such action by going over the secretary's head and appealing directly to Congress. This "everyone's out of step but me" provision, he said, undermined civilian authority as well as the "concept of flexibility of combatant functions." In like fashion he attacked another provision in the bill that allowed any member of the JCS or service secretary to appeal any decision taken by the secretary of defense directly to Congress. This, he said, was a form of "legalized insubordination" that would further undermine the defense secretary's authority. "It invites inter-service rivalry, insubordination to the President and Secretary of Defense; endorses the idea of disunity and blocking of defense modernization; suggests that Congress hopes for disobedience and inter-service rivalries; is a bad concept, bad practice, and bad influence on the Pentagon."[71]

Eisenhower's hard-hitting press release touched off an angry partisan debate. The Texas Democrat, Paul Kilday, told Stuart Symington that he was truly miffed. He had worked with Harlow and Vinson to produce a bill Ike could sign, and believed he had succeeded until the president publicly denounced their work. House Democrats became even more incensed at what followed. First, Harlow sent every Republican member of the House a copy of the bill, a set of proposed amendments designed to meet the president's criticisms, and a plea from Eisenhower for party solidarity. Immediately after this House Republicans caucused. The Republican floor leader, Joseph P. Martin of Massachusetts, then announced that 95 percent of the Republicans in the House would vote in favor of the president's amendments.

The decision to transform the debate over Pentagon reorganization into a partisan issue turned out badly for the president. Sam Rayburn of Texas accused the Republicans of "corralling votes on a partisan basis to crush the Armed Services Committee." Carl Vinson added to the furor by charging that it was the first time in his forty years in the House that a national security issue had become "a subject of partisan politics." It is not surprising, then, that each of the president's proposed changes in the Armed Services Committee's bill went down to defeat by an almost strict party vote of 211–192. Only twenty Democrats supported the president while 15 Republicans went the other way.[72]

On June 17, one day after the House passed its version of the Defense Department Reorganization Act, the Senate Armed Services Committee, chaired by another powerful Georgian, Senator Richard Russell, opened hearings on the measure. This would be the administration's final chance to make changes in the House-passed bill. The opportunity was there since, despite the recent political debacle in the House, Russell wanted a bill the president could sign, one that would pass muster as a work of bipartisanship. The Senate hearings were hardly under way, however, before a long-smoldering issue suddenly caught fire. From the beginning, it had been rumored that the president was attempting to prevent high-ranking military officers from offering their honest opinions regarding reform. The issue had come up during the House hearings and it arose again during Secretary McElroy's testimony before the Senate Armed Services Committee. Senators Henry Jackson of Washington, Margaret Chase Smith of Maine, and Sam Ervin, Jr., of North Carolina all appeared to be concerned about this. "Frankly," Jackson told McElroy, "it is a pretty difficult situation right now to get information directly from the services because they are under compulsion not to talk to you about it." When an apparently startled McElroy reacted by saying that he had no intention of muzzling the military, Jackson replied that the threats came not from him but from the White House.[73]

Two days after this, with the issue out in the open, Chief of Naval Operations Admiral Arleigh Burke testified in support of the House-passed bill and in opposition to amendments recommended by the president. Burke told the committee that he believed the defense secretary should be required to exercise his authority "through the service secretaries" and that Congress would be wise to place strict limitations on the secretary's power to merge, transfer, or abolish "major combatant functions." Congress, he said, should "leave the business of strategic planning and operational guidance to the Joint Chiefs of Staff—the business of fighting to the combatant commanders, and the business of administration and support to the military departments." He thought that in these regards the bill passed by the House "can work well."[74]

Immediately following Burke's appearance before the Senate Committee the *New York Times* published the first of two stories that caused an eruption on Capitol Hill. Hanson Baldwin, the military columnist for the *Times* whose connection to high-ranking naval personnel was well known, reported on the substance of a recent private meeting that took place between McElroy and the JCS.[75] At this meeting, Baldwin reported, the defense secretary informed the chiefs that the president was extremely angry about the changes the House had made in his reorganization proposal and that during the upcoming Senate hearings he expected them to provide "active" and not merely "passive support" when testifying. The rest of Baldwin's story detailed other ways in which the administration had allegedly attempted to influence witnesses appearing before the House and Senate committees. He described the Gale committee's "little black books" in which were summarized "arguments and statistics" that witnesses were to use in support of the president's plan. He also noted that the administration monitored the hearings and claimed that in some instances witnesses had been asked to change their testimony. Some officers, Baldwin claimed, were considered so unreliable that they had been placed under surveillance "by civilian intelligence operatives." The pressure on officers to conform to the administration line, he wrote, was "without any recent precedent."[76]

One day after Baldwin's piece appeared, the *Times* reported on a press conference McElroy held during which he told reporters that he was "disappointed" in Admiral Burke's recent testimony. "I think he is a fine officer," he said, but "he is mistaken in this respect." McElroy would have been wise to stop there. According to the *Times*, while he denied that he had any plans to discipline Burke, he added that he was "not the only one responsible for the admiral's future." He reminded the reporters that the president, who was the commander in chief, wanted amendments to the House bill. "The Chief should make his own decision about his testimony in the light of that fact."[77]

When accused of attempting to intimidate Burke and discourage other officers from expressing their honest convictions, McElroy claimed that he had been misquoted. However, Senator Russell, who read the entire transcript of McElroy's news conference, thought that the "clear implication" of his remarks was that officers "must conform or be purged." He suspended the hearings and refused to reconvene them until he had received written assurances from McElroy and the White House that witnesses would be allowed to testify "in complete candor without being threatened overtly or covertly."[78] McElroy's blunder transformed the issue of "legalized insubordination" into the most controversial of the three proposed changes that Eisenhower sought in the House-approved measure. After this, neither house of Congress was in any mood to give in to the president on this issue.

At a meeting of Republican legislative leaders held immediately following these developments, Senators William Knowland of California and Leverett Saltonstall told the president that he was not going to get all the changes he sought in the House-passed measure. Eisenhower, who judged that the moment for compromise had arrived, replied that the first two of his three proposed changes "were the ones with real substance," that the third "was more a matter of 'the spirit' than it was really essential." [79]

Four days later, this message having been carried to the Democratic leadership in the Senate, Ike received a call from McElroy. Stuart Symington, a member of the Senate Armed Services Committee and a firm advocate of unification, wanted to bring him back for further Senate testimony. According to Symington, a majority of the committee was prepared to support other changes the president sought in the House-passed bill if he would abandon his call for an end to "legalized insubordination." McElroy wanted instructions. Ike authorized him to make the necessary concession.

Once the president indicated his willingness to abandon the third of the three points then in dispute, Senator Russell adjourned the hearings and together with Harlow and Dechert got down to the business of negotiating a compromise Eisenhower could support.[80] The issue that most concerned the president was a stipulation in the House version of the bill that stated that the secretary of defense would, as in the past, exercise his power "through the respective secretaries of the departments." Administration witnesses claimed that this clause in the law had been repeatedly used by service secretaries to disrupt the proper functioning of the department, to sidetrack and/or undermine the policies of the secretary of defense. However, they had never been able to provide compelling evidence of this. Never that is until, Charles Coolidge recalled, an assistant secretary of defense produced "the complete chapter and verse on several instances where the services used this aspect of the law to defeat constructive moves by the Secretary of Defense." According to Coolidge, Russell, who was impressed, said: "Why, this is mutiny! We can't have this go on!"[81] Whether this story is true or not, Russell's committee removed the offending clause from the

House version of the bill thus removing the service departments from any role in policy formulation. "We tried to make it very clear," Russell told the press, "that the Secretary of Defense is the supreme officer in the Department of Defense."[82]

Russell was less willing to give ground on the remaining issue, the question of the secretary's right to change or alter "major combat functions." This clause in the Senate bill, which some viewed as more stringent than the House version, stipulated that any proposal to "merge, transfer, or abolish a major combatant function" would have to be submitted to the two armed services committees. The proposal would die if, within thirty days, a majority of either committee objected and if within the next forty days one house of Congress passed a resolution opposing the move. Moreover, the Senate version of the bill sought to quiet the fears of those who suspected that some future secretary of defense would use his power to threaten the Marines, the Navy's air arm, and the National Guard by adding language to the bill specifically protecting these organizations.[83]

On July 18 the Senate voted 80–0 in favor of the Senate version of the reorganization plan. A few days later a Senate-House Conference Committee produced a bill considerably closer to the Senate than the House version. While not ecstatic, Eisenhower was willing to sign the bill, which he said "adequately meets every recommendation I submitted to the Congress on this subject."[84]

The Defense Reorganization Act of 1958 fell considerably short of the president's true ambitions. At the same time, it was a major legislative achievement, the culmination of years of effort on Eisenhower's part to bring a greater degree of unity to the military establishment by focusing power in the hands of the secretary of defense while weakening the individual services. First, the law made it absolutely clear that the services, though "separately organized," operated under the "direction, authority and control of the Secretary of Defense." Service secretaries no longer had any basis upon which to oppose or place obstacles in the way of policies decided upon at a higher level. They had become mere administrators with no role to play in policy formulation.

The power of the secretary was further enhanced by three other complementary provisions of the law. The first established a set of unified commands whose commanding officers had absolute authority over all ground, naval, and air forces under their control.[85] The second denied the services and individual members of the JCS any authority over the unified commands by eliminating the service secretaries from the chain of command, which, under the new law, ran directly from the defense secretary to the individual commands. The third granted the secretary the power, admittedly subject to congressional review, to abolish, modify, or consolidate "major combatant functions." In effect the secretary, not the separate services, had the power to determine down to the last detail the force structure of each of the unified commands.

Among the most important aspects of the new law was a provision designed to end waste and duplication in the expanding area of weapons research and development. In his book, *The Race to Oblivion*, Dr. Herbert York, Eisenhower's first director of Defense Research and Engineering, observed that in the mid-1950s the services were engaged in a fierce struggle to determine "who would get the juiciest and sexiest roles and missions in long range missilry and, ultimately, in space." As a result of this uncontrolled competition, by the time Sputnik came along, the services were working on six separate missile programs where three—Titan, Minuteman, and Polaris—would have been appropriate. At the same time each service was also working independently on its own artificial satellite program. "As a result," York has written, "we spent about twice as much money and we employed about twice as many people on these development programs as we should have." The 1958 Defense Reorganization Act was designed "to cope with the kind of frantic struggles for new roles and missions that had followed in the wake of Sputnik." It created the post of director of Defense Research and Engineering whose responsibility it was "to supervise and direct all research that required central direction." He alone had the power to approve and disapprove research and development projects and to decide which of the services could undertake a given project.

If, acting through the director, the secretary could end competition in the areas of research and development, the law also gave him the power to decide which of the "departments or services" would control "the development and operational use of new weapons or weapons systems." This provision gave the secretary the last word on an issue that in the past had always been the sole prerogative of professional military men. He had the power to decide how the individual services would be armed.

This is not to say that the 1958 law produced all of the changes that Eisenhower believed essential to sound and economical military planning. Congress made it clear almost from the start of the debate that it would not turn control over funding for defense to the secretary. Moreover, the Joint Chiefs of Staff system, with all of its inadequacies, continued in place. While the act strengthened the chairman of the JCS, by no means did it transform him into the powerful chief of staff that Eisenhower thought so vital.

How significant were the changes brought about by the Defense Reorganization Act of 1958? If one were to make a judgment based on the remaining thirty months of Eisenhower's second term, one might be tempted to say, very little. In fact, however, Eisenhower had managed to create a highly centralized organization that placed enormous power in the hands of the secretary of defense. The fact that this power went largely unused during the remainder of his tenure in office had more to do with the men who held the office of secretary of defense than with the power at their disposal. Neil McElroy glided through the remainder of his two years in office, a charming but ineffective man anxious to avoid making enemies. Thomas Gates, the former secretary of the navy who followed him, showed somewhat more interest in exercising these new powers. Thus, for example, in 1959 when the Air Force and the Navy proved unable to agree on an integrated targeting policy as part of an overall Integrated War Plan, Gates imposed a new command arrangement that, much to Admiral Arleigh Burke's annoyance, subordinated the Navy to the Strategic Air Command.[86] However, Gates did not hold office long enough, nor did he have the personal and intellectual skills, to truly test the expanded powers of the office. That was left for Robert S. McNamara, who, courtesy of years of effort on the part of Dwight Eisenhower, for better and worse, came to the Pentagon fully empowered to bring about what came to be known as "the McNamara Revolution."

NOTES

1. For the best and most complete analysis of Eisenhower's reaction to the Sputnik crisis see Robert A. Divine, *The Sputnik Challenge* (New York: Oxford University Press, 1993). See also Richard A. Aliano, *American Defense Policy from Eisenhower to Kennedy* (Athens: Ohio University Press, 1975).

2. Andrew Goodpaster, memorandum of a White House conference, 26 Oct. 1957, Whitman File, Diary Series, Box 27, Eisenhower Library (hereafter cited as Goodpaster Memcon, and EL). See also Goodpaster Memcon, 8 Oct. 1957, White House Office of the Staff Secretary, Defense Department Sub-series, Box 1, EL. During his last private meeting with outgoing Defense Secretary Charles Wilson, the president remarked that "the probably sound course of action would be to abolish the Army, Navy, Air Force and Marines and go to task forces under defense." Ike thought it would probably take another twenty years to achieve this, however. Other fine histories of the Reorganization Act of 1958 are Robert J. Watson, *The History of the Office of Secretary of Defense*, vol. 4 (Washington, DC: Historical Office of the Office of Secretary of Defense, 1997) and Divine, *The Sputnik Challenge*, 128–143. See also Dwight David Eisenhower, *Waging Peace: The White House Years, 1956–1961* (Garden City: Doubleday, 1965),

244–54; Douglas Kinnard, *The Secretary of Defense* (Lexington: University of Kentucky Press, 1980), 62–65.

3. Divine, *The Sputnik Challenge*, 19–21, 68–70; Watson, *History of the Office of the Secretary of Defense*, 4:148. Ultimately Eisenhower felt compelled to increase his 1959 budget recommendation to $39.6 billion.

4. Goodpaster Memcon, 31 Oct. 1957, White House Office of the Staff Secretary, Defense Department Sub-series, Box 1, EL.

5. Ibid.; Neil McElroy, Oral History, 74, EL.

6. Goodpaster Memcon, 28 Oct. 1957, White House Office of the Staff Secretary, Miscellaneous Series, Box 1, EL; Rockefeller, "Notes on the Reorganization of the Department of Defense," ibid. This paper was part of a Rockefeller Brothers Fund Report on National Security Issues that was published in full in April 1958. See the *New York Times* (hereafter cited as *NYT*), 6 Jan. 1958.

7. Notes on the Reorganization of the Department of Defense, n.d., in White House Office of the Staff Secretary, Miscellaneous Series, Box 1 EL, 8–14; Goodpaster Memcon, 31 Oct. 1957, Whitman File, Diary Series, Box 27, EL. The Joint Staff suffered from the same problem that often paralyzed the JCS, vicious partisan infighting that often made it impossible to arrive at a consensus. Ike wanted it replaced by a staff that would be organized functionally. Each section would be headed by a single individual. This officer would provide the JCS with "a single recommendation" but might also take note of an objection by other staff officers if the view was strongly held. The point, though, was that the staff should be able to produce consensus recommendations—not split papers. The object, Ike said, was to develop a staff with a "national outlook so that when the Chiefs ask for an answer they get, not what each service thinks, but what highly selected, highly intelligent men think to be the best solution."

8. Goodpaster, memorandum for the record and attachments, 28 Oct. 1957, White House Office of the Staff Secretary, Miscellaneous Series, Box 1, EL.

9. Goodpaster Memcon, 4 Nov. 1957, Whitman File, Diary Series, Box 28, EL; "Defense Organization: Propositions and Questions," ibid.

10. Rockefeller and Brundage to Eisenhower, 15 Nov. 1957, Whitman File, Administration Series, Box 25, EL. Rockefeller and Brundage recommended Dr. James Killian, White House science advisor, former Secretary of Defense Robert Lovett, former Deputy Secretary of Defense William Foster, General Alfred Gruenther, former Chairman of the JCS Admiral Arthur Radford, and General James McCormack to be members of the advisory committee.

11. Brundage and Rockefeller to Eisenhower, 15 Nov. 1957, Whitman File, Administration Series, Box 25, EL.

12. Goodpaster, memorandum for the record, 27 Nov. 1957, White House Office of the Staff Secretary, Miscellaneous Series, Box 1, EL; Eisenhower, memorandum for the record, 4 Dec. 1957, Whitman File, Administration Series, Box 25, EL.

13. Watson, *History of the Office of the Secretary of Defense*, 4:249.

14. *The Public Papers of the Presidents: Dwight David Eisenhower, 1958* (Washington DC: GPO, 1960), 8–9; Divine, *The Sputnik Challenge*, 80–89.

15. Whitman, memorandum for the record, 31 Dec. 1957, Administration Series, Box 10, EL. Supplementary notes on a legislative leadership meeting, 14 Jan. 1958, Whitman File, Diary Series, Box 30, EL.

16. Goodpaster Memcon, 6 Nov. 1957, Diary Series, Box 28, EL; *NYT*, 6 Jan. 1958. A complete copy of the report may be found in the Harlow Papers, Box 20, EL.

17. *NYT*, 5, 6, and 26, Jan. 1958.

18. H.R. 11001 was introduced on February 26, 1958. Vinson and Arends introduced similar proposals (H.R. 11002 and 11003) immediately thereafter.

19. *NYT*, 3, 5, 12, and 16 Jan. 1958. For the thinking of the Coolidge Commission on the question of a single chief of staff and reforming the JCS, see Coolidge, "For the President," 27 Feb. 1958, White House, Office of the Staff Secretary, Department of Defense Sub-series, Box 1, EL.

20. *NYT*, 12 and 15 Jan. 1958. The fact that the chiefs opposed any changes in their organization came as no surprise to Eisenhower, who discovered that firsthand at a White House stag dinner on November 4. See Goodpaster Memcon, 6 Nov. 1957, Whitman File, Diary Series, Box 28, EL.

21. Charles Coolidge, Oral History, 6, EL. For Rockefeller's notes on some of these meetings, see Memoranda for the record for the meetings of 22, 25, and 27–28 Jan. and 4 Feb. 1958, in the President's Advisory Committee on Government Organization, Box 18, EL.

22. Goodpaster Memcon, 10 Jan. 1958, Whitman File, Diary Series, Box 30, EL; Telephone conversation between Rockefeller and Eisenhower, 20 Jan. 1958, ibid.; Rockefeller to McElroy, 24 Jan. 1958, White House Office of the Staff Secretary, Miscellaneous Series, Box 1, EL.

23. Ibid.; see also Diary entry, 20 Jan. 1958, Ann Whitman Diary, Box 9, EL.

24. Ibid., 21 and 28, Jan. 1958. According to Whitman, General Bradley was in favor of going further in the direction of unification than Eisenhower thought feasible at the time.

25. Diary entry, 25 Jan. 1958, Ann Whitman Diary, Box 9, EL; Harlow, memorandum for the record, 30 Jan. 1958, Whitman File, Diary Series, Box 30; Legislative Leadership Meeting, 28 Jan. 1958, ibid.; Douglas Kinnard, *Secretary of Defense* (Lexington: University of Kentucky Press, 1980), 212.

26. Charles Coolidge, Oral History, 6, EL.

27. Coolidge's memorandum for the president, 27 Feb. 1958, White House, Office of the Staff Secretary, Box 1, EL; NSC discussion, 28 March 1958, Whitman File, NSC Series, Box 10, EL.

28. Goodpaster Memcon, 28 Feb. 1958, White House Office of the Staff Secretary, Box 1, EL; Goodpaster Memcon, 12 March 1958, Whitman File, Diary Series, Box 31, EL; Rockefeller, notes, 26 March 1958, Presidential Advisory

Committee on Defense Department Reorganization, Box 1, EL; Charles Coolidge, Oral History, 7, EL.

29. Eisenhower to Lodge, Whitman File, Administration Series, Box 24, EL; Diary entries, 29–30 March 1958, Ann Whitman Diary, Box 9, EL; Diary entry, 2 April 1958, ibid., Box 10, EL.; Adams, *First Hand Report* (New York: Harper, 1961), 418–21.

30. Diary entry, 28 and 31 March 1958, Ann Whitman Diary, Box 9, EL; Legislative Leadership Meeting, 1 April 1958, Whitman File, Legislative Meeting Series, Box 3, EL.

31. *Public Papers of the Presidents: Dwight D. Eisenhower, 1958,* 274–88.

32. Adams, *Firsthand Report,* 405.

33. *Public Papers of the Presidents: Dwight D. Eisenhower, 1958,* 274–88.

34. Ibid., 282–86; *Newsweek,* 14 April 1958, 34.

35. Ibid.; see also Charles Coolidge, Oral History, 11, EL.

36. Ibid.; *NYT,* 5 April 1958; McElroy, memorandum for General Goodpaster, 16 April 1958, Papers of Bryce Harlow, Box 2, EL.

37. NSC discussion, 27 March 1958, Whitman File, NSC Series, Box 10, EL.

38. *NYT,* 6 and 23, Feb. and 7 April 1958; *Wall Street Journal,* 19 Feb. 1958; *New York Mirror,* 20 March 1958.

39. *New York Herald Tribune,* 18 April 1958; *Los Angeles Times,* 4 April 1958; *Kansas City Star,* 12 April 1958.

40. *NYT,* 7 April 1958.

41. *NYT,* 5 April 1958.

42. *Newsweek,* 14 April 1958.

43. *NYT,* 21 April 1958.

44. *Newsweek,* 21 April 1958.

45. Ibid.; *New York Daily News,* 11 April 1958.

46. Stans, memorandum for the president, 16 April 1958, White House Central Files, Office Files, Box 111, EL; Dechert to Stans, 10 April 1958, Papers of Bryce Harlow, Box 1, EL.

47. Goodpaster Memcon, 10 April 1958, Papers of Bryce Harlow, Box 2, EL; *Public Papers of the Presidents, 1958,* 313; *NYT,* 17and 19 April 1958. At a press conference held on the day the bill was submitted to Congress, Eisenhower observed that his April 3 message had been misinterpreted, that he was seeking only greater flexibility for the secretary of defense regarding the use of funds.

48. Harlow to Robert T. Stevens, 12 April 1958, Harlow Papers, Box 1, EL; undated form letters from Postmaster General Arthur Summerfield and Commerce Secretary Sinclair Weeks may be found in ibid., Box 2; Harlow to Clarence Francis, 9 May 1958, ibid.; Harlow to Louis H. Renfrow, undated draft, ibid.; Goodpaster Memcon, 24 April 1958, Whitman File, Diary Series, Box 32, EL. For the letter that the president sent to his many business friends see the *NYT,* 12 May 1958.

49. Memorandum for the record, n.d., Papers of Bryce Harlow, Box 2, EL; Suspense memorandum, ibid. For a copy of the speaker's manual see ibid., Box 1. The book was divided into thirteen parts: Background Material, Actions under Presidential Directive, General Policy and Intent, Strength and Authority of the Secretary of Defense, Establishing Unified Commands, Strengthening the Military Staff for Planning and Operations, The Administrative Role of the Three Military Departments, Reorganizing Research and Development Functions, Inter-service Transfer of Officers, The Roles of Assistant Secretaries, Miscellaneous Questions, Specific Congressional Questions, and Summaries of Hearings.

50. "Speech to the American Society of Newspaper Editors," 17 April, in *Public Papers of the Presidents, 1958*, 327–33.

51. Congressional Record, 85th Cong., 2nd sess., vol. 104:4, 3903–3904; *Newsweek*, 28 April 1958.

52. *NYT*, 23 April 1958.

53. U.S. Congress, House Committee on Armed Services, *Hearings on the Reorganization of the Defense Department*, 85th Cong., 2nd sess., 6048.

54. Ibid., 6037–39. See also a summary of McElroy's testimony as viewed by Bryce Harlow's observer at the hearings, 22–25 April 1958, Harlow Papers, Box 2, EL.

55. U.S. Congress, House Committee on Armed Services, *Hearings on the Reorganization of the Defense Department*, 85th Cong., 2nd sess., 6037–39; Harlow, memorandum for the record, 27 April 1958, White House, Office of the Staff Secretary, Box 7, EL.

56. Ibid., 25 and 26, April 1958. When Eisenhower, who was on vacation at the time, discovered what McElroy had done, he called the secretary. The two men agreed that there could be no "compromise on or retreat from the essentials of this legislation." McElroy issued a clarification that was apparently drafted for him by General Goodpaster. See Memorandum, n.d., White House Office of the Staff Secretary, Miscellaneous Series, Box 1, EL.

57. Ann Whitman Diary, 25 April 1958, Box 10, EL.

58. Unsigned memorandum, White House Office of the Staff Secretary, Miscellaneous, Series, Box 1, EL; Memorandum for the record, 27 May 1958, Papers of Bryce Harlow, Box 2, EL; *NYT*, 27 April 1958; Adams, *Firsthand Report*, 418–21.

59. Unsigned memoranda, n.d., White House Office of the Staff Secretary, Miscellaneous Series, Box 1, EL; Adams, *Firsthand Report*, 418–20. For a different view of McElroy, see Divine, *The Sputnik Challenge*, 134; *Public Papers of the Presidents, 1958*, 30 April 1958, 362–65; ibid., 6 May 1958, 373–74, 379–380.

60. U.S. Congress, House Committee on the Armed Services, *Hearings on the Reorganization of the Defense Department*, 85th Cong., 2d sess., 6037–39; *NYT*, 12 May 1958.

61. *NYT*, 1 and 2 May 1958; E. B. Potter, *Admiral Arleigh Burke* (New York: Random House, 1990), 414–25.

62. Col. F. B. Bounds, memorandum, n.d., Papers of Bryce Harlow, Box 2, EL; Notes on reorganization hearings before the House Armed Services Committee, ibid.; Harlow to Bendetsen, 12 May 1958, Papers of Bryce Harlow, Box 2, ibid. See also *NYT*, 29 April 1958.

63. Ibid.

64. Diary entry, 16 May 1958, Ann Whitman Diary, Box 10, EL.

65. Ibid., 14 May 1958; Harlow to Stevens, 20 May 1958, Papers of Bryce Harlow, Box 2, EL; outline summary of Dechert's memorandum, n.d., Papers of Bryce Harlow, Box 1, EL.

66. *NYT*, 17 May 1958.

67. Diary entry, 24 June 1958, Ann Whitman Papers, Box 10, EL.

68. *NYT*, 17 May 1958; Diary entry, 20 June 1958, Ann Whitman Papers, Box 10, EL; Eisenhower to Arthur Krock, 30 May 1958, Whitman File, Diary Series, Box 33, EL.

69. *NYT*, 17 and 28 May 1958; Harlow to Stevens, 20 May 1958, Papers of Bryce Harlow, Box 2, EL.

70. *NYT*, 30 May 1958. In his column of this date the well-known columnist, Arthur Krock, suggested that Dechert, Foster, and Harlow had convinced Eisenhower to fight for the changes he sought. Harlow seems unlikely to have been instrumental in this. Dechert clearly had problems with the amended bill, and William Foster, who was close to Eisenhower, shared his views on the importance of reform.

71. Press release, 28 May 1958, Whitman File, Diary Series, Box 32, EL; *NYT*, 29 May 1958; *Newsweek*, 9 June 1958.

72. *NYT*, 13 June 1958.

73. U.S. Congress, Senate Armed Services Committee, *Hearings on Defense Department Reorganization*, 85th Cong., 2nd sess., 50.

74. Ibid.

75. Goodpaster Memcon, 23 June 1958, White House, Office of the Staff Secretary, Box 4, EL.

76. *NYT*, 21 June 1958.

77. Ibid., 22 June 1958.

78. Ibid., 24 and 25 June 1958; *Wall Street Journal*, 25 June 1958.

79. Legislative Leadership Meeting, 24 June 1958, Whitman File, Diary Series, Box 33, EL.

80. Stuart Symington's relationship with the president had its ups and downs over the years. They had been close until Eisenhower became president. Then, Symington became one of Ike's foremost partisan critics. However, Symington, a successful businessman before turning to politics, had always believed the military could be run much more efficiently and proved a staunch supporter of the president's reorganization proposal.

81. Charles Coolidge, Oral History, 9, EL; Symington to Amberg, 3 July 1958, Symington Papers, Alphabetical/subject list, Box 32, Western Manuscripts Division, Missouri State Historical Society.

82. *NYT*, 16 July 1958.

83. Ibid. The act also granted members of the JCS and the service secretaries the right of appeal. Moreover, assistant secretaries of defense could only issue orders to military departments if such authority was first delegated by the secretary of defense.

84. Ibid., 24 July 1958.

85. Sad to say, in the years that followed the individual services found means of undermining the power of the unified commands.

86. Thomas Gates, Oral History, EL.

Epilogue

"In Our System Clausewitz Would Probably Make Full Colonel, Retire in 20 Years, and Go to Work for a Think Tank."

The 1958 Reorganization Act did not produce all of the changes that Eisenhower thought essential. He took what he could get from a Congress that, on this issue, was dominated by Carl Vinson and Richard Russell, men not yet ready to accept many of the changes he advocated. Thus, the JCS went unreformed while the services remained distinct and separate, their roles and missions ill-defined and the subject of ongoing dispute. The struggle between the services for resources continued, and interservice cooperation remained more fantasy than fact. Nevertheless, if Ike failed to achieve all of the changes he sought, he left a legacy in the form of a set of ideas that a later generation of reformers found compelling.

Twenty-four years after the enactment of the 1958 Reorganization Act, Air Force General David Jones, the first sitting chairman of the JCS to do so, picked up the torch that Eisenhower had left burning. In February 1982, over the objections of Secretary of Defense Caspar Weinberger and much of the rest of the Pentagon establishment, Jones issued a blistering critique of the JCS as an organization, which, because of service parochialism, was incapable of providing the president with sound military advice. While denying that it was his intent to destroy the JCS per se, he nevertheless argued that Congress should endow the chairman with considerably more power than he then enjoyed. Like Eisenhower before him, Jones warned that decision making by committee was not in the national interest and called for the abolition of a system that granted each service a veto over decisions taken by the military leadership. He warned, too, that the members of the JCS spent too much time fighting over budget allocations and available resources, and too little time on joint strategic planning. "In our system," he acidly remarked, Carl von Clausewitz, the great nineteenth-century Prussian military strategist, "would probably make full colonel, retire in 20 years, and go to work for a think tank." It was time, Jones believed, for the services to break down the barriers that separated them. Officers from all branches, he argued, should work together planning and preparing for the joint missions in which all would inevitably participate.[1]

Jones was joined in his criticism of the JCS by Army Chief of Staff General Edward Meyer, who also called for sweeping changes. Echoing the thinking of Eisenhower and other reformers who had searched in vain for some method of providing the secretary of defense with advice that did not represent narrow service interests, or was not the result of interservice log-rolling, Meyer sought to reignite interest in an idea that had been first proposed in 1952 by Robert Lovett. He called for the creation of a new independent military advisory group for the secretary, a panel of four-star officers who would, on completing their tour, go into permanent retirement and would therefore, at least theoretically, be less inclined to represent their service interest when offering counsel.[2]

Neither Jones's scathing review of the JCS system nor Meyer's recommendations had any immediate impact. However, by 1985 circumstances had changed. First, in the early 1980s the Pentagon experienced a series of procurement scandals involving some highly publicized corrupt practices on the part of defense contractors. For a time the press was filled with stories of ashtrays that cost the taxpayers hundreds of dollars, $640 toilet seats, and the like. These reports, combined with the fact that the Reagan administration was running huge deficits while at the same time lavishing money on the military, produced increased support for reform.

During this same period the military experienced a series of embarrassing fiascoes that raised questions about its ability to function effectively and further encouraged the impulse toward reform. In 1980 came the aborted attempt to rescue the American hostages being held in the American embassy compound in Teheran, Iran. Operation Eagle Claw fell apart not only because of difficulties implicit in the operation itself, but also because of inadequate coordination and planning on the part of the services involved. In 1983 two more embarrassing incidents occurred. The first was the successful terrorist attack on a Marine barracks in Beirut, Lebanon, that left 241 marines dead. The second was the botched invasion of the little Caribbean nation of Granada in which more than 7,000 soldiers and Marines took more than three days to overcome fifty Cuban troops and a few hundred lightly armed construction workers.

Another factor strengthening the reform movement had to do with a change that took place in Congress. In January 1985, Republican Senator Barry Goldwater of Arizona, a champion of reform, became chairman of the Senate Armed Services Committee. Georgia's Sam Nunn, the ranking minority member and the leading Democratic expert on military affairs, also supported change. "Nunn and I concluded," Goldwater later wrote, "that so long as the JCS continued with a weak joint system—a single-service rather than a joint perspective—our divided planning and structuring of the armed forces could lead the nation into terrible trouble in the future."[3]

Over the strong opposition of the Navy Department, Goldwater and Nunn forged legislation that picked up where Eisenhower had left off in 1958. The Goldwater-Nichols bill, which passed the Senate and House almost unopposed, strengthened the secretary of defense by granting him "sole and ultimate power within the Department of Defense on any matter on which the Secretary chooses to act." More important, the bill took a significant step toward creating the chief of staff of the armed forces that Eisenhower had argued for thirty years before. Under the new law many functions formerly performed by the JCS were vested in the chairman. For example, he alone became the principal military advisor to the president and the secretary, thus freeing him from service parochialism when advising the civilian leadership. The act also provided the chairman with the staff support he required by granting him absolute control over the Joint Staff. The law thus forged a partnership between a secretary of defense who was supreme on the civilian side of the Pentagon and a new and more powerful chairman, and gave to the secretary what Eisenhower had long advocated, an advisor who would bring unambiguous advice to the executive branch and who would, hopefully, be above narrow service prejudices.

If there was a single theme that Eisenhower had emphasized over all others, it had been that the days of separate land, sea, and air operations were over and that in future the services would have to work and plan together as a team. Goldwater and Nunn advanced this cause in a variety of ways. First, the 1986 Defense Reorganization Act provided the unified commanders with far greater control over the military resources they would require than they had previously enjoyed. They were further strengthened by a change in the Defense Department's organizational structure that had them bypass the JCS entirely and report directly to the secretary of defense.

The law was also designed to foster joint planning and cooperation. In 1958 Ike had issued an executive order making joint work a requirement for promotion to flag rank. After he left office the idea of interservice cooperation languished. By the mid-1980s as Sam Nunn put it, the military was "a group of all-stars who are not accustomed to planning together and playing together on the same team."[4] Now Congress made it a binding rule. The Goldwater-Nichols Act actually created "a career specialty for officers on joint duty assignment," stipulated that future promotions would depend on a record of joint duty, and required that when officers on joint duty assignment came up for promotion, senior officers already serving on joint duty must sit as part of the panel considering the candidate's record. The law also stipulated that no officer lacking such a record could be appointed to a top position. The law further required the services to engage in joint planning for a series of clearly defined missions including "nuclear deterrence, maritime superiority, general power projection superiority, defense of NATO Europe, defense of East Asia, and defense of Southeast Asia." The object was to create a military establishment that, as Eisenhower had hoped, would focus on proposed missions, not individual services. It was with a good deal of pride as well as an awareness that he was following where Eisenhower had led, that Barry Goldwater remarked in 1988, "Our separate ground, sea and air warfare by individual services is gone forever." [5]

NOTES

1. *New York Times* (hereafter cited as *NYT*), 18 and 25 Feb. 1982; Peter J. Roman and David W. Tarr, "The Joint Chiefs of Staff: From Service Parochialism to Jointness," *Political Science Quarterly* (Spring 1998): 97.

2. *NYT*, 31 March 1982.

3. Barry M. Goldwater, with Jack Casserly, *Goldwater* (New York: Doubleday, 1988), 351.

4. *NYT*, 8 May 1986.

5. Goldwater and Casserly, Goldwater, 355. For a complete description of how the Goldwater-Nichols Act has changed things, see Roman and Tarr, "The Joint Chiefs of Staff," 102–11.

Selected Bibliography

MANUSCRIPT AND ARCHIVAL MATERIALS

Eisenhower Library

Manuscript Collections

Eisenhower, Dwight D.: Pre-presidential Papers

Papers as President (Ann Whitman File):

  Administration Series

  Ann Whitman Diary Series

  Cabinet Series

  DDE Diary Series

  Legislative Meetings Series

  Miscellaneous Series

  NSC Meeting Series

  Records as President (White House Central Files), Confidential File

Papers of Oliver Gale

Papers of Bryce Harlow

Papers of Meyer Kestnbaum

Papers of Neil McElroy

Papers of Kevin McCann

Papers of Gerald Morgan

Papers of Lauris Norstad

Papers of William Robinson

U.S. President's Committee on Government Organization

White House Office of the Staff Secretary:

> Subject Series, Department of Defense Subseries
>
> Subject Series, Staff Research Group

Oral Histories

Evan Aurand

Edward Beach

Arleigh Burke

Charles Coolidge

James Douglas

Thomas Gates

Bryce Harlow

Robert Lovett

Edward McGuire

Neil McElroy

Lauris Norstad

Leverett Saltonstall

Nathan Twining

Truman Library

Manuscript Collections

Papers of Clark Clifford

Papers of Robert Dennison

Papers of George Elsey

Papers of John L. Sullivan

Papers of Stuart Symington

Oral Histories

Clark Clifford

Marx Leva

Milfred McNeil, Jr.

Stuart Symington

Western Manuscripts Collection, University of Missouri

Papers of Stuart Symington

Manuscript Division, Library of Congress

Papers of Robert Patterson
Papers of Carl Spaatz
Papers of Nathan Twining
Papers of Hoyt Vandenberg

National Archives, Modern Military Branch

American-British Conversations (ABC)
Combined Chiefs of Staff (CCS)
Office of the Army Chief of Staff (COS)
Office of the Secretary of Defense (OS/D)
Papers of Robert Patterson (OS/D)

PUBLISHED DOCUMENTS

Cole, Alice C., et al., eds. *The Department of Defense: Documents on Establishment and Organization, 1944–1978.* Washington, DC: Office of the Secretary of Defense, Historical Office, 1978.

Public Papers of the Presidents: Dwight D. Eisenhower, 1953–1958. Washington, DC: GPO, 1960–1961.

Public Papers of the Presidents: Harry S. Truman, 1945–1947. Washington, DC: GPO, 1961–1964.

U.S. Congress. House of Representatives. Committee on the Armed Services. *Hearings on the Reorganization of the Defense Department.* 85th Cong., 2nd. sess. Washington, DC: GPO, 1958.

U.S. Congress. House. Committee on the Armed Services. *Hearings: Investigation of the B-36 Bomber Program.* 81st. Cong., 1st. sess. Washington, DC: GPO, 1949.

U.S. Congress. House. Committee on Appropriations. *Hearings: Department of Defense Appropriations for 1955.* 83rd. Cong., 2nd. sess. Washington, DC: GPO, 1954.

U.S. Congress. House of Representatives. Committee on Expenditures in the Executive Departments. *Hearings on H. R. 2319.* 79th Cong., 1st. sess. Washington, DC: GPO, 1946.

U.S. Congress. House of Representatives. Committee on Expenditures in the Executive Departments. *Hearings, National Security Act of 1947.* 80th Cong., 1st. sess. Washington, DC: GPO, 1947.

U.S. Congress. Senate. Committee on the Armed Services. *Hearings before the Subcommittee on Airpower.* 84th Cong., 2nd. sess. Washington, DC: GPO, 1956.

U.S. Congress. Senate. Committee on the Armed Services. *Hearings on Defense Department Reorganization.* 85th Cong., 2nd. sess. Washington, DC: GPO, 1958.

U.S. Congress. Senate. Committee on the Armed Services. *Hearings on the National Defense Establishment.* 80th Cong., 1st. sess. Washington, DC: GPO, 1947.

U.S. Congress. Senate. Committee on Appropriations. *Hearings, Department of Defense Appropriations for 1955.* 83rd Cong., 2nd. sess. Washington, DC: GPO, 1954.

————. *Hearings: Department of the Army Appropriations for 1955.* 83rd Cong., 2nd. sess. Washington, DC: GPO, 1954.

U.S. Congress. Senate. Committee on Military Affairs. *Hearings on S. 84 and S. 1482, Department of Armed Forces, Department of Military Security.* 79th Cong., 1st. sess. Washington, DC: GPO, 1946.

U.S. Congress. Senate. Naval Affairs Committee. *Hearings: Unification of the Armed Forces.* 79th Cong., 2nd. sess. Washington, DC: GPO, 1946.

U.S. Congress. Senate. Subcommittee on Appropriations. *Hearings on Defense Appropriations for 1954.* 83rd Cong., 1st. sess. Washington, DC: GPO, 1954.

U.S. Department of State. *Foreign Relations of the United States, 1952–1958.* Washington, DC: GPO, 1984–1990.

PUBLISHED DIARIES, LETTERS, AND MEMOIRS

Adams, Sherman. *Firsthand Report.* New York: Harper, 1961.

Chandler, Alfred D., Jr., Stephen E. Ambrose, Louis Galambos, et al., eds., *The Papers of Dwight D. Eisenhower.* 17 vols. Baltimore: Johns Hopkins University Press, 1970–1996.

Clifford, Clark, with Richard Holbrook. *Counsel to the President: A Memoir.* New York: Random House, 1991.

Collins, J. Lawton. *Lightning Joe: An Autobiography.* Baton Rouge: Louisiana State University Press, 1979.

Eisenhower, Dwight D. *Crusade in Europe.* Garden City: Doubleday, 1948.

————. *Mandate for Change.* Garden City: Doubleday, 1963.

———. *Waging Peace: The White House Years, 1956–1961*. Garden City: Doubleday, 1965.

———. *At Ease: Stories I Tell My Friends*. Garden City: Doubleday, 1967.

Eisenhower, John S. D. *Strictly Personal*. Garden City: Doubleday, 1974.

Ferrell, Robert A., ed. *The Eisenhower Diaries*. New York: Norton, 1981.

Gavin, James. *War and Peace in the Space Age*. New York: Harper and Brothers, 1958.

Griffith, Robert, ed. *Ike's Letters to a Friend*. Lawrence: University of Kansas Press, 1984.

Hughes, Emmet John. *Ordeal of Power*. New York: Atheneum, 1962.

Jurika, Steven, Jr., ed. *From Pearl Harbor to Vietnam: The Memoirs of Admiral Arthur Radford*. Stanford: Hoover Institution Press, 1980.

Killian, James R. *Sputnik, Scientists, and Eisenhower*. Cambridge: Massachusetts Institute of Technology Press, 1977.

Millis, Walter, ed. *The Forrestal Diaries*. New York: Viking Press, 1951.

Ridgway, Matthew. *Soldier, the Memoirs of Matthew B. Ridgway*. New York: Harpers, 1956.

Stimson, Henry L., and McGeorge Bundy. *On Active Service in Peace and War*. New York: Harper and Brothers, 1947.

Taylor, Maxwell. *An Uncertain Trumpet*. New York: Harper and Brothers, 1959.

———. *Plowshares into Swords*. New York: Norton, 1972.

Truman, Harry S. *The Memoirs of Harry S. Truman: Years of Trial and Hope*. Garden City: Doubleday, 1955.

Twining, Nathan. *Neither Liberty nor Safety: A Hard Look at U.S. Military Policy and Strategy*. New York: Holt, Rinehard and Winston, 1966.

York, Herbert. *Race to Oblivion: A Participants View of the Arms Race*. New York: Simon and Schuster, 1970.

UNPUBLISHED DOCTORAL DISSERTATION

Tarr, Curtis W., "Unification of America's Armed Forces." Stanford University, 1962.

NEWSPAPERS AND PERIODICALS

Newsweek

New York Times

Time

SECONDARY SOURCES

Albion, Robert G., and Robert H. Connery. *Forrestal and the Navy*. New York: Columbia University Press, 1962.

Aliano, Richard A. *American Defense Policy from Eisenhower to Kennedy*. Athens: Ohio University Press, 1975.

Alsop, Joseph, and Stuart Alsop. *The Reporters Trade*. New York: Reynal and Co., 1958.

Ambrose, Stephen. *The Supreme Commander: The War Years of General Dwight D. Eisenhower*. Garden City: Doubleday, 1969.

———. *Eisenhower: Soldier, General of the Army, President Elect, 1890–1952*. New York: Simon and Schuster, 1983.

———. *Eisenhower: The President*. New York: Simon and Schuster, 1984.

Art, Robert J., Vincent Davis, and Samuel P. Huntington, eds. *Reorganizing America's Defense: Leadership in War and Peace*. New York: Pergamon, 1985.

Bacevich, A.J. *The Pentomic Era: The U.S. Army between Korea and Vietnam* Washington, DC: National Defense University Press, 1986.

Caraley, Demetrios. *The Politics of Military Unification: A Study of Conflict and the Policy Process*. New York: Columbia University Press, 1966.

Coletta, Paolo. *The U.S. Navy and Defense Unification, 1947–1953*. Newark: University of Delaware Press, 1981.

Condit, Doris. *The History of the Office of the Secretary of Defense*. Vol. 2. Washington, DC: History Office, Office of the Secretary of Defense, 1988.

Condit, Kenneth W. *A History of the Joint Chiefs of Staff, 1947–1949*. Vol. 2. Wilmington: Michael Glazier Inc., 1979.

Davis, Vincent. *Postwar Defense Policy and the United States Navy, 1943–1946*. Chapel Hill: University of North Carolina Press, 1965.

Desmond, James. *Nelson Rockefeller, a Political Biography*. New York: Macmillan, 1964.

Divine, Robert A. *Eisenhower and the Cold War*. New York: Oxford University Press, 1981.

———. *The Sputnik Challenge*. New York: Oxford University Press, 1993.

Dockrill, Saki. *Eisenhower's New Look: National Security Policy, 1953–1961*. New York: St. Martin's Press, 1996.

Donovan, Robert J. *Conflict and Crisis: The Presidency of Harry S. Truman, 1945–1948*. New York: Norton, 1977.

———. *Eisenhower*. New York: Harper, 1956.

———. *Tumultuous Years: The Presidency of Harry S. Truman, 1949–1953*. New York: Norton, 1982.

Freedman, Lawrence. *The Evolution of Nuclear Strategy*. New York: St. Martin's Press, 1981.

Gaddis, John L. *Strategies of Containment: A Critical Appraisal of Postwar American National Security Policy*. New York: Oxford University Press, 1982.

Geelhoed, E. Bruce. *Charles E. Wilson and the controversy at the Pentagon*. Detroit: Wayne State University Press, 1979.

Graebner, Norman, ed. *The National Security: Its Theory and Practice*. New York: Oxford University Press, 1986.

Halberstam, David. *The Best and the Brightest*. New York: Random House, 1969.

Hammond, Paul Y. *Organizing for Defense*. Princeton: Princeton University Press, 1961.

Hastings, Max. *Overlord D-Day & the Battle for Normandy*. New York: Simon and Schuster, 1984.

Hayes, Grace P. *The History of the Joint Chiefs of Staff in World War II: The War against Japan*. Annapolis: Naval Institute Press, 1982.

Haynes, Richard F. *The Awesome Power*. Baton Rouge: Louisiana State University Press, 1973.

Hitch, Charles J. *Decision Making for Defense*. Berkeley: University of California Press, 1965.

Hoxie, R. Gorden. *Command Decision and the Presidency*. New York: Readers Digest Press, 1977.

Huie, William Bradford. *The Case against the Admirals*. New York: E. P. Dutton & Co., 1946.

Huntington, Samuel. *The Common Defense*. New York: Columbia University Press, 1961.

Kahan, Jerome. *Security in the Nuclear Age*. Washington, DC: The Brookings Institution, 1975.

Kaplan, Fred. *The Wizards of Armageddon*. 1983. Reprint. Stanford: Stanford University Press, 1991.

Kinnard, Douglas. *President Eisenhower and Strategy Management*. Lexington: University of Kentucky Press, 1977.

―――. *The Secretary of Defense*. Lexington: University of Kentucky Press, 1980.

Koladziej, Edward. *The Uncommon Defense and Congress*. Columbus: Ohio State University Press, 1966.

McClendon, R. Earl. *Changes in Organization for National Defense, 1949–1953*. Maxwell Air Force Base: Air University Press, 1956.

McCullough, David. *Truman*. New York: Simon and Schuster, 1992.

McNamara, Robert S. *The Essence of Security*. New York: Harper, 1968.

Parmet, Herbert S. *Eisenhower and the American Crusade*. New York: Macmillan, 1972.

Patterson, James T. *Mr. Republican: A Biography of Robert A Taft*. Boston: Houghton Mifflin, 1972.

Pogue, Forrest C. *George Marshall, Education of a General*. New York: Viking Press, 1957.

―――. *George C. Marshall: Ordeal and Hope*. New York: Viking Press, 1965.

————. *George C. Marshall, Organizer of Victory.* New York: Viking Press, 1973.

Potter, E. B. *Nimitz.* Annapolis: Naval Institute Press, 1976.

————. *Admiral Arleigh Burke.* New York: Random House, 1990.

Rappaport, Armin. *The Navy League of the United States.* Detroit: Wayne State University Press, 1962.

Raymond, Jack. *Power at the Pentagon.* New York: Harper, 1964.

Rearden, Steven L. *The History of the Office of the Secretary of Defense: The Formative Years.* Vol. 1. Washington, DC: Historical Office, Office of Secretary of Defense, 1984.

Ries, John C. *The Management of Defense: The Organization and Control of the U.S. Armed Forces.* Baltimore: Johns Hopkins University Press, 1964.

Schilling, Warner R., Paul Y. Hammond, and Glenn H. Snyder. *Strategy, Politics, and Defense Budgets.* New York: Columbia University Press, 1962.

Schnabel, James F. *The History of the Joint Chiefs of Staff.* Vol. 1. Wilmington: Michael Glazier Inc., 1979.

Sherry, Michael. *Preparing for the Next War: American Plans for Postwar Defense, 1941–1945.* New Haven: Yale University Press, 1977.

Stein, Harold. *American Civil-Military Decisions: A Book of Case Studies.* Birmingham: University of Alabama Press, 1963.

Stockfisch, Jacob A. *Plowshares into Swords: Managing the American Defense Establishment.* New York: Mason and Lipscomb, 1973.

Watson, Robert J. *A History of the Joint Chiefs of Staff.* Vol. 5. Wilmington: Michael Glazier, Inc., 1979.

————. *The History of the Office of the Secretary of Defense: Into the Missile Age*, Vol. 4. Washington, DC: Historical Office, Office of the Secretary of Defense, 1997.

Weigley, Russell F. *A History of the United States Army.* New York: Macmillan, 1967.

Index

About the Author

GERARD CLARFIELD is Professor of American Diplomatic History at the University of Missouri. He is the author of numerous books, including *Nuclear America*, which he co-authored with William Wiecek of Syracuse University, and a two volume history of United States foreign policy.

ISBN 0-275-96445-0

90000>

EAN

9 780275 964450

HARDCOVER BAR CODE